ENDURING POSTWAR

ENDURING POSTWAR
YASUOKA SHŌTARŌ
AND LITERARY
MEMORY IN JAPAN

KENDALL HEITZMAN

VANDERBILT UNIVERSITY PRESS
NASHVILLE

© 2019 by Vanderbilt University Press
Nashville, Tennessee 37235
All rights reserved
First printing 2019

Library of Congress Cataloging-in-Publication Data
Names: Heitzman, Kendall, 1973– author.
Title: Enduring postwar : Yasuoka Shotaro and literary memory in Japan / Kendall Heitzman.
Description: Nashville : Vanderbilt University Press, 2019. | Includes bibliographical references and index. |
Identifiers: LCCN 2019006668 (print) | LCCN 2019011281 (ebook) | ISBN 9780826522573 ( ) | ISBN 9780826522559 (hardcover) | ISBN 9780826522566 (pbk.)
Subjects: LCSH: Yasuoka, Shōtarō, 1920-2013—Criticism and interpretation.
Classification: LCC PL865.A7 (ebook) | LCC PL865.A7 Z65 2019 (print) | DDC 895.6/35—dc23
LC record available at https://lccn.loc.gov/2019006668

To the memory of my grandparents,
who lived the war and postwar in very different ways

Contents

	Acknowledgments	ix
	A Note on Names, Translations, and Citations	xiii
	Introduction: Yasuoka Shōtarō and the Histories of Shōwa	1
1	Politics by Other Means: Allegories of Resistance and the Endless War	23
2	The Generation of Deception: Canon and Archive in the Fiction of the Long Postwar	61
3	Local History, Global History, and the Triangulation of Memory	98
4	Long Shots in *Tokyo Olympiad*	130
5	Bakumatsu, Postwar, and Memories of Survival	155
	Conclusion	183
	Appendix: Works by Yasuoka Shōtarō in English Translation	189
	Notes	191
	Bibliography	201
	Index	211

Acknowledgments

This book has accrued many debts over many years. John Treat, my PhD advisor at Yale University and someone known to resist facile collective memory himself, supported this project from beginning to end. Over the course of my graduate career, Aaron Gerow provided me with a stellar education in film and a model for working with passion and good cheer. Before Yale, I made the transition from English literature to Japanese literature during a year at Dartmouth College in the Comparative Literature master's program, a wonderful, fully funded one-year program that more people should know about. There, I studied with Dennis Washburn and Ikuko Watanabe and benefited from the constant kindness of Jim and Yukari Dorsey.

In Japan, I benefited from the advice and hospitality of Kōno Kensuke at Nihon University in Tokyo for the academic years 2007–2009. Two fellow auditors in Professor Kōno's class, Kameda Hiroshi and Yamanaka Chiharu, and a small crew of graduate students including Kitano Jun'ichi, Komine Hiroyoshi, and Koizumi Kōta provided me with a wealth of information and advice on modern Japanese literature and helped me to explore Yasuoka's Tokyo haunts. I spent the 2014–2015 academic year at Waseda University, where Toba Kōji provided me with access to three valuable resources: the university library, the larger academic community, and his own endless knowledge of the field. A month at Osaka University in 2016 gave me an opportunity to discuss issues relating to memory and Japanese literature with a terrific group of undergraduate and graduate students, which helped shape this book. I am grateful to Unoda Shōya for the opportunity. In the summer of 2018, I desperately needed a place to work through some rewrites on this volume; I thank my old friend Jordan A. Y. Smith and Jōsai University for library access. Late in the process, I benefited from kind advice from Murakami Katsunao and Kim Jiyoung. Along the way, two teachers who taught me all kinds of things about Japanese language and literature despite the fact that I was *not* their charge have become great friends: I thank Hanzawa Chiemi and Akizawa Tomotarō, whom I first met at Middlebury and the Inter-University Center for Japanese Language Studies (IUC), respectively, for their longstanding dedication to a wayside student.

Before I knew any of these people, two decades ago, on my very first trip to Japan, I met three members of the English Club of Sukumo City, Kōchi Prefecture, five minutes after I arrived in town. I am so happy that I am still in regular touch with all of them. For my very first education in Japanese language and culture, I am grateful to Matsumoto Miho, Miki Mika, and Fujisaki Aki. I miss Matsumoto Yasuhiro, my self-appointed Japanese father, every day.

I was able to meet with Yasuoka Shōtarō himself in the summer of 2006, at his home in Tokyo. For making this happen, and for generous assistance provided over the years since, I am deeply grateful to his daughter, Prof. Yasuoka Haruko. Yasuoka Shōtarō's cousin, Yasuoka Fumi, allowed me to visit her at the Yasuoka ancestral estate in Kōchi-ken, the *o-shita*, now designated as an Important Cultural Property. More recently, her son Yasuoka Masatoshi has welcomed me to the newly restored estate and has been of great help to me in determining the proper pronunciation of family names. Prof. Minoo Adenwalla, emeritus of Lawrence University, provided me with information relating to his friendship with Shōno Junzō during their time at Kenyon College. Tokushima Takayoshi was kind enough to reminisce about his days as Yasuoka's editor and to send me a copy of the essay he wrote over half a century later about the experience.

I am grateful to the following funding sources: A grant from the Blakemore Freeman Foundation took me to the Inter-University Center for Japanese Language Studies in Yokohama in 2003–2004, and the Council on East Asian Studies at Yale provided me with Summer Travel & Research Grants in the summers of 2004–2007. A Monbukagakushō (MEXT) Fellowship brought me to Nihon University in 2007–2009, and the Japan Society for the Promotion of Science (JSPS) provided funding that allowed me to conduct further research at Waseda University in 2014–2015. The Center for Asian and Pacific Studies (CAPS), International Programs, and the Old Gold funding, all at the University of Iowa, funded multiple trips to Japan over the past seven years. A faculty research award from the Japan Foundation's Institutional Project Support (IPS) 2016–2019 grant to the University of Iowa gave me funding at a key point in the project.

Acknowledgments

During the Great Recession, I taught at three liberal arts colleges as I continued to work on this study. Thanks to my colleagues who supported me during those years and made it—if I am allowed to admit this—such a pleasant period of my life: Mariko Kaga, Bardwell Smith, Katie Sparling, and Noboru Tomonari at Carleton College in 2009–2010; Hoyt Long and Michiko Baribeau at Bard College in 2010–2011; and Satoko Suzuki, Christopher Scott, Ritsuko Narita, and Frederik Green at Macalester College in 2011–2012.

Colleagues at the University of Iowa who have helped me in one way or another over the years are certainly too numerous to name, but I want to thank those who have devoted significant time to mentoring me, perhaps without even realizing it: Russ Ganim, Katina Lillios, Philip Lutgendorf, Scott Schnell, Fred Smith, and Stephen Vlastos. I thank my colleagues in the Japanese Program, Yumiko Nishi and Kendra Strand, for their good company and extraordinary collegiality. Thanks as well to my current and former colleagues who have read or discussed portions of this project: Amber Brian, Corey Creekmur, Melissa Curley, Roxanna Curto, Jennifer Feeley, Denise Filios, Brian Gollnick, Lisa Heineman, Jiyeon Kang, and Ana Rodríguez-Rodríguez. Luis Martín-Estudillo channeled my sensibilities and suggested the title for this book in its entirety. During my time at Iowa, I have benefited from the support of two of the great librarians in the field, Chiaki Sakai and Tsuyoshi Harada. My co-PI on the Japan Foundation grant and dear friend Morten Schlütter has been there for me and my family in ways large and small.

One of the pleasures of the Inter-University Center for Japanese Language Studies is getting to know people in other fields studying Japanese for various reasons: Rebecca Nickerson, Gene Park, Lorraine Plourde, Sam Porter, Jamie Ravetz, and David Wolitz have all shaped my broader understanding of Japan. During my first extended research period in Tokyo, I got to know a group of scholars who have been there for me over the years, as friends and as sounding boards: Susan Furukawa, Nick Kapur, Kari Shepherdson-Scott, Ben Uchiyama, and Kirsten Ziomek. Without the willingness of these two groups of intellectuals to work long evenings and occasionally through the night, the discipline of karaoke studies would not be the rich, burgeoning field of inquiry it is today. Thanks as well to those who over the years have shared their knowledge and advice, practical and theoretical, with someone a stage or two behind them: Charles Exley, Sarah Frederick, Alisa Freedman, Joe Hankins, Kyle Ikeda, Anne McKnight, Steve Ridgely, Colin S. Smith, and, really, the field as a whole. Finally, I was always fortunate to be surrounded by smart, thoughtful people who had an effect on my thinking at every school I attended, researched at, or taught at; I fear that if I try to name them all there will be no end and too many inadvertent omissions, so a simple thank you to all of my cohorts along the way.

At Vanderbilt University Press, this project first caught the eye of Michael Ames; I am in his debt. Zack Gresham and Joell Smith-Borne cared immensely about details on this project. For assistance with many of the images in this book, I am grateful to the Kanagawa Museum of Modern Literature and especially staff member Saitō Yasuko. I am honored to use with permission Tamura Yoshiya's famous lettering of Yasuoka Shōtarō's name on the front cover of this book.

Finally, thank you to family in the United States and Japan. For their own act of endurance, my greatest thanks go to my wife Yuri and to our son Kaoru, who has been a Perfectly Patient Gentleman throughout. Let's go play, guy.

A Note on Names, Translations, and Citations

Japanese names in this book are given in Japanese name order, family name first. This does not apply to scholars who happen to have Japanese names who work primarily in English.

In order to create a unified voice for Yasuoka in this study, and because of the simple reality that one reader-translator will gloss over or elide things that another reader-translator chooses to emphasize, I have translated everything of Yasuoka's that I cite, even when an English translation exists. We are fortunate that excellent translations have been published of a number of Yasuoka stories and one novella; in order to help the reader access these works, I have provided a list of works available in English translation in the appendix. Unless otherwise noted, when a story has been translated into English, I defer to the translator's English title for the work.

For texts by other authors, I have attempted to defer to English translations when they exist. Texts mentioned only in passing are included in the Bibliography only when an English translation exists, for the reader's convenience.

A list of abbreviations used in citations is given at the beginning of the Bibliography.

Introduction

Yasuoka Shōtarō and the Histories of Shōwa

It is not often that we can speak of a writer representing both center and margin. After he won the Akutagawa Prize in 1953, however, Yasuoka Shōtarō (1920–2013) spent over five decades as a surprisingly subversive voice at the center of the Japanese literary establishment. Much of this is the result of a life lived on the cusp of respectability: He was the son of an army veterinarian and descendant of a low-ranking Tosa samurai family, but the family moved from region to region in the Japanese Empire, and he faced difficulties both academically and socially. The winnowing process to enter one of the prestigious higher schools, a brutal ratio that left the vast majority of Japanese citizens without more than a middle-school education, left him stranded for three long years from 1938 to 1941 as a *rōnin*, a would-be student without a school, biding his time in preparatory school hoping that the next year would offer him a chance to advance. Although advancement would fulfill his status-obsessed mother's academic ambition for him, failure offered him a means of deferring the draft during World War II. He eventually went to war in 1944, passed much of it in the sickbay, and was returned to Japan shortly after the firebombing of Tokyo in the spring of 1945 wiped out the family home and left Yasuoka and his parents utterly destitute. His wartime bout of pleurisy led to spinal caries, which left him bedridden for years during the early postwar period. He wrote his first stories on his stomach on a futon, two or three literally painful sentences at a time.

Yasuoka came to early fame as a member of the literary coterie formed by the editors of *Bungakukai* that became known as the Third Generation of New

Writers (*Daisan no Shinjin*), a group that included such authors as Kojima Nobuo (1915–2006), Shimao Toshio (1917–1986), and Yoshiyuki Junnosuke (1924–1994). Van Gessel has written persuasively about the coterie members' shared themes —a tendency toward autobiographical fiction combined with a new sense that one could no longer write the truth with any authority.[1] Yasuoka merits a reading outside the framework of a group, however, if for no other reason than that his most representative protagonists are people apart from society. A number of Yasuoka's early autobiographical stories depict a young man at odds with authority, whether in the form of schoolteachers, the Japanese wartime government, or the American Occupation. In December 1959, Kōdansha published what many consider to be Yasuoka's masterpiece, the short novel *A View by the Sea* (*Kaihen no kōkei*), an unsparing depiction of his mother's death in an insane asylum. The following year, Yasuoka left for the United States on an award from the Rockefeller Foundation; in his memoir of the experience, Yasuoka focuses on his sudden awareness of himself as something other than "White" or "Colored" in a city roiled by the Civil Rights Movement. Yasuoka later co-translated Alex Haley's *Roots* into Japanese, an experience that in turn would lead him to explore his own family roots in the massive family history *A Tale of Wanderers* (*Ryūritan*) and become one of the faces of social justice among writers in Japan, despite having no family and few personal connections to *hisabetsu burakumin* "outcast" or other oppressed communities. For fifteen years in the 1970s and 1980s, he served as a judge for the Akutagawa Prize, becoming an arbiter of literary taste and a gatekeeper to the guild, though he never quite felt at home in the world of Japanese letters himself.

Yasuoka's stories of radical isolation, I will argue, are impossible to read outside of his proclivities toward counterhistory and countermemory. By the time Yasuoka set to work in the 1980s on *My Shōwa History* (*Boku no Shōwa-shi*, serialized in *Hon*, 1980–1988; published in book form, 1984–1988), his three-volume memoir *and* history of the period from 1926 to the 1980s, he was an elder statesman of the Japanese *bundan*, or literary establishment. He continued to write autobiographical fiction, but more and more his stories grew to resemble the bevy of personal and historical essays he continued to produce until after the turn of the millennium. *My Shōwa History* operates somewhere in the middle of these modes of writing and serves as a compelling introduction to and microcosm of both Yasuoka's life and writings. In this lengthy memoir, all the themes of Yasuoka's career are brought to bear. We can use it as an introduction to the author's life, as well as a touchstone to the career of one of postwar Japan's most engaging, necessary voices.

The covers of the three volumes of *My Shōwa History*, using the package designs of cigarette brands popular in each era: Golden Bat during wartime, Peace during the early postwar, and Seven Stars in late Shōwa. Yasuoka smoked as many as one hundred cigarettes a day before quitting during a hospitalization in 1986.

Memory and Its Markers in *My Shōwa History*

Time and Space

In the opening pages of *My Shōwa History*, Yasuoka tells us that he was born in 1920, and he is therefore six when the Taishō emperor dies on December 25, 1926, a year that corresponded in the Japanese calendar to Taishō 15 and then became the first year of Shōwa with the change of emperor. He says that his first memories involve the lead-up to the imperial funeral on February 7, 1927 (Shōwa 2), when children slightly older than he are taught the funeral song, but he is not, because he has not yet entered elementary school. Yasuoka reminds us that in World War II an age difference of two or three months determined when men were drafted and could mean the difference between life and death. When he does start school in the spring of 1927, he enters wearing mourning clothes and with a black armband, although he doesn't remember how long the mourning period lasted. In the summer of 1927, he notes, the writer Akutagawa Ryūnosuke commits suicide, and around the same time Yasuoka's mother's older sister's husband shoots himself after a stock loss, but for Yasuoka the beginning of Shōwa is a happy time; he is in Seoul (then known as Keijō and part of Japan), where his father is posted as an Imperial Army veterinarian, and the family enjoys not only a middle-class existence but also the rights and prestige that are accorded to occupying forces (BSS 1: 3–7).

This is the beginning of a book that is not quite an autobiography and not quite a history—and one that incorporates the techniques of fiction—and the

Yasuoka, age six, with his father and mother when the family was living in present-day Seoul. Photograph courtesy of Yasuoka Haruko.

opening sequence lays bare many of the tensions that are inherent in a text that negotiates between modes of writing. Yasuoka deliberately raises a number of questions. First, how are his memories constituted in relationship to the history he tells? The historian Jay Winter has written that history establishes "the boundary conditions of possibility," the range within which memory can function (10). Of the general impressions that Yasuoka claims belong to the opening of the Shōwa era—the brick houses of the Japanese settlement in Honmachi; Korean children begging for change in the streets and freezing to death in winter; his mother straightening her hair; the chocolate, ham, sausages, and Westminster cigarettes his family cherishes (BSS 1: 7–9)—surely some of them predate the end of Taishō. Yasuoka's memory of the Taishō emperor dying is likely not his first memory, then, but simply the first that can be dated definitively; the historical fact of the emperor's death serves to reinforce and order his memory.[2]

Second, how do time and place function in this work? By contemporary reckoning, Yasuoka's opening scene is set in the winter of 1926–1927. To Yasuoka at the time, however, the calendar changed from Taishō 15 to Shōwa 1 on December 25, 1926, and to Shōwa 2 on January 1, 1927, meaning that the so-called first year of Shōwa was really only one week long. Yasuoka notes that it was jarring to go through a whirlwind week which culminated in the second year of Shōwa, as though the events he had just experienced were already distanced in the official calculation of time. Moreover, while we would say that he was six at the time, under the *kazoedoshi* system then in use, in which one's age was calculated as the number of calendar years in which one has been alive, he was seven when the Taishō emperor died and turned eight with the advent of Shōwa 2, on January 1, 1927. Yasuoka later mentions that the system of counting ages as *mannenrei*, the number of full years one has been alive beginning with one's own birthdate (the system used in the West) started in Japan on January 1, 1950. With that, Yasuoka suddenly went from being thirty-one to a youthful twenty-nine. The only thing the change served to do, he writes, was to make him feel like something of a fraud, going back to his twenties a full year after he had left them behind (BSS 2: 102–3).

Place is an equally fraught concept for Yasuoka, who throughout his career demonstrated a keen interest in the locations of his past. In *An Autobiographical Journey* (*Jijoden ryokō*, serialized in *Bungei shunjū* in 1971), a sort of trial run for *My Shōwa History*, Yasuoka traces the history of his family around the Japanese Empire, with an essay for each location. In *My Map of Tokyo* (*Boku no Tokyo chizu*, serialized in *Misesu* in 1985), he does the same for the places he haunted around the metropolis. When he walks through Kanda, for example, he is reminded of what he saw when he rode the Chūō Line along the Outer Moat after the firebombing of Tokyo: outside the moat the city had been obliterated; from Ochanomizu looking north, nothing was left all the way to the stone steps of Kanda Shrine—about three hundred meters away. Inside the moat, however, Meiji University and Suzuran-dōri in the heart of Jinbochō had been left completely intact (116). This was the exception, however: when he returned from the war and came into Tokyo through Ueno Station, he was disoriented by the empty open space in front of it where the city had been (103).

My Shōwa History starts with an even bigger spatiotemporal paradox: It is a memoir-cum-history of the Japanese Shōwa era that begins in present-day South Korea. At that time Korea was part of Japan, having been annexed in 1910, and Yasuoka is careful to remind us that the Seoul he knew as a child bore little resemblance to the Seoul we know today. It was a city of only five hundred thousand when Yasuoka lived there (as opposed to five million at the time of his writing in the mid-1980s and over ten million today), but that number still doesn't give an accurate portrayal of the city as he experienced it, because the number of people who were Japanese, the only people with whom he would have had meaningful contact, was even smaller, as was the Japanese settlement where he lived. The Japanese population in Seoul was about sixty-five thousand in 1920, rising to nearly one hundred thousand in 1930 (Uchida 65). The Japanese in Seoul, to varying degrees, held themselves apart from the general population; they feared adopting too many Korean customs and "falling into that hazy, intermediate realm *between* colonizer and colonized" (Uchida 89).³ Moreover, this distant point in Japan was in a linguistic sense more central than Tokyo itself: Yasuoka remembers his time in Seoul as being the only place he fully understood what his fellow Japanese were saying. The Japanese people that Yasuoka encounters there are educated and speak a language he (naturally) understands. Both his parents are from Kōchi Prefecture in Shikoku, but they have not passed on the Tosa dialect of that place to Yasuoka, their only child, and he thus cannot communicate with his relatives. In May 1929, the family moves back to Japan proper, bouncing back and forth between the country's rural north and the migrant sections of Tokyo. Linguistically, Yasuoka's Japanese becomes a hodge-podge; he cannot understand what his classmates or teachers are saying to him in the *Tsugaru-ben* dialect of Aomori Prefecture, and by the time he gets to Tokyo, no one there can understand what *he* is saying. Yasuoka becomes an isolated, lonely boy, an awful student who dreads school, but this is not because he grew up in the far reaches of the Japanese Empire; rather, the disparate elements of the Japanese "mainland" themselves do not add up to a single linguistic space that Yasuoka can inhabit.

Introduction 7

What connects these fragments of place and time is a literary impulse. Yasuoka's mention of the suicides of the writer Akutagawa Ryūnosuke and Yasuoka's uncle in the summer of 1927 is one good example of this. The uncle's death, after a financial problem, is another temporal dislocation, a foreshadowing of the bodies that will plummet to the ground along with stock prices around the world in the crash of 1929. Taken together with Akutagawa's death, however, it also represents the reconciling of history and personal memory through a literary turn. Yasuoka was not reading Akutagawa as a seven year old; this is the first of many historical intrusions into the flow of memory that appear with variations on the caveat "not that we knew that at the time" or "not that we understood the significance of that at the time." The pairing can be considered literary, in several senses. It is a foreshadowing—these are only the first spectacular deaths in Yasuoka's lifetime, the template for many more to follow. We could call it a motif, not only because of the suicides of literary greats that follow it (such as those of Dazai, Mishima, and Kawabata, all of which are mentioned in *My Shōwa History*), but also because it pairs the famous with the anonymous, shadowed by a similar pairing—the death of the emperor and the homeless and hungry Koreans—in the background. Yasuoka will go on to receive the award named after Akutagawa, lifting Yasuoka from anonymity and establishing him as a literary force. And it is a palimpsest, a personal history written over both collective memory and institutional histories to the point that they become mere traces; it is a reminder that events as they are lived are often at a variance with how they are recorded in histories or in the collective memory: famous people are not yet famous, deaths go unnoticed, wars go unexplained, societal problems go unquestioned.

The Personal in the National

Throughout his life, Yasuoka had the sense that his own personal narrative was connected to a national narrative of the Shōwa era. Yasuoka made much of the fact that he was a terrible student, perhaps owing to the vagaries of his father's career as much as anything else, but in some ways, it could be considered the hallmark of a literary career: the subgenre of childhood memoirs in Japanese literature appears to be awash in stories of sensitive children, mostly boys, whose failings make for excellent stories. To take two examples from among the writers of a previous generation that Yasuoka admired, Murō Saisei (1889–1962), in *Childhood* (*Yōnen jidai*, 1919),[4] writes of his poor academic record and the doubts he felt from being shuttled off by his birth mother to live with another family, while Satō Haruo (1892–1964) writes in *Wanpaku jidai* (*Wild Days*, 1958)[5] of failing in school and spending solitary days reading borrowed books and magazines.

During his *rōnin* years, trying to land a spot in a higher school, 1939, in front of the family home. Photograph courtesy of Yasuoka Haruko.

Yasuoka, however, may have been unique in the way his childhood shortcomings resonated with greater political events: in one amazing sequence, Hitler occupies a new country every time Yasuoka fails an entrance exam, and the young Yasuoka begins to suspect "that Hitler was a figure with a terrible connection to me" (BSS 1: 75). The relationship Yasuoka draws between Hitler and his own test scores is capricious, to be sure, but the situation is a reminder that the apprehension of history is to some extent always personal.

Moreover, later events justify his perceptions of powerful forces at work in very immediate ways in his education. In the spring of 1940, Yasuoka fails the entrance exam for Waseda University, his fourth failure in three years. On the application, Yasuoka attempts to curry favor with his examiners by naming as his most admired person Wang Jingwei, who has just formed a puppet government in Nanjing in opposition to Chiang Kai-shek. The examiner calls his answer "pretty journalistic," but Yasuoka notes that he couldn't bear to give the answer all the other applicants were giving: Kusunoki Masashige, who in the fourteenth century led his warriors into certain death rather than question Emperor Go-Daigo's mindless battle plan (BSS 1: 105). Yasuoka may be right that his academic career is being dictated by, well, dictators. In April of 1941, after three years in a holding pattern, Yasuoka at last begins at Keiō University, which, regardless of the sterling reputation it holds today, was considered a much easier target than the national universities at that time. No sooner is he in than he reverts to his old ways, skipping classes almost as often, he says, as his professors. Despite the low standards, his inability to take the July mid-year examinations means that there is no way he can pass the year. Students at the time had draft deferments; it isn't clear whether flunking and needing to repeat a grade, dragging out one's deferral, was a terrible move or a brilliant one. In March of 1942, he waits for the messenger bearing a Keiō-branded lantern who comes at night to tell students that they have failed for the year; Keiō students at the time referred to flunking as being *chōchin*-ed, or "lanterned" (BSS 1: 172). But by chance, the war is going well for Japan, which has taken control of both Singapore and Corregidor, and in the general celebration, even failing students are allowed to pass and continue on to the next year (BSS 1: 173). By the following year, the war effort isn't going as well, and all students at public and private schools alike lose their draft deferments, regardless of how they are performing. Yasuoka finally finishes his degree in 1948 by copying word for word an English essay he finds and turning it in as his own work. The gross plagiarism hardly matters, however; he is graduated not owing to anything he has done (and he has really done nothing at Keiō after the war, either), but because universities need to clear a backlog of students in order to make way for new ones. "The truth is," he writes, "I was able to graduate thanks to the confusion that resulted from losing the war" (BSS 2: 56). In this way, Yasuoka becomes the tragicomic hero in his own rendition of the great national failure—the text is at one and the same time autobiographical and allegorical.

Active Forgetting and Active Remembering

Yasuoka's memory of the Taishō emperor's death is in some sense a memory because it stands out among other things half remembered or forgotten altogether; in that sense, memories—and by extension, memoirs—are only made possible through the process of forgetting. In *On the Genealogy of Morality* (*Zur genealogie der moral*, 1887), Nietzsche argues that there is such a thing as "active forgetting," which allows one to take control of the past, "an active and in the strictest sense positive faculty of suppression [. . .] a little stillness, a little *tabula rasa* of consciousness so that there is again space for new things" (Nietzsche 35). Memoirists may generally assume that what has stayed in their memory is naturally the most important, but Yasuoka seems keen to draw attention to the gaps in his narrative, and to construct meaning out of them.

He doesn't remember what he did in the month before he reluctantly took his first postwar trip abroad, to the United States, and points out that in a similar fashion, he doesn't remember what he did in the month before he went into the army (BSS 2: 255). The parallel is clear for Yasuoka. He points out that accepting a Rockefeller grant was somewhat akin to being drafted for the army: they sought him out in order to send him to a foreign place, and he didn't see any way to refuse (BSS 2: 242). This active forgetting allows Yasuoka to make connections that would otherwise be lost in the shuffle of history.

Another example among many: in the middle of 1942, he is riding on the Yamanote Line, traveling from Sugamo to Nihonbashi. Next to him, a man and a woman with a traditional hairstyle are speaking about nothing meaningful, but the conversation has stayed with him all of these years:

> "So I hid the sweets I had received on the shelf. I thought that I would eat them later. But when I went to get them, they were gone. The sweets I had placed right there on the shelf . . ."
> "Kids sure are fast on the draw these days." (BSS 1: 175)

The train suddenly stops at Akihabara Station; the air-raid sirens go off, and people flood onto the platform to see smoke rising in the distance. Yasuoka understands instinctively that the Americans have managed, already, to bomb Japan. (Although it is not mentioned by name, the incident in question is the Doolittle Raid of April 18, 1942.) Yasuoka doesn't remember what happened to the couple, nor does he remember whether the train started moving again or whether he walked on foot from Akihabara to Nihonbashi; the halo of memory surrounding the moment extends its rays no further.

Over three years later, on August 15, 1945, Yasuoka hears the emperor announce the end of the war from a train platform where his train is being held for the speech; he is so annoyed by having to stand in the hot sun that he goes back onto the train, following a mother with a crying baby (BSS 1: 253). Yasuoka's narrative of Tokyo's experience of the war thus begins and ends on a train. When the war comes to Tokyo, it interrupts the passengers' everyday lives, but when it ends, the passengers' everyday lives interrupt it. In both scenes, sustenance during times of privation—children stealing sweets, a baby crying to be fed—is a central element. Although the scenes are far removed in the narrative sequence, Yasuoka's "failing" memory has created a structure so that the parallel appears.

Forgetfulness is more than tactical. It is necessary to the construction of meaning; it sutures narratives and salves trauma. At times, another narrative threatens to emerge from its dormant state just beneath the surface of his consciousness. "I'm forgetting something. Surely I'm forgetting something—but what could it be?" Yasuoka suddenly announces at one point in the narrative (BSS 3: 156). It is 1966, and Yasuoka is watching the student strikes in Japan turn oppressive. He sees them as doubles of the Red Guard in the Chinese Cultural Revolution and of the young American soldiers in Vietnam: young people who, in a variety of political situations, are doomed to replicate the depravities of the powers against whom they fight. Yasuoka has no doubt that Mishima Yukio—who wrote an open letter condemning the oppression of academic and artistic freedom in the Cultural Revolution—ultimately took inspiration from the Red Guard in creating his own ultranationalist Shield Society. The chain of signifiers is endless for Yasuoka: "Everything I see around me has been double exposed, but I sense a strange emptiness because there is something underneath but I don't know what, and at that moment I suddenly feel uncomfortable, as though I have completely forgotten something" (BSS 3: 157).

At key points, memory comes rushing back, as a scene in Paris reveals. The France Yasuoka had imagined as a young man in 1944 is very different from the France he encounters in 1963 when he finally gets there, but the two times and the "two Frances"—one imaginary, one all too real—collide in *My Shōwa History*. In Paris, Yasuoka goes to a café along the Seine. In a sure sign that Yasuoka's memory is allusive, he meets a younger version of himself: a young Asian man who sits in the café slowly sipping a beer to conserve money, who greets every young woman who enters the café but receives nothing but cold shoulders in return. Normally shy, Yasuoka feels a pan-Asian sense of racial solidarity with the man and brings him a beer. The man is a Vietnamese exchange student in a situation that doubles Yasuoka's, but with a twist: whereas a war in his homeland prevented Yasuoka from going to Paris as a young man, a war in this student's homeland has stranded him in Paris as a young man (BSS 3: 81–83). Shōwa history, it appears, crosses time and place, especially for Yasuoka, and the scenario evokes a long-submerged memory:

> I remembered how my friends and I had said to one another on the eve of our enlistment, "We'll meet on the Pont des Arts on July 14, 1950. Of course, at the time none of us knew how long the war would continue, or who among us would survive to 1950. In those circumstances, saying that we should meet at the base of a bridge in Paris was, put bluntly, nothing more than empty, crazy, drinking talk, and I had completely forgotten about that promise until right now. But now, in August 1963 here I was, on the banks of the Seine drinking a beer like this. Now, in addition to the young Vietnamese man I had never seen before in my life sitting next to me, I couldn't help but picture in turn the faces of Kobori Nobujirō, who I heard had died in the mountains of Luzon just before the end of the war; Kurata Hiromitsu, who had fallen in Manila; and Takayama Akira, who, it had been reported, had died in battle somewhere in China. (BSS 3: 83–84)

He is thirteen years late in remembering his promise, but by the time the agreed-upon date rolled around, some of the others had been dead for five years. Yasuoka's friends and companions died in various occupied territories, while Yasuoka remembers them in another, France, albeit one from a different theater of the war. The past intrudes on his reverie when he brings his Vietnamese friend to a Japanese restaurant in Paris. It is filled with expatriate Japanese, and the Vietnamese man is visibly uncomfortable; an American war is being fought in Southeast Asia, but Japan's occupation of French Indochina lingers even now, even here.

The Endless Postwar

Debating whether or not the postwar is over in Japan is one of the great parlor games of modern Japan studies (see Gluck, "The 'End' of the Postwar," for multiple conceptions of "postwar Japan"). The question returns to Yasuoka's narrative again and again. The most famous declaration of the end of the postwar came in July 1956, when the government issued an economic white paper declaring, in a famous turn of phrase, "it is no longer the postwar" (*mohaya sengo de wa*

Introduction

nai). In *My Shōwa History*, Yasuoka proclaims the end of the postwar as though it is an incantation, the expression of something longed for rather than a *fait accompli*. At various points, he wonders whether the postwar has ended or fundamentally changed, including when Truman replaced MacArthur as Supreme Commander of the Allied Occupation in 1951 (BSS 2: 122–23), when Kurosawa Akira's *Rashōmon* won the Golden Lion at the Venice Film Festival in 1951 (BSS 2: 126), when a good friend committed suicide in 1956 (BSS 2: 181), when he and his friends hear in the late 1950s that in the United States people say "postwar" to mean post *Korean* War (BSS 2: 187), when he institutionalized his mother (BSS 2: 188), when the coverage of the 1960 US–Japan Security Treaty protests (commonly known in Japanese as *Anpo*, an abbreviation of the term for the treaty itself, the *Anpo jōyaku*, itself an abbreviation of the full treaty title) gave way to news about the 1960 Rome Olympics (BSS 2: 247), when the economy boomed in the mid-1960s (BSS 3: 130), when a number of literary giants passed away in 1965 (BSS 3: 141), and when the worldwide unrest of 1968 appeared to usher in a "new postwar" (BSS 3: 166–67). One realizes along the way that the postwar never truly ends.

If the postwar is located between the personal and the public, it is also somewhere between the national and the international. In 1960 Yasuoka prepares to head for Nashville, Tennessee, on a grant from the Rockefeller Foundation and notes that William Faulkner had once said that he understood Japan's pain, because his people, too, had suffered defeat at the hands of the Yankees. Yasuoka is stunned that there is a place that has been struggling with a postwar mentality for nearly a century:

> I had no idea what to make of the fact that this wound suffered a hundred years earlier hadn't healed. But really, I didn't even know what to make of the fact that I personally had been on the losing side of the Second World War.
>
> To be sure, it was no longer the postwar. But all that meant was that the shock of losing the war had at last dissipated. What sort of thing was it to lose a war? I still wasn't able to grasp the meaning of it, nor was I able to clearly parse the bitterness of it. (BSS 2: 254–55)

This casual remark by Faulkner that the two regions share a specific bond will become the driving force for Yasuoka's memoir of his time in Nashville, *A Sentimental Journey to America* (*Amerika kanjō ryokō*, 1962), but here the South merely issues a reminder that the postwar, like Paris, is a moveable feast. It follows Yasuoka through time and space and offers as proof of its ongoing existence the numbing repetitiveness with which it is declared to be over. Is it possible that this is trauma? Andreas Huyssen describes trauma as "located on the threshold between remembering and forgetting, seeing and not seeing, transparency and occlusion, experience and its absence in repetition" and suggests that "both memory and trauma are predicated on the absence of that which is negotiated in memory or in the traumatic symptom. Both are marked by instability, transitoriness, and structures of repetition" (8). Yasuoka's history of Shōwa, "marked by instability, transitoriness, and structures of repetition," bears all the hallmarks of a traumatic text. But is it?

To be sure, there are wounds that have not healed. The narrative is riddled with suicides that are, in one way or another, blamed on the enduring postwar: Dazai Osamu's, literary critic Hattori Tatsu's, and Mishima Yukio's among them. Yasuoka himself considers suicide at least twice in the narrative. At one point, he asks a veterinary student visiting his father to bring him some poison, ostensibly to take care of a screeching cat in the neighborhood. When the student obliges Yasuoka on his next visit, Yasuoka realizes what he is actually plotting in his heart and, chilled, refuses to accept it (BSS 2: 95–97). And yet, all memory is not trauma, Huyssen himself concludes, for that would treat it "too exclusively in terms of pain, suffering, and loss. It would deny human agency and lock us into compulsive repetition. Memory, whether individual or generational, political or public, is always more than only the prison house of the past" (8). For Yasuoka, as we have seen, the past informs the present, creates bonds between people of different races and nationalities, and serves as a wedge *against* despair and the isolation he has felt throughout much of his life. If anything, the difficulty for Yasuoka is in retaining his individual voice in the face of the collective understandings of history.

Memory in Literature, Literature in Memory

Although public memory in Japan has had a volatile history, a number of historians have noted its monolithic tendencies. For Akira Iriye, public memory "serves an important function as a cognitive glue of the community, subsuming under it a host of private memories" (89). In her essay "The Past in the Present," Carol Gluck points out that in spite of the numerous and diverse factions that have battled for control of modern Japanese history, "public memory is hegemonic": "Collective national history tends to produce a canonical past that excludes variant voices" (Gordon, *Postwar Japan* 65, 88). Later scholarship has clarified that this is not to say that a single acknowledged understanding of historical events has taken root in contemporary Japan. Akiko Hashimoto goes so far as to say that "there is no 'collective memory' in Japan; rather, multiple memories of war and defeat with different moral frames coexist and vie for legitimacy" (Hashimoto 4). Even in a fragmented society, however, there are camps, and to construct one's individual memory is a great feat of resistance. Yasuoka has struggled to talk about popular history without being subsumed by the hegemon, to remain one of the "variant voices."

In his essay "The History within Me" ("Watashi no naka no rekishi," 1988), Yasuoka points out that "some things make strong claims to be history despite the fact that they have not been recorded, and even *because* they have not been recorded" (*Yasuoka Shōtarō zuihitsu shū* 7: 317). The anthropologist Michel-Rolph Trouillot calls these things that have not been recorded "silences" and notes, "professional historians alone do not set the narrative framework into which their stories fit. More often, someone else has already entered the scene and set the cycle of silences" (26). Yasuoka's efforts to retrieve the memory in these interstices makes his work similar in some ways to the *jibunshi* "self-history" boom of the 1970s and 1980s that Gerald Figal has explored in his essay "How to Jibunshi: Making and Marketing Self-Histories of Shōwa among the Masses in Postwar Japan." The idea, inspired by the work of ethnologist Yanagita Kunio, of having ordinary people write out their memories of Shōwa would seem to offer the hope of a massive, heterogeneous archive, but the routes down which the memoirists were encouraged to funnel their memories and the control their writing groups exercised over them ultimately led to "the homogenization and trivialization of these personal historical narratives as their production [became] commodified" (Figal 916).

Yasuoka has at his disposal a deep and abiding suspicion of other people's narratives, especially retrofitted nostalgic representations of wartime and postwar Japan, and in *My Shōwa History* he counters this impulse by writing from the double perspective of the present and the past. What appears is a world that is morally muddled and lost deep in the fog of the immediate moment. His hatred for the war effort stemmed not from any principled belief in freedom or democracy, but because a French film he had been looking forward to seeing, Jean Renoir's *Grand Illusion* (*La Grande Illusion*, 1937) had been banned shortly before its Japanese release (BSS 1: 67). It is one instance of many in the text in which Yasuoka resists established institutional or collective narratives in favor of personal ones. To the notion that the Japanese general population knew little or nothing of what was happening on the front, he points out that he is amazed later in the war to find that the carpenters and shop owners at home know more about the minutiae of the war than Yasuoka ever did when he was in the army: that the Shinano had sunk, that Truk had been lost, and so on (BSS 1: 224).

In Yasuoka's resistant history, the major events commonly enshrined as turning points in the war are silenced by personal narrative. In Japanese, many call World War II the Fifteen-Year War, but the first six years of this period, between the Manchurian Incident of September 18, 1931, and the Marco Polo Bridge Incident of July 7, 1937 (itself considered the starting point of the Second Sino-Japanese War, euphemistically called the "China Incident" by the Japanese government at the time), are a long placid time that simply doesn't feel like war to Yasuoka (BSS 1: 34–36). Even after it is clear that the "China Incident" is much more than an incident, and even after Japan's ruinous battle against Soviet forces at Nomonhan in 1939, life feels peaceful. Yasuoka's father, in the military in China, spends his days drinking, while Yasuoka's mother, flush with money, spends her time at the theater, shopping, and with friends (BSS 1: 89). The war for Yasuoka starts in earnest in 1940, with the fall of France and the commemoration of the 2600th anniversary of Japan's mythical founding. When war with the United States does come, he hears about it through his friends, who have heard about it from someone else, and he claims feeling "a confusion that comes from not being surprised in the least," and despite his misgivings, readily admits that "it would be a lie to say that we weren't excited" (BSS 1: 167). But he also lays claim to a moment of prescient skepticism and resignation: "There was probably no one who thought Japan could beat the United States in a war, and yet the war had become a reality. Despite this astonishing fact, we weren't the least astonished" (BSS 1: 167–68). In Yasuoka's telling, the war ends for him not with the emperor's speech but rather, about an hour later, when the black-marketers begin to ply their goods in the open without fear of reprisal (BSS 2: 3–5).

Yasuoka's resistance to powerful narratives extends to the postwar as well. When the US–Japan Security Treaty comes into effect in 1952, Yasuoka sees it as the end of Japan's so-called neutrality and pacifism (BSS 2: 136), but at the same time, he bristles at "the countless times afterward I had to hear [exaggerated] tales of bravery" from the students involved in the protests of 1960 against the treaty's renewal (BSS 2: 137). Although he is sympathetic to the protesters' desires, he wonders if they themselves understand the nature of their counter-narrative: "If asked whether they were for or against the revised security treaty, the natural answer was 'against.' But if you were to ask people 'What part of the new treaty are you against?' almost no one would have had an answer. How many people had read the provisions of the treaty and had a thorough understanding of it?" (BSS 2: 235). Yasuoka again sees a trauma being repeated: in this case, the student protests bear a striking resemblance to the *sonnō jōi* ("Revere the Emperor, Expel the Barbarians!") rabble-rousers of the 1850s and 1860s who decried the unequal treaties Japan was forced to sign at that time. Both groups fooled themselves into thinking that there were legitimate alternatives to signing the respective treaties, but at neither point in history were the protestors willing to say that Japan should go it alone as an unarmed country, Yasuoka argues (BSS 2: 236–37).

For the students, it may well be a traumatic repetition of history, an inability to write over what has been written, but for Yasuoka, the return to the past informs the present rather than restricts it. He points out that the postwar educational system is very different from the one he largely opted out of. It was made possible in part by educational reforms during the American Occupation, but in Yasuoka's mind, if you want to talk about societal levelers in education, you need to start with the wartime draft: When student deferments ended, so did all of the special treatment that students—generally the children of wealthy, powerful families—were used to receiving. "If we believe that the foundation for Meiji modernization was really laid during the Edo period, then we can say that the drive to a postwar 'democratic' society was really started during the war" (BSS 1: 188). Yasuoka is telling a history that is not generally acknowledged, using one commonly accepted narrative to bolster another. The parallel he is pointing out is a rhetorical one, not a causal one. Far from being mired in a repetitive or circular view of history, Yasuoka is quick to point out that there is no going home again. In order to understand the present we may return to the past, but it is not a return to any past we have known; the creative impulse has already shaped it into something new.

On the surface, Yasuoka's narrative ends where it begins. As he writes at the end of the Shōwa era, Seoul is preparing to host the 1988 Summer Olympics (BSS 3: 234). Yasuoka only appears to be going back to his own beginnings, however; Seoul is now a city with a different name, in a different country, in a different postwar, with a different history. It is virtually unrecognizable from the Seoul he knew, which is visible now only in the narrative of its history, and the history of its narrative.

Sites of Memory

In Europe and the United States, the study of collective memory originated, several times over, in studies of experiences of World War I. Paul Fussell's *The Great War and Modern Memory* (1975) is often thought to be the opening salvo in contemporary studies of memories and war, but surely the war was not far from Maurice Halbwachs's mind when, in *On Collective Memory* (*Les cadres sociaux de la mémoire*, 1925, literally "the social frameworks of memory"), he argued for a memory that can never be individual, that is "a part or an aspect of group memory, since each impression and each fact, even if it apparently concerns a particular person exclusively, leaves a lasting memory only to the extent that one has thought it over—to the extent that it is connected with the thoughts that come to us from the social milieu. One cannot in fact think about the events of one's past without discoursing upon them" (53). In this reckoning, individual memory is always connected to the collective memory.

The other privileged site in the West for memory studies is, of course, the Holocaust. Jay Winter sees a very different kind of collective memory emerging in the 1970s and 1980s, when a generation of young Europeans sought to resist their parents' generation's false narratives of World War II, which consisted of "heroic narratives of resistance to the Nazis and their allies"; around the same time, Holocaust accounts began to gain import as central narratives in remembering the war (26–27).

This book examines one writer's conception of individual and collective memory, which requires a reworking of the way we approach contemporary memory studies. Many of the assumptions that memory studies makes—about canon and archive, about generation, about social and cultural memory—do not apply to an individual writer's engagement with collective memory and institutional history, nor do they apply in this particular Japanese context. At the same time, new modes of engaging with memory emerge—some of these modes originate with Yasuoka, and others are my own, informed by Yasuoka's individual take on his historical moment.

In the study of Japanese literature and memory, scholarship in English and Japanese has often focused on the literature and cultural production of privileged memory sites—what Pierre Nora would call *lieux de mémoire*, such as Hiroshima and Okinawa—both as actual, physical sites and as abstract conceptualizations of memory.[6] This study is unusual in that it concerns a writer who might not be expected to be a font of variant memory. That said, part of the argument to be made about Yasuoka is that he cultivated a radical apartness that prevented him from ever feeling comfortable anywhere, which made him uniquely qualified to comment on and resist mainstream understanding of the war and postwar. Yasuoka himself has been discussed as part of larger projects, but a study of Yasuoka Shōtarō's career as a *lieu de mémoire* requires us to consider the entire span of his work. This book breaks from traditional practice in single-author studies, however, in that I devote a large portion of each chapter to analysis of Yasuoka's predecessors and contemporaries, to contextualize and make clear where he is engaging with his milieu and where he breaks from it. Because this is the first full-length study of Yasuoka in English, I do not shy away from close readings of key works. Yasuoka's contemporaries and friends Endō Shūsaku and Shimao Toshio have been the subject of monographs, and it is my hope that this study adds to our understanding of this still-underappreciated generation of writers.[7]

Introduction

Although this book negotiates thousands of pages of the Yasuoka canon, most of it not in English translation, I have attempted, particularly in the first chapter, to engage with work by Yasuoka and others that is available in English and has—to my thinking—much to offer memory scholars outside of a Japanese context as well. I have indicated in the Appendix where this small but key selection of stories and a single novella can be found in English.

This work is informed by contemporary global memory studies, which relies on a central framework that has been elucidated most clearly by Aleida and Jan Assmann. Although memory is often placed in opposition to history, the post-World War II era has seen a reconsideration of oral testimony and witnessing in the absence of written records that has made memory studies a critical part of contemporary historical practices, what Aleida Assmann has called "the new rapprochement between history and memory" (Aleida Assmann, *Shadows* 32). The Assmanns have identified three "dimensions" of memory: neural, social, and cultural. The neural dimension is that of the individual, whose memory of events extends back to childhood and only lasts until the end of that individual life. The social dimension belongs to those present and interacting in the sliding window of time that is presently between eighty to one hundred years long; if there are those who directly experienced the event still living, it remains within the realm of the social. Within families, this social memory is often that of three generations, occasionally four, and very rarely five. One person's memory is affected by the memory of others, and the average person's understanding of the world is under constant pressure from that of others; social memory is a process of synthesizing disparate memories of events into a usable whole, even at the expense of denying individual memory. Finally, cultural memory is a means of communicating across generations, what Jan Assmann calls "that body of reusable texts, images, and rituals specific to each society in each epoch, whose 'cultivation' serves to stabilize and convey that society's self-image" ("Collective Memory" 132). Objects of memory stored in archives gain the "stability and duration that are secured through institutions," but must also be reimagined anew in each generation (Aleida Assmann, *Shadows* 19).

In Chapter One, I use the distinctions Aleida Assmann makes between neural memory and social memory in my discussion of Yasuoka's individual memory resisting the collective understanding of the war and postwar, and her work on canon and archive informs my discussion of Yasuoka and his literary cohorts (plural) in Chapter Two. I make use of her paradigm of the varieties of witnesses in my Chapter Three discussion of Yasuoka's witnessing the Civil Rights Movement, and her work on memory as art versus memory as force offers me a way of approaching the documentary of the 1964 Tokyo Olympics in Chapter Four.

The sliding timeframe Jan Assmann has identified, during which social memory yields to cultural memory as the living memory of a time period dies out and gives way to something that can only be constructed from the archive, is key to my understanding of Yasuoka's relationship to the Japanese late-Edo *bakumatsu* period discussed in Chapter Five. Throughout, I have employed the work of a number of other memory scholars to further develop my argument.

Enduring Postwar

In contrast to previous studies that see Yasuoka and his coterie as apolitical, I argue that he is deeply political in the only way he could be: through individual, unallied resistance. In the first chapter, "Politics by Other Means: Allegories of Resistance and the Endless War," I look at Yasuoka's short fiction set during the war and postwar as works that suture the break of World War II by presenting themselves as allegories that resist common understandings of the war and postwar. Despite the overwhelming sentiment among the writers of the day across all schools that the end of the war represented a convincing break from the past, Yasuoka consistently sees life under the Occupation as being of a part with life during wartime. I argue that Yasuoka sees continuity and repetition, where others see historical ruptures and change, as a function of his deep-rooted isolation, one that fractured and conflated a sense of time and space for Yasuoka, such that the isolation of the nation was synecdochically reflected in the personal experiences of his protagonists. In his stories set in wartime, the protagonist's relationships with older women are imbricated with the constant pressure he feels from the state. In those set in the postwar, the so-called emasculation of the nation is reflected in his powerless, childish characters. Through a close reading of Yasuoka's masterful novella *A View of the Sea* (*Kaihen no kōkei*), I argue that even as fundamental a fact as the end of the war can be called into question through individual experience and memory.

In the second chapter, "The Generation of Deception: Canon and Archive in the Fiction of the Long Postwar," I consider Yasuoka's conception of narrative as deception, arguing that it is a function of his "generation," a narrowly defined cohort born around 1920 that suffered through the long war and postwar with dim memories of the greater freedom of "Taishō democracy" and a deep skepticism of authority and accepted ideologies of all stripes. Yasuoka's approach to literature was shaped less by the Third Generation of New Writers and more by a forgotten group of friends with literary ambitions that formed in wartime Tokyo. Rather than seeing Yasuoka as the one who happened to "strike it big," we can consider his work as canonical only thanks to the archive from which it draws and on which it relies. Yasuoka is widely regarded to be a writer of autobiographical "I-novels" (*shishōsetsu*), part of a specific tradition in Japanese letters that goes back to the beginning of the twentieth century. Yasuoka's stories, however, are often variations of the same personal experiences, stories that differ in the details and thus mutually undermine one another. Yasuoka is not the first writer to tell his story multiple times or even to call attention self-reflexively to the fictionality of his enterprise, but Yasuoka's work is significant for the way he connects his ostensibly isolated protagonists to the broader sweep of postwar Japanese history. Looking at these autobiographical stories, as well as others he based on well-known stories from the Bible and fairy tales, it becomes obvious that "deception" for Yasuoka is both theme and narrative strategy. Yasuoka felt that his cohort was triply deceived: by the war, by the Occupation, and by the fact that neither would ever end. To show this circularity, I discuss three novels about infidelity Yasuoka wrote in the 1950s, 1960s, and 1970s, in which variations of the same story of marital infidelity are a product of the postwar's psychological toll, the sum total of which calls into question both histories of postwar *shishōsetsu* and the role of deception in the ongoing postwar.

The third chapter, "Local History, Global History, and the Triangulation of Memory," treats Yasuoka's travelogues of his 1960–1961 stay in Nashville, Tennessee, during the Civil Rights Movement, and the effect it had on his writing. I argue that through a process of what I call "historical triangulation," Yasuoka used these experiences to reconcile his own feelings about the seemingly never-ending Japanese postwar. In Nashville, Yasuoka finds himself in a region, the American South, that in some senses has been in a postwar mode since the 1860s—a period contemporaneous with the history of modern Japan since the *bakumatsu*, the last days of the Tokugawa shogunate in the 1850s and 1860s. Through Yasuoka's rare American experience (no other major Japanese writer of the period spent significant time in the South during the Civil Rights Movement and wrote about it to such an extent), the post-Tokugawa moment and the post–World War II moment come to occupy the same temporal space for Yasuoka. Yasuoka makes sense of the present in Japan by casting it against the American South, which in turn makes it possible to access the *bakumatsu* and the beginnings of the Japanese nation-state, a period just as fraught for the nation but crucially different in the way that he personally relates to it. His time as a witness (in at least two senses of the word) to the Civil Rights Movement in Nashville makes it possible for him to find a way forward from the endless repetition of a seemingly endless postwar, one that is only available to him by "triangulating" through the prism of a separate place. Finally, I discuss the new outward-looking meaning Yasuoka draws from this: Yasuoka's experiences in Nashville sparked an interest in questions of discrimination and human rights, which resulted in his series of *zadankai* (conversations for public consumption) with Noma Hiroshi and others on social-justice issues in Japan in the 1970s.

I discuss Yasuoka's growing interest in race in the fourth chapter, "Long Shots in *Tokyo Olympiad*," in the context of Yasuoka's participation in the filming of Ichikawa Kon's documentary *Tokyo Olympiad* (*Tokyo Orinpikku*, 1965). The 1964 Tokyo Olympics represented Japan's symbolic return to the community of nations, the event that normalized Japan in the eyes of the world and—with its bullet trains, world-class facilities, and star architecture—served as a harbinger of a new image for Japan as a high-tech wonderland. For Yasuoka, the life-long film buff, the massive 1964 documentary was a cherished opportunity to move to the other side of the camera. The Ichikawa documentary stands in contrast to Leni Riefenstahl's famed film of the 1936 Berlin Olympics not only aesthetically, but also in terms of its production, which privileged a multitude of voices. Yasuoka's contribution to the project—a depiction of a lonely runner from Chad, one with no hope of winning a medal—is both the literal and figural centerpiece of the film. Yasuoka's efforts to make an African athlete the paragon of the "ordinary participant" for Ichikawa's film serves as a collective counterpoint to Jesse Owens's place in Riefenstahl's film, just as the technical limitations of the production allowed the filmmakers to "forget" collective visions of the Olympics and remember things that would normally be discarded or quickly overwritten.

In the fifth chapter, "Bakumatsu, Postwar, and Memories of Survival," I discuss Yasuoka's exploration of the mutual dependence of literary narrative, transgenerational memory, and history, this time in the broad sense, through a discussion of his translation into Japanese of Alex Haley's Pulitzer Prize–winning family history *Roots* and his own family histories. In researching his end-of-the-shogunate (*bakumatsu*) ancestors for his multi-generational dramatization of his own family history, *A Tale of Wanderers* (*Ryūritan*, 1976–1981), Yasuoka painstakingly examines the historical record to find that much of what has commonly been considered family history—and even memory—is in fact based in popular fiction of the Meiji period. In his 2000 follow-up *The Kagami River* (*Kagamigawa*), Yasuoka rescues the reputation of a literary-minded ancestor, long savaged by family memory. The silences that were perpetuated on his family and the manner in which lines of communication were cut between people bear parallels to and ongoing influence in his own life. As he reads into the gaps in letters, diaries, and other fragmentary records, Yasuoka inserts himself into the narrative to find a way for literary narrative and history to move forward via the process of creative memory.

1

Politics by Other Means

Allegories of Resistance and the Endless War

When Yasuoka Shōtarō was awarded the Akutagawa Prize for the first half of 1953 for the short stories "Bad Company" ("Warui nakama," 1953) and "Gloomy Pleasures" ("Inki na tanoshimi," 1953), it was the culmination of a quick rise in his career. It was the fourth time he had been nominated, after "The Glass Slipper" ("Garasu no kutsu," nominated for the first half of 1951), "Homework" ("Shukudai," first half of 1952), and "Prized Possessions" ("Aigan," second half of 1952). The Akutagawa Prize, Japan's most famous literary award, is offered twice a year; it has traditionally been given to writers early in their careers, often as much to acknowledge the promise of their careers to come as the honored work itself.[1] Yasuoka was the first of a group that came to be known as the Third Generation of New Writers (*Daisan no shinjin*) to win the award, soon followed by Yoshiyuki Junnosuke in 1954; Kojima Nobuo, Shōno Junzō, and Endō Shūsaku in 1955; and Kondō Keitarō in 1956.[2]

The "Third Generation" was from the start a contrived appellation. The first generation of postwar writers was simply known as the Sengo-ha ("postwar writers"). Associated with the literary magazine *Kindai bungaku*, their numbers included writers such as Noma Hiroshi (1915–1991) and Haniya Yutaka (1909–1997), known for their philosophical heft and political engagement. They were the giants of the Occupation, attempting to reconcile the national experience of the war head-on. An otherwise forgotten article by Usui Yoshimi in the January 1952 issue of *Bungakukai* attempted to identify "The Second Generation of New Writers," which led to a follow-up in the January 1953 issue, "The Third Generation of New Writers." Van Gessel provides the standard history in English for the construction of the Third Generation: A monthly gathering that developed out of this article was put together at the behest of *Bungakukai* by Yasuoka Shōtarō and two others; this group, the One-Two Association (*Ichi-ni-kai*), met for a year starting in early 1953, to be replaced by the Conceptions Society (*Kōsō no kai*) in the spring of 1954. The Conceptions Society lost a number of literary critics from the One-Two Association but added the critic Hattori Tatsu and Yasuoka's acquaintance from Keiō, Endō Shūsaku. When *Bungakukai* withdrew its sponsorship of the group in 1954, it turned into a group of friends, some closer than others. After a few years in the wilderness during the mid-1950s, they triumphantly returned with longer works that established their preeminence in Japanese letters (Gessel 41–60).

The Third Generation was famously described by the literary critic Hattori Tatsu in a way that has determined nearly all subsequent scholarship on them: they are writers of small-scale, autobiographical "I-novel" fiction; they don't hold to any particular critical doctrine; and politics is largely absent from their work (Hattori, "Shinsedai no sakka-tachi"). In his survey of the Third Generation, Van Gessel notes how they were mocked by the critics associated with *Kindai bungaku* (47), who themselves were not as orthodox as the leftist intellectuals of *Shin nihon bungaku* but clearly not willing to cede the political entirely.[3] When a subsequent generation of flashier, more politically aggressive writers came on the scene in the late 1950s—Ishihara Shintarō, whose right-wing politics were already on display in *Season of the Sun* (*Taiyō no kisetsu*, 1955, translated as *Season of Violence*), Kaikō Takeshi, and future Nobel laureate Ōe Kenzaburō—critics claimed it was the end for the Third Generation (BSS 2: 192). Gessel sees the Third Generation writers as important in their own right but also transitional in the way they opened up new avenues for the I-novel, pointing to "transformations" in "the relationship between author, text, and reader" that subsequent Japanese writers would make use of (73).

All of this downplays the act of political resistance that Yasuoka's writing represents. The Third Generation lived lives constrained by the difficulties of wartime and postwar. Yasuoka felt that his youth had been stolen by the excesses of the 1930s, but his disillusionment with the wartime government did not translate into a fondness for the new Occupation government. If anything, the cynicism he learned as a youth translated all too easily into a continued radical individuality as a young adult. His protagonists find it difficult to build alliances with people of any political stripe, and like their author they do not readily subscribe to collective understandings of the past. But this does not make Yasuoka apolitical. One of the central tenets of this study is the insistence that Yasuoka's rejection of all existing political allegiances is itself a deeply political act.

The relationship of the individual and the community is perhaps the central concern of scholars of memory working in the humanities and social sciences. Aleida Assmann's paradigm of memory posits an individual memory and a social memory that come into contact with one another (*Shadows of Trauma* 11–16). The fact that there is no memory outside of the human brain, and that the use of the word "memory" in the phrase "social memory" can only be metaphorical, has given some scholars pause in their attempts to identify what is meant by collective memory. Jeffrey Olick has proposed the opposition of "collected memory," the societal framework as it impinges on an individual mind, and "collective memory," which he sees as the "symbols, media, social institutions, and practices which are used to construct, maintain, and represent versions of a shared past" (338–43). Astrid Erll's synthesizing semiotic model of cultural memory shows the collective level "shaping" the individual level, while the individual level "actualizes" the collective level (99). In all of these conceptions, there is no collective memory without individual memory, and vice versa.

But what happens when an individual deliberately resists the allure of the collective and the way it silences contradictory narratives? One cannot simply stand apart from the collective entirely. Generations of scholars have refined, resisted, and outright rejected the principles of collective memory that Maurice Halbwachs first theorized in 1925 in *On Collective Memory* (*Les cadres sociaux de la mémoire*), but the undeniable connection of individual memory and group memory has stood the test of time: "One may say that the individual remembers by placing himself in the perspective of the group, but one may also affirm that the memory of the group realizes and manifests itself in individual memories" (40). A writer is compelled to simultaneously engage the collective and resist it.

Many of Yasuoka's early stories demand readings on multiple levels, as though in acknowledgement of this double task. These stories are clearly autobiographical, and are generally read as such; at the same time, they often serve as allegories for the nation, allegories that more often than not resist collective understandings of the period. This effort to integrate his narrative with others, even while resisting, is the story of his early career. This chapter begins by comparing stories of August 15, 1945, demonstrating that Yasuoka did not feel the epistemic break of the end of the war in the same way his contemporaries overwhelmingly did. Yasuoka's own experiences resist commonly accepted understandings of the war and postwar, and he wrote allegories of resistance into his largely autobiographical works. For the purposes of this discussion, we can look at the way Yasuoka used different stages of his life to call into question the collective memory of the nation, from the physical and temporal dissonance of his childhood, to the frustrated desire of his wartime adolescence, to the postwar feeling of "emasculation" in which the country as a whole has been brought to his level of despair. Although I have divided these stories into groups following a rough chronological order with regard to autobiography, as opposed to order of composition, the child becomes the man against a backdrop that, in Yasuoka's reckoning, stays the same the more it changes. The war is present long after it has ended in common reckoning; the absurdities of his own military experience, as related in the novel *Flight* (*Tonsō*, 1957), continue into the postwar. It is this that allows him to say that his mother's death over a decade later, depicted in his greatest work of fiction, *A View of the Sea* (*Kaihen no kōkei*, 1959), was yet another war death.

The Single Shōwa

To date, Yasuoka is one of only three Akutagawa Prize recipients to win for multiple works.[4] Moreover, whether the prize judges realized it or not—and they make no mention of it in their comments accompanying the announcement in *Bungei shunjū*—they awarded him the prize for one story set in wartime and one set in the postwar.[5] It would be easy to overlook the fact: Yasuoka's protagonists, at odds with authority and fumbling their way through the world, seem to hardly be aware themselves whether it is wartime or peacetime. But this is the very thing that makes the stories call into question the meanings of wartime and postwar that calcified during the Occupation and beyond.

In "Bad Company" ("Warui nakama," 1953), which takes place sometime after the "China Incident" (the egregious euphemism for the start of the Second Sino-Japanese War in 1937), the narrator meets the worldly Fujii Komahiko in French class, where Fujii is attempting to seduce the teacher. The narrator falls in with Fujii, who introduces him to two important customs: skipping out on restaurant tabs (*kuinige*) and visiting the red-light district. When the protagonist and his friends go their separate ways in the pleasure quarters, he is immediately picked up by a cop on the lookout for juveniles; his friends later "console" him by explaining that during the hour or so that he was hounded and beaten by policemen, they had been watching the entire time (YSS 1: 172).

Yasuoka's wartime protagonists are alienated to the second degree, from society at large and from their own peers. There is no means by which those opposed to the imperial order can resist it—the disintegration of the left and the overwhelming number of writers who have "converted" to the cause have proven that the system will brook no resistance.[6] Moreover, there is no means by which those who would resist can collaborate with others; the directionless resistance of the bad company, although certainly a product of their resistance to the state, soon turns on itself when the authorities come in pursuit.

Part of this may well be a function of Yasuoka's own personality. Nevertheless, it is striking how little has changed in the psychic space of his postwar alter egos. In "Gloomy Pleasures" ("Inki na tanoshimi," 1953) the postwar narrator is too ill to work a regular job. He receives two thousand yen a month in disability but is required to receive it in person. Fearing that he will appear too healthy, he constantly feels the need to play up the part. He has a particular dislike of the young woman, around eighteen years old, who watches him from her desk during the time his paperwork is being processed at the government office. On one perfect day, the young woman is not in the office, and he unexpectedly, perhaps mistakenly, receives a full three thousand yen from the clerk. It is the first spending money he has had in years, and he intends to spend it on luxuries, but a chance encounter in a sweets shop with the young woman from the city office derails his plans. Suddenly required to play the part of the invalid he is supposed to be, he soon loses the urge to spend his windfall.

Although the circumstances of Japan had changed drastically between the late 1930s and the early Occupation, the central narrative arc is strikingly similar: after an initial shady success—skipping out on paying a bill, getting away with an overpayment—a young man finds himself at the mercy of the authorities. Yasuoka made an early career out of stories about young men oppressed by political circumstance, and it is clear that he is rendering the same judgment but on very different authorities: the wartime police and the postwar bureaucracy.

This disregard for the differences between wartime and the Occupation is striking when compared to the overwhelming depiction of the break in postwar Japanese letters. In the common conception of things, on August 15, 1945, at noon, everything changed forever in Japan. The argument has been made that long before the emperor's speech was broadcast, the empire had been lost, the homeland laid to ruin, and soldiers and civilians alike scattered and stranded, living and dead, across a stretch of nearly three million square miles, from Manchuria and Sakhalin Island in the north to the Dutch East Indies and the Solomon Islands in the south, from Burma at its farthest point west to the Aleutian Islands and Marshall Islands at its farthest reaches in the east. Political, social, and economic histories have often engaged in an ongoing effort to acknowledge hidden continuities across the obvious, cataclysmic break of war's end: a political system with largely the same bureaucratic structure and a host of familiar figures, and their scions, both before and after the promulgation of the new constitution in 1947; deprivation and its attendant black-market supply lines that were in place before the end of the war; and collapses in class structure and gender roles that owed as much to the exigencies of wartime as to the subsequent efforts of the GHQ idealists.[7] Yet, despite these historical and social trends, the *lived* experience of the end of the war, as recorded in memoirs, diaries, and by those involved in the work of Japanese culture and letters, the contradictory moment at which the emperor implored his subjects to "endure the unendurable" was nearly universally recognized as the starting point of a new era.

However one characterizes the different schools of writers in the scrum of the early postwar, one theme dominates above all else: the end of the war as fundamental break. The recognition of the enormity of the moment was almost immediate. Nagai Kafū, who had actually been with Tanizaki Jun'ichirō on the morning of August 15, at Tanizaki's mountain retreat of Katsuyama in Okayama Prefecture, returned to his home in Okayama in the afternoon to find that the war had ended. He promptly gathered friends to celebrate (Keene 92). The magazine *Shinsei* acknowledged as early as the fall of 1945 that they were living in "historic days that divide the century" (Gluck, "Long Postwar" 65). For writers emerging from self-imposed silences, including Tanizaki, Kafū, and Ibuse Masuji, the end of World War II represented a chance to begin publishing anew.[8] The recognition of a break crosses all boundaries of school, theme, and literary "generation." Shin Nihon Bungakukai (New Japan Literary Society) leader Kurahara Korehito called in the *Tokyo shinbun* in November 1945 for a return to realism in narrative (Koschmann 43–44), while the less programmatic writers who organized around the magazine *Kindai bungaku* saw an opportunity for a more open, egalitarian system to emerge. In his essay in the first issue of *Bungaku jihyō*, Ara Masahito is downright messianic about this new age: "The stones will cry out again! At last, light has come to the dark night of despair that we had feared would never end. We have endured the miserable pain and humiliation of over a decade of the reactionaries' rule, and we rejoice in our souls at being able to stand in the light of freedom today, saying, 'Our lives have meaning'" (5).

August 15, 1945, looms large in stories of the war. A full catalog of responses to the war's end would be seemingly infinite, but we can get a sense of the overwhelming paradigm shift by examining just the treatment of the moment of defeat itself, when the emperor's voice was broadcast to the nation announcing Japan's acquiescence to the Potsdam Declaration's call for unconditional surrender.[9] In the modernist Ishikawa Jun's "The Legend of Gold" ("Ōgon densetsu," 1946), the narrator is onboard a train on August 15, 1945, when word about the announcement begins to spread among the passengers. Just then, an old man loses his balance and clunks his rucksack against the protagonist's chest, stopping his watch (Ishikawa 58). The fact of the postwar literally assaults the protagonist, and time symbolically stops at the moment of rupture. In Ibuse Masuji's "The Sutra Case" ("Kyōzutsu," 1946) an old man, Ryūsaburō, unearths a sutra case, and at that moment the impenetrable voice of the emperor is played over the radio. John Treat has pointed out that Ryūsaburō's response—to set down his burden—is in concert with "the rest of his countrymen" (*Pools of Water* 134). In Shimao Toshio's "This Time That Summer" ("Sono natsu no ima wa," 1967), the residents of O. Village in the Amami Islands just north of Okinawa are taking to the hills in fear of what the enemy will do when they land, and the protagonist, a lieutenant in the now-defeated army, is asked to reassure them. The narrator decides to read the Imperial Proclamation to them, assuming that part of the confusion stems from the fact that they haven't heard "an accurate version." In reading the emperor's speech to them, however, the narrator soon discovers just how confusing it is: "After hesitating for a minute trying to decide how to pronounce the first word, I proceeded, but all confidence had deserted me. [. . .][10] Unfortunately, I had had no forethought and was being swept away unprepared, ricocheting off difficult vocabulary words along the way" (Shimao 40). Only when he has finished the speech does he realize that he still needs to explain the very thing that the speech purports to verify but inexplicably does not say: "Japan has surrendered unconditionally to the Allied Armies" (41). The protagonist realizes it is no longer enough simply to repeat the words of the divine—to allow the divine to speak through him; he himself must offer an interpretation and take individual responsibility for it, and to a group of people who no longer feel the need to pay him any deference.

All of these individual responses to the precise moment of the war's end, the individual, local details—a watch stopping, an old man setting down his work, a man suddenly responsible for his own speech and actions—stand in metonymic relationships to national, universal feelings of rupture at the end of the war: that the flow of time has been interrupted, that work has been rendered meaningless, that hierarchies will change. The feeling lasted: Thirty years after the war, when Nosaka Akiyuki published a collection of twelve children's stories, each one was set on August 15, 1945 (Nosaka 2003).

Even for writers in Hiroshima and Nagasaki, August 15 holds a powerful meaning—as a capitulation that came too late to save them. For Hara Tamiki, August 15 functions as a moment of ultimate regret. On that day, Hara's narrator in *Summer Flowers* (*Natsu no hana*, 1947, 1949) hears the national anthem playing on the radio: "I went straight to the radio in the main house. I couldn't hear the voice of the newscaster distinctly, but the words 'cessation of hostilities' were unmistakable. Shocked so deeply I couldn't sit still, I went outside again and set off for the hospital. At the entrance to the hospital, Seiji was still waiting, a vacant look on his face. On seeing him, I said: 'What a pity! The war's over, but . . .' If only the war had ended a little sooner—these words became a common refrain thereafter" (Minear 62).

Ōta Yōko's narrator in *City of Corpses* (*Shikabane no machi*, 1948) imagines that the August 15 radio broadcast will expand on a theme found in the newspapers on August 14: that Japan will carry on despite the Soviet Union's entrance into the war. The radio at the doctor's office where they intend to listen to it is broken, but the bigger impediment is life in the wake of the bombing of Hiroshima: "I was so overwhelmed I even forgot the announcement about the important broadcast, and having lost track of its importance I could think of nothing but what was before my eyes. In addition to the people I saw every day, there were the new patients who were leaving Hiroshima and coming here in a steady stream" (Minear 239). The information comes to them third-hand, via the doctor's wife, who announces, "They say Japan's capitulated! The children heard it on the two o'clock broadcast" (240). The narrator wonders if Japan has agreed to terms "[t]he same as Germany's" (240).

Yasuoka resists this master narrative. Not out of respect for the emperor or the undying nation—not that he has particularly spoken out against either—but out of a sense of singular, individual experience that does not align with the agreed-upon history of wartime and postwar Japan. In "The Medal" ("Kunshō," 1953), his protagonist doesn't believe the emperor:

> For as long as I could remember, the war had determined everything in my life. So when I heard the Emperor's speech, my first instinct was not to believe him. [...] In fact, I had a theory after the speech that the world would plunge even deeper into war, and so the next day I headed to where my mother had taken refuge from the war on Mount Minobu. There wasn't anything to eat there, but there also wasn't any worry the enemy would come there, either. (YSS 1: 230–31)

In *My Shōwa History*, Yasuoka offers his reaction to the actual moment of the emperor's speech; it is quite similar to the fictionalized version. Having been repatriated earlier in the year, he is on a train at midday on August 15, 1945, heading from his family's temporary lodgings in the countryside back into the bombed-out Tokyo, where he moves from friend's house to friend's house, his own home having been destroyed in the firebombing. Along the way, at noon, the train stops at a station, and the passengers file onto the platform; the station loudspeaker crackles to life, and everyone gathers around it to hear the emperor announce Japan's surrender.

> It was the first time we were hearing the Emperor's voice, but there was a great deal of static, so it was very difficult to understand. All I understood

was that he was announcing the end of the war, but the crowd around me was impatient. Suddenly, a baby was bawling somewhere behind me, and the midsummer sun beating down directly on our heads was starting to become unbearably hot. The important broadcast was still going on, but the mother, clutching her baby, went back on the train. And I did the same thing. (BSS 1: 253)

Yasuoka isn't interested in the moment that defined the end of the war for millions around the world. In Yasuoka's telling, the war ends for him not with the noon broadcast of the emperor's speech, but rather, about an hour later, at 1:00 p.m. Yasuoka slips some money to an old man in the burned-out area in front of Shinjuku Station, which is swarming with homeless people and swimming in excrement. The man gives him real cigarettes, and Yasuoka decides that if this old guy can hawk rationed cigarettes in the middle of the day in front of Shinjuku Station without fear of punishment, then at *this* moment the war is truly over (264). Yet from "The Medal," we can assume that even this sense of an ending was only provisional for Yasuoka.

This complete refusal to acknowledge fundamental political change was a hallmark of the first decade or so of Yasuoka's career. Yasuoka continued to write short stories at a fairly rapid pace throughout the rest of the 1950s and into the 1960s. He alternated between those set in the long wartime (often starring an alter ego named Juntarō) and those set after the war, further proof that for Yasuoka it was all part of the same continuum. Regardless of setting, the war is everywhere in Yasuoka's work, and the postwar is merely its continuation by other means. In "Humid Morning" ("Mushiatsui asa," 1961), set in wartime, the protagonist Juntarō watches children outside the window being made to do calisthenics:

"One-two, three-four, one-two, three-four!"
The tempo of the march gradually increased, and the children in their white shirts sped up their actions to match it. *Oh, when the children grow up, will they do what we are doing?*
Juntarō rested his head on his arms on the windowsill, and absently homed in on the voice giving commands as it echoed up toward him. (YSS 3: 317)

Although the schoolchildren are doing calisthenics in much the same way people of all ages in Japan continue to do them today, it meant something different during wartime, and in Juntarō's mind, of course, the children are being militarized in a way that he has resisted. The story resonates in part because it was written after the war. Juntarō has been gifted with prescience; he seems to know that his generation—for all of their resistance—will go off to war, and he hopes that the children he is watching will be spared that experience. It is an elegy for war set in a time before war comes to the main character. Like Tanizaki's *The Makioka Sisters* (*Sasameyuki*, 1943–1948), a story of prewar Osaka rendered elegiac for the chasm that separates the elegant world it depicts and the obliteration its readership knows is coming for it, Yasuoka's story gains rhetorical force from the circumstances of its publication. Ken Ito has argued that *The Makioka Sisters* is one of those texts that "derive their significance from their relationship both to time itself and to their times": "By contrasting the sisters' youthfulness, their momentary immunity from time, against the insistent pace of history, Tanizaki foreshadows the tragic and inevitable loss" (Ito 192, 193). Unlike Tanizaki's narrative, however, the story of Yasuoka's Juntarō betrays an awareness of where the militarization will lead them, an awareness, Yasuoka has argued, the nation as a whole shared; the gulf that divides prewar and postwar Japan is effaced by his double consciousness.

The narrator of "Jingle Bells" ("Jinguru beru," 1951), set in the early postwar, marches across the same gulf, in the opposite direction. The narrator crosses Tokyo by train, starting at Tamagawa-en (present-day Tamagawa Station) in the west of the city and heading toward Mitsukoshi-mae, where a woman named Mitsuko waits for him; through a combination of train breakdowns and his own lethargy, it becomes obvious that he won't make it on time. As he walks to the station, "Jingle Bells" starts to play over a radio, and he marches to its beat just as he marched in the army during the war. To the narrator, there is very little difference between the oppression he felt during his time in the Imperial Army and the oppression he feels under the Allied Occupation. The song is ubiquitous; he hears it again on the crowded train, perhaps coming from a radio at a coffee shop. It is stuck in his head as he navigates Shibuya station. It plays over a loudspeaker as he walks from Mitsukoshi-mae, where his date has apparently given up on him, to Tokyo Station. The next day, Mitsuko asks the narrator over for ice cream, if he can get to Meguro; he sets off all over again, and once again "Jingle Bells" plays in his head. Earlier he had heard a version of "Jingle Bells" in which the singer seemed to be imitating a black jazz singer—it sounded "just like the voice of one of those people born into slavery" (YSS 1: 37). Here, marching in the rain, he imagines himself a reindeer tied to St. Nicholas's sleigh, asking for a little rest. The constraints that he feels—piped-in American culture, life on the margins in postwar Tokyo—are at once tied to his failure to connect with Mitsuko and partially the result of his own literal inability to navigate the confusion of Occupied Japan. The homophony of the name of the woman he is trying to locate, "Mitsuko," and the location he is trying to reach, "Mitsukoshi-mae" (literally "in front of Mitsukoshi," named for the great department store), is probably no coincidence. If the wartime narrator of "Humid Morning" looks down at the children and imagines himself to be old before his time, the narrator of "Jingle Bells" reverts to being a child of sorts, trapped under the cruel gaze of a Santa Claus who bears more than a passing resemblance to the wartime Japanese military authorities: he is sadistic, racist, ubiquitous. The space of wartime has been collapsed into the postwar.

Physical and Temporal Dislocation

In all of these stories, the narrators are out of sorts with the world around them, both temporally and spatially. Movement is a constant of life for them, and happiness—or at least, satisfaction—lies at a distance from the masses: in a red-light district across the river, at a government office in downtown Yokohama, down in a schoolyard the narrator sees from his window, and, in "Jingle Bells," always somewhere *other* than where the narrator currently is within the frenzied, chaotic terrain of postwar Tokyo. All of these physical spaces are also layered with temporal dimensions: prostitutes succor the boys for only a set period of time in "Bad Company" and other stories, disability payments mark the passing months in "Gloomy Pleasures," and the boy who has grown up too soon in "Humid Morning" becomes the man who reverts to boyhood in "Jingle Bells." In Yasuoka's stories, time is space, and space is time, and the interaction between the two merits discussion for the ways the two operate in conjunction to isolate his narrators.

In *Re-Inventing Japan: Time, Space, Nation*, Tessa Morris-Suzuki explores the relationship of time and space in the construction of a Japanese center and periphery. In her reading of history, premodern conceptions of Ryūkyū and Ainu territories as spatial "frontiers" were displaced by modern temporal conceptions of Okinawan and Ainu people as Japanese "marooned in some earlier phase of national history": "The modern transfer of difference from the dimension of space to the dimension of time was closely linked to the emerging sense of ethnicity as the chief construction of nationhood" (Morris-Suzuki 31, 32). The geographer David Harvey sees a profound connection between space and time in the construction of modernity; he has demonstrated the ways that ever-increasing speed in communications and travel diminished the sense of the saliency of space following the Industrial Revolution (Harvey 240–59). In the Japanese postwar, however, notions of linear, progressive time and space—the very Enlightenment project itself—are called into question. In his essay "The Double-Layered Occupation" ("Senryō no nijū kōzō"), Isoda Kōichi discusses a passage from Dazai Osamu's "Winter Fireworks" ("Fuyu no hanabi," 1946) that was censored by the Occupation: "The country of Japan is occupied from one corner to another, and we are all, every single one of us, captives" (Isoda 38). It is clear what Japan's new authorities would find offensive in Dazai's text, but Isoda points to a parallel that Dazai perhaps did not have in mind:

> Dazai's formula, that occupation is tantamount to captivity, belongs to 1946. But I can perhaps be forgiven—for the sake of my argument [*sagyō kasetsu*, literally "working hypothesis"]—for taking the liberty of reading this passage through the lens of the ten years of history prior to its composition. Not only did Dazai have the experiences of participating in prewar left-wing movements and surrendering to the police, to those people, "being arrested" was nothing other than "being taken captive," and the break-up of their movement was to them a kind of war defeat. Accordingly, we can conceive of 1935–1945 Japan as being an era in which "Japan was occupied from one corner to another" and the people, "every single one of them, were captives"—to the Imperial Japanese Army and Navy (38).

For Isoda, writing from a long-postwar, long-Security-Treaty position, the situation of wartime is echoed in the situation of the postwar. This essay and the others Isoda wrote for *Shinchō* in 1981 and 1982 were collected in a volume entitled *The Space of Postwar History* (*Sengoshi no kūkan*, 1983). Like the English word "space," the Japanese *kūkan* can delineate both physical and temporal terrain (and in Japanese academic writing, it is often used in titles to signify exactly nothing). Although he never directly problematizes it, the space of occupation for Isoda extends both physically—"from one corner to another" (*sumi kara sumi made*) of Japan—and temporally, in the connection he draws between wartime "occupation" and postwar Occupation. The nexus of time and space pulls Isoda's conceptualization away from Dazai and toward something more universal in the Japanese wartime and postwar experience.

All of these frameworks operate on the level of the nation-state, and naturally focus on a rupture between present and past: for Morris-Suzuki, the double displacement of Okinawan and Ainu cultures; for Harvey, the advent of the Industrial Revolution and modern communications and transportation; and for Isoda, the end of the war. The war was an exception to the modern impetus toward crossing boundaries and borders; the war set limits on the movements of people in the form of blockades and frontlines, even as the movement of troops and materiel created a new, revised impetus to build new and faster routes to previously distant places around the Pacific and occupied parts of the continent. As the United States and Europe grew impossibly distant, places such as Palau, Burma, and much of China drew unexpectedly closer. After the war ended, narratives both historical and fictional emphasized efforts to return to what had become the everyday of the modern; displaced people returned to cities to start again, writers and editors rushed to create new publications and alliances, families on the home front searched lists of returning soldiers for loved ones.

The construction of the new social order occupies a central place in postwar narratives, from novels such as Dazai's *The Setting Sun* (*Shayō*, 1947), Osaragi Jirō's *The Homecoming* (*Kikyō*, 1949), and Hayashi Fumiko's *Floating Clouds* (*Ukigumo*, 1951) to films such as Kinoshita Keisuke's *Morning for the Osone Family* (*Ōsone-ke no ashita*, 1946) and the three-part *What Is Your Name?* (*Kimi no na wa*, dir. Ōba Hideo, 1953–1954). The war operates as a drag on these characters, pulling them back in time and away in physical distance. The goal, always, is to find a way past the war. Characters in postwar literature who did not manage to relocate physically and temporally in the social order were not long for postwar Japan. In Dazai's *Setting Sun*, the son Naoji surrenders to a life of dissipation and commits suicide, in part because he is unable to adjust to a leveling of class distinctions in the postwar. In Takeyama Michio's *Harp of Burma* (*Biruma no tategoto*, 1946), the deep-feeling Mizushima refuses to return to Japan with his fellow troops, preferring instead to stay behind in Burma to bury the dead.

The unbroken Shōwa of Yasuoka's fiction, on the other hand, is a function of radical individuality, of a consciousness that is socially ostracized and at odds with the spirit of the age, whatever the age. Yasuoka's protagonists are dislocated in space and time, but if the war has anything to do with it, it is perhaps a result not of rupture but of the blurring of wartime and postwar. For Yasuoka's protagonists, the isolation of the postwar has little to do with a failure to adjust to a new order. The direct relationship between the mutually ever-diminishing time and space in David Harvey's description of modernity is gone. For Harvey, a sense of space is bound to a specific conception of time, and when one is attenuated, the other inevitably collapses with it. In Yasuoka's wartime and postwar Japan, however, one finds a broken framework; just as the narrators find themselves isolated spatially from their peers, they are isolated temporally as well. The example par excellence of this may be Yasuoka's somewhat rambling early short story "Homework" ("Shukudai," 1952, in YSS, vol. 1). The narrator skips school to spend time by himself in the Aoyama cemetery, spreading out his books on the grave markers. He is physically isolated, but the poignant way he finds solace among the dead casts him temporally away from the living as well. His sense of time is withered to the point that he does not understand the ramifications of neglecting his summer homework until the night before it is due.

Yasuoka's schoolboy protagonists never learn. In "Handstand" ("Sakadachi," 1954), the narrator has been out of middle school for two years and is struggling to get a spot in a higher school. He goes on a summer hike with young people his own age who have entered various higher schools and colleges, but the other children soon leave him behind. A girl has been dropped from the pack with him, and as the two of them walk together, the narrator tells her his only skill: he can walk sixty meters on his hands. They catch up to the others and have a wonderful afternoon, during which the girl hangs upside down from a tree—here appears to be someone who is also at her best when she is literally acting contrary to the crowd. Months later, in the fall, the narrator thinks he spots her in Ueno Park. He does a handstand on the grass, thinking that if she sees someone doing a handstand she will immediately know it is him. Instead, like generations of acts in Ueno Park before and after him, he draws a crowd that treats him as a performer. "I looked wildly across the mass of people, which appeared to be suspended upside down" (YSS 1: 356). The relationship between the narrator and his peers begins as a rather straightforward gesture: he and the girl he meets are out of step, literally and metaphorically, behind the other students and struggling to catch up. The ending moves in a different direction, literally: the narrator stands on his head, an indication that his alienation is something more than linear, but the reversal makes everyone else appear to be upside down. From being behind them, he shifts to being deliberately at odds with them. He is in despair, but the action of moving in an oblique direction is also his sole source of liberation. The child protagonist of Yasuoka's 1972 "Where the Ball Went" ("Tama no yukue") is even more removed from society at the story's conclusion, alone in a tree surrounded by his mother and a gang of baseball players who have eased him off of the team but kept his equipment (YSS 4: 161–63).

As the war grows ever more dire, the already tenuous relation of time to space for Yasuoka's protagonists becomes increasingly contradictory, paradoxical. In "Same Old, Same Old" ("Ai mo kawarazu," 1959), the narrator goes out carousing with friends the night before an entrance exam. When a young woman in whom his friend Gotō had been interested loudly spurns his quiet advances such that all of his friends hear, he turns it into a joke and wrestles her for a kiss in front of them. The next day, exhausted and unable to think his way through the test problems, he walks out in the middle of the exam, dooming himself to another year off track educationally. His reasoning for how things have come to this pass is surprising:

He himself couldn't even explain what he had done. . . . But everything seemed to come out of a feeling of responsibility. Meaning, out of a sense of duty to his friends, he had gone out on the town last night. And caught between his obligations to the woman and his loyalty to Gotō, he had done those things. Out of responsibility to his mother he had gone to the test, and out of obligation to the proctor he had tried to answer the questions, but again out of duty to his friends he had thrown it all away halfway through and walked out of the exam. (YSS 3: 106)

He imagines that his mother will be outraged again, but his cousin tells him that he is pretty sure she is pleased he is limbo: "Deep down, your mother is happy that you're failing year after year. Because if you become a college student, it'll mean that she's an old lady, whether she likes it or not" (114). He is growing older without growing up, converging with his mother's generation, perhaps with all of the Oedipal distress that portends, via a strange sense of duty that compels him to treat everything serious as a farce.

In a number of stories set in wartime, the dissonance between Yasuoka's protagonists and the world around them appears to be a commentary not only on life during wartime, but also on the way wartime is remembered—namely, the furious misdirection of early postwar Japanese culture that glossed over the degree to which nearly everyone was complicit in the war effort. In "Music Class" ("Ongaku no jugyō," 1955), the schoolboy narrator finds reason to overcome his isolation: He is in love with Ōtama Yuriko, the music teacher at his elementary school in Tokyo. Until he met her, he had no sense that there was any shame in not doing one's homework and being forced by his teachers to stand in the hallway; now, he keeps thinking of excuses for what he is doing out there when she walks by (YSS 2: 97). His love for Miss Ōtama is out of the ordinary, but so is she: She has her students sing a French song that isn't in the government textbook, one that probably would have been banned a few years later. For his final exam in the music class, he is required to sing the French song alone. Despite his long hours of practicing, he misses all of the notes, is hounded by Ōtama for the rest of the hour to sing high notes he cannot possibly hit, and is given the only C (*hei*) of his lower-school academic career (YSS 2: 107). Again, the narrator finds his identity in spatial and temporal isolation—he stands alone without feeling shame, and the object of his affection is well out of his age range.

At first blush, the story would seem elegiac: Miss Ōtama is teaching non-sanctioned material, and French itself will fall out of favor starting with the ban on French films in December 1937. She is an individual riding against the wave of the times, and in that sense, to readers in 1955 she may have conjured up images of the teacher Miss Ōishi in Tsuboi Sakae's sentimental novel *Twenty-Four Eyes* (*Nijūshi no hitomi*, 1952). Miss Ōishi is a modern woman; she rides a bicycle around town, she sings incessantly, and she does not hide her disapproval of the war effort. In the postwar "liberal humanist" rewriting of wartime history, she is a paragon of the passive, suffering masses; for James J. Orr, Tsuboi's novel "offers a prime example of Japanese innocents victimized by the vast anonymous forces of war and serves as a model for the artistic foundations for victim mythologies" (107).

Kinoshita Keisuke's enormously popular film version of the story was released in 1954, a year before this story's publication, and it is not difficult to imagine that Yasuoka is responding at least in part to the wave of sentimentality about individualistic, wartime teachers. Yasuoka's narrator, although he longs for his teacher's affection, holds *her* responsible for the victimization he feels. What Miss Ōtama likely considers to be good pedagogy Yasuoka's narrator takes with the grudge of a spurned lover, deciding, "the people in this world who are closest to being madmen are neither politicians, nor theologians, nor dancers, but actually musicians" (YSS 2: 92). Perhaps readers are being reminded that teachers such as Tsuboi's gently subversive, nurturing Miss Ōishi are romantic notions more easily found in popular fiction and film than in the reality through which Yasuoka's generation lived.

The pathos of Yasuoka's characters' desire to find something to feel sentimental about in wartime is also at the heart of "A Room in Tsukiji" ("Tsukiji Odawara-chō," 1953). The protagonist and his friends dream of returning to the Edo period, free of the entire modern trajectory of Japan. "There is no beauty left in our era," the narrator's friend Komai mourns. "If you want to live the aesthetic life, first you need to surround yourself with the mores of the Tokugawa Period or earlier" (YSS 1: 247). As we have seen elsewhere, a change in space is tantamount to a change in time, and the boys decide to look for Tokugawa Japan in the *shitamachi*; they take up residence in various houses near one another in the low city. The author settles in with a family in Tsukiji Odawara-chō, but his attempts to render his lifestyle an Edo one are stymied by the basic reality of his situation: He lives in a modern house built since the beginning of the war with China, and the family insists on displaying calligraphy by Tōgō Heihachirō, the commander-in-chief of the Imperial Japanese Navy during one of the defining moments of Japanese modernity, the Russo-Japanese War.

The boys' exercise in aestheticism comes to an ugly end—they are covered in bedbug bites from their "pure" Edo lodgings, and their attempt to blackmail a woman by mail comes to naught when she cannot understand the letter the narrator has painstakingly and dreamily written in the almost-extinct *sōrōbun* literary style. When they finally see an actual remnant of the pre-industrial past, a single firefly, the narrator gets as far as "Ah, the Edo Period—" before stopping himself (YSS 1: 263). The Edo Period is long gone, he decides, even as he wonders what the firefly is doing in this modern urban setting. Here again, a notion of the future may intrude on the world of the story. The flicker of light signifies the past for these boys, not simply because the natural environment has disappeared as the city has grown, but also because the lights of Japanese cities were extinguished at night to protect from air raids. Blackout drills began as early as 1933 in Tokyo (Daniels 120). The illuminated city, the past that they hold in such high regard, is so long gone to them that it may as well be the Edo Period. What will become of Tokyo the boys cannot possibly imagine, but here again, the story is an ironic elegy that may have brought its original readers back to the present: Odawara-chō actually survived the various waves of firebombing—which destroyed large swaths of Tokyo all around it—completely intact,[11] and the adjacent Tsukiji Fish Market would go on to serve as an American distribution hub during the Occupation (Bestor 117).[12] The Odawara-chō (now merged with Tsukiji) that Yasuoka sought out in wartime was too new to provide him the solace he was looking for; by the time of writing, it could have acquired the patina of age and the cache of being one of the few portions of eastern Tokyo that survived the war intact, but probably not, given its location. Yasuoka's narrative of disjointed dreaming warns against any inchoate romanticism about wartime "Old Tokyo."

The physical and temporal isolation of childhood never end, for author or his protagonists. Even adult protagonists can quickly be brought back to their hapless youths. In "The Fortune Teller" ("Uranaishi," 1954, in YSS, vol. 1), the narrator visits a fortune-teller in Shinjuku who tells him he will have a long life and find love, but he will ultimately have bad luck. His friend Yamano is out drinking with a woman named Kurihara while her husband the judo master is away. Yamano and Kurihara engage in a wild flirtation, but the narrator, partly to test the fortune-teller, outlasts Yamano and ends up being the one to escort her home. They arrive to find the woman's husband at home; she is quick-thinking enough to introduce him as an earnest student who has walked her home, even though the narrator is actually over thirty. The husband graciously allows the "student" to spend the night. They lay out bedding for him in the middle of their own, and he sleeps between them like a child between his parents, a would-be threat to the family who is not recognized as such, or even as an adult. The middle-aged narrator on a trip to North America in "Fly, Tomahawk!" ("Hashire tomahōku," 1972) is as adrift as the protagonists of "Handstand" or "Where the Ball Went." At the end of the story, he is left desperately hanging on when the aging horse he has been ambling along on decides to live up to its name for a wild stretch back to the ranch, taking him away from companions and guide (YSS 4:

146). Yasuoka's stories glide across space and through time, always whirling away from the hapless figure at the center.

Wartime Desire and the Body Politic

On a practical level, it makes perfect sense that Occupation-period Japanese literature was obsessed with the body; one imagines the horizon for possible subjects shrank to one's immediate physical survival for any number of writers in Japan in the late 1940s. At the same time, however, these works reveal an intellectual class in open revolt against the state. In his study of early postwar Japanese literature, Douglas Slaymaker finds its focus on "the body, carnality, and sexuality" to be inherently political "because it defies the primacy of the national body," the wartime body politic (*kokutai*) that placed the emperor at the head (*The Body* 11). The writer best known for the Occupation-era "literature of the flesh" (*nikutai bungaku*), Tamura Taijirō, saw his writing as "a subversive political agenda to overturn the collective and still-resonant *kokutai*" (Slaymaker, *The Body* 44). The war had produced a nation more concerned with an abstract "body politic" than with the actual bodies of its constituent citizens; for Yoshikuni Igarashi, the proliferation of images of the body in the Japanese postwar "must be read against the official narrative's impulse to construct an ahistorical body" (14).

Yasuoka's stories of adolescent boys during the war represent a contrapuntal melody to postwar *nikutai bungaku*, an ex post facto attempt to reconsider the relationship of the individual body to the body politic in wartime. There is no freedom from the body for Yasuoka's wartime protagonists. His characters are victimized, denied individual agency, and about to be placed into the service of the emperor, but at the same time, they are made to represent wartime Japan. Their individual plights serve as metaphors for the plight of wartime Japan. Far from being forced to grow up too soon—a near-universal trope of stories set in wartime—his protagonists are trapped in a perpetual state of adolescent unrequited desire, with all of the sexual tension that entails. Their longings are complicated by the stunting forces of their mothers and the authorities, and by their own feelings of responsibility toward both. Unlike Yasuoka's idol Nagai Kafū's hedonism-as-escape, an image of resistance that brought him great fame (and fortune) in the postwar, Yasuoka's wartime protagonists often find their relationships to both sex and the state to be similarly oppressive and mutually entangled.[13]

In "Thick the New Leaves" ("Aoba Shigereru," 1958), Abe Juntarō has just failed his higher-school entrance exams for the fourth year in a row, this time to Z. University.[14] In the 1930s, the tightest bottleneck in the Japanese education system lay between middle schools and higher schools. For financial reasons, the vast majority of elementary-school students would not go on to middle school, or even attempt to. Due to this self-selection, over half of students attempting to continue their studies from elementary school to middle school were accepted, but the same did not hold true for the next level of testing: fewer than 8 percent of middle-school students were able to enter a higher school, and only 4 percent gained admission to the numbered higher schools that provided the only avenue to study at the imperial universities and thus to the highest class of jobs that drew exclusively from the top public universities (Keenleyside 193, 209). Middle-school students unable to access higher schools had the option of matriculating directly at one of the less competitive private universities.[15] Juntarō's mother, convinced he would be able to pass a private-school exam, if not a public higher-school one, has prematurely had a uniform for Z. University made for him. To further exacerbate the situation, his cousin five years younger than him has been admitted to a higher school. As in "Same Old, Same Old," the protagonist's testing inadequacies are compounded by his perceived sexual inadequacies. "Thick the New Leaves" is carefully crafted, matching sexual embarrassment for educational humiliation throughout: Juntarō dreams of having the maid crawl into bed with him, but instead she is the one who—somewhat gleefully—brings him the postcard announcing his rejection from Z. For the first time in years, he is able to go down the hall to the facilities without having to worry about hiding a morning erection; the testing defeat has rendered him flaccid. To celebrate signing up for a cram school that will keep them out of the draft another year, he and his friends Yamada and Takagi go to a café; a woman at the door lures customers in, but once inside they find they can't talk to her. Juntarō is reminded of the maid bringing him the rejection postcard and determines that "he had fallen into the same trap as all of the customers around him, who all seemed to be held in confinement" (YSS 2: 413–14). The twinning of sexual and institutional failings appears to reach a spectacular (anti-)climax at the end of the narrative. Juntarō and his friends apply for positions in the Navy Accounting Bureau, an enlistment that would allow them to evade front-line action as well as give them a slightly more desirable position in the military hierarchy. As part of the application, they are required to submit "undressed full body" photos of themselves (YSS 2: 426); in the photo, "the thing in his crotch was visible through his fresh underwear, squeezed and sadly contorted" (YSS 2: 428). The bullish Navy examiner mocks him, and after he fails the exam he spitefully heads for a red-light district, Tamanoi. There the prostitute chides him for dilly-dallying—"Why aren't you taking your pants off? Come on, them and your underwear, too. Chop chop"—and he is surprised to find that she reminds him of the military examiner (YSS 2: 434).

Van Gessel offers a compelling close reading of "Thick the New Leaves," together with a number of other Yasuoka works, as being primarily about the protagonist's relationship with his mother; Juntarō "is being pulled in many directions at once, but consistently the strongest attraction comes from within the home" (87). At the same time, it is difficult to read the story without seeing the Navy examiner and the prostitute as occupying the same space; the dread Juntarō feels about his own sexual inadequacies is duplicated by the dread he feels about his physical inadequacies. By extension, his personal dread is overlaid with the dread that wartime Japan felt collectively. There was no one who thought the war could be won, Yasuoka claims in *My Shōwa History*; collective memory of the war has effaced the intuitive understanding immediately following Pearl Harbor, among top brass and ordinary people alike, that declaring war on the United States was a breathtakingly foolish endeavor (BSS 1: 167–68).

The feeling of wartime isolation is perhaps visible in the fact that what Juntarō fears more than anything else is to be *seen*. Sharalyn Orbaugh has described the intrusion of both the wartime and Occupation authorities into personal life as a "panoptic model of power" in the Foucaultian sense—both groups worked to be all-seeing and all-knowing (*Japanese Fiction*, 93). Here, although he has managed to escape state detection and give further range to his desires than the narrator of "Bad Company" does, Juntarō falls victim to another gaze: that of the brisk prostitute. He is far less interested in consummating his relationship with her than he is in reversing the power dynamic between the gazer and the gazed that has put him at both her mercy and the state's. The prostitute lets him look at her for a while, reversing the dynamic of the gaze and bringing him a sense of temporary relief.

The relationship between protagonist, mother, and unrelated older woman is most clearly delineated in "The Pawnbroker's Wife" ("Shichiya no nyōbō," 1960), one of Yasuoka's underappreciated masterpieces and one of the great short stories of postwar Japanese literature. The teenaged narrator is spending what he knows to be his last months of freedom before being drafted visiting the licensed quarters:

> My mother pretended not to have any idea what I was up to when I went out. Not about my skipping school to head over to friends' boarding houses, where we spent our time writing all kinds of strange things, nor about our overnight visits to Yoshiwara and Tamanoi, which we referred to as "going on trips" . . . And yet, for some reason, she would do things like go through my scattered drawers, pull out something incriminating when I

wasn't around, and with nary a change in her expression leave it sitting out somewhere I was sure to see it. I could never be exactly sure with how much knowledge she was doing this. (YSS 3: 208)

It is impossible for him to determine whether his mother is actually scolding him or he is projecting onto his relationship with her his feelings of guilt for visiting the pleasure quarters. But his relationships with the older prostitutes and his own mother are commingled; in spite, and in confusion, the narrator decides to hock a good winter coat to the local pawnshop. Inside, a woman without makeup sits facing the door. She refers to the burly pawnbroker as "Father" (*otōsan*), which a married Japanese woman would naturally call her husband when they have children, but it is clear to him that this is no ordinary housewife. Then as now, one could roughly calculate a woman's age from the color of the kimono she wore, from bright colors when she is young to more demure hues for older women. The narrator is stumped by her clothes: "Hers was a plainer kimono than even the kimono my mother wore, which itself was probably too plain for a woman of her age. I was sure that 'Father' wasn't her own father. But she didn't seem to be the married lady of the house in any normal sense of the term" (YSS 3: 210–11). Later the woman admits that a venereal disease had prevented her from having children, leading the narrator to wonder if she is a former geisha and the bearish man her patron. At least three destabilizing elements are at play here: the ambiguity of the language as it comes to the use of *otōsan* for father/husband; the fact that his own mother is literally cloaked in ambiguity herself, thus rendering comparison difficult or impossible; and the unmentioned fact that, due to the exigencies of the war, the rules governing clothing designs tended toward the notion of "self-restraint," i.e., duller, darker colors.

One can read this story as the narrative of a boy's transferral of feelings from his mother to an unrelated older woman.[16] But there is a second doubling in the story. The war enters its late stages, and students around the narrator are drafted left and right. The pawnbroker's wife asks him to sort some books that a student has left behind, and the narrator finds himself imagining what sort of person would have collected these books:

Never reading them, never selling them, just accruing interest, and in order to pay it off always buying another volume, consigning it to the pawnshop, and using that money to buy yet another volume, over and over. I couldn't help but feel a kind of closeness to him all of a sudden. My whole body seemed to be caught up by a vexing illusion: that this boy who had never done anything other than this mechanical repetition, who had never *thought* to do anything else, was sitting right across from me in this chicken-wire storeroom. (YSS 3: 217)

The drafted boy is his doppelgänger, one who has mechanically come to the same pawnshop over and over again to entrust the fragments of his library, of a future that will never exist in which he has both the money to liberate his books and the time to read them. In *My Shōwa History*, it was Yasuoka himself who could not imagine life not surrounded by his books (BSS 1: 211–12). Yasuoka has written eloquently of what the young men of his generation did before they were drafted, of the "mechanical repetition" with which they attempted to compress their everyday lives into the time they had left—collecting books, writing novels, pursuing women (BSS 1: 196–204). As a symbol, the pawnshop represents the futility of the ways in which the mass of men lead their lives of quiet despair; as a business, it is a repetition of exchanges in which the customer must always commit more money to the process just to stay even on his accounts.

In this sense, the drafted boy's actions bear a synechdochic relationship to the draft that took him away; the Japanese army at this point was throwing the living after the dead, increasing the numbers in an effort simply to hold even. The narrator's visits to this mysterious woman stand in for the whole of his own act of mechanical repetition—his increasing visits to the prostitutes in Yoshiwara and Tamanoi. When the narrator realizes that the older woman has feelings for him, and the die is cast that will result in a single night of passion between the two, he feels himself slip free of "the illusion of this 'repetition'" that had entangled him (YSS 3: 218).

The state's mass consignment of its youth to the vagaries of war and the boy's equally desperate individual search for affection cross paths at the end of the story. He returns home expecting to be scolded for having been out so late at the pawnshop, but his mother is distraught for a different reason: his draft card has arrived, rendering up his individual experience to the war. The woman shows up at his house bearing a gift: the coat he had originally consigned to her. "So that you don't catch a cold along the way," she says, before adding, "And, maybe I shouldn't say this, but consider the rest of it to be a parting gift from me" (YSS 3: 221). "The rest of it" (*ano hō*) goes unnamed, deliberately so. One imagines that she is speaking about the remainder of the money owed on the coat, but one can just as easily imagine the narrator taking it to mean their single night of passion. His individual experience with her is threatened by the possibility that it is nothing more than a transaction, a contribution to the war effort (in whose name she has come to see him, after all), another act of "mechanical repetition" for them both. In this way, the state controls not only the fact of their relationship but also the meaning of it. The one thing he most wants to know—was it love or simply charity?—is subsumed by Imperial Japan.

Postwar "Emasculation" and National Allegory

Immediately following the war, with millions of adult males missing in action or stranded overseas and millions of women responsible for navigating households through the physical and societal ruins of the postwar, the tropes of absent men and longsuffering women became powerful elements in Japanese creative culture. The melodramatic "mother films" (*hahamono*) of the late 1940s and early 1950s depicted an absent father and a suffering mother, who perform metonymic roles for the nation; among the most notable of these is Kinoshita Keisuke's *A Japanese Tragedy* (*Nihon no higeki*, 1953), in which the children turn their backs on their single, self-sacrificing mother as a means of moving forward into the postwar. As men returned home, emasculation narratives flourished. Kurosawa Akira's film *Stray Dog* (*Norainu*, 1949) is ostensibly about a young detective searching for his stolen gun, a plot that can easily be read as a returned soldier searching for his manhood, as Mitsuhiro Yoshimoto has argued. The gun may be a phallic symbol, but the detective is obsessed with the man who stole his gun, an ex-soldier like himself; Yoshimoto argues that the perpetrator "appears as a return of the repressed, something many Japanese simply wanted to forget, and what the official discourse tried to erase" (178). Even in this film about one man searching for another, the search hinges on the liminality of their very existence.

Men continue to be demeaned in narratives of the war defeat throughout the 1950s. The middle-aged male English teachers in Kojima Nobuo's "American School" ("Amerikan sukūru," 1954, in Hibbett, *Contemporary* 119–44) are literally left by the wayside when they are forced to walk to an American base school and their female colleague is plied with cheese and chocolate by soldiers passing by in a jeep; the men are either incapable of carrying on conversations in English or ignored when they try, and they are made to feel like children by the base teachers. Despite the raucous, dark comedy at play in the work, it represents no less an incisive critique of Japanese masculinity than an entire genre of war novels that proliferated after the defeat. James J. Orr has detailed how Gomikawa Junpei's long novel *The Human Condition* (*Ningen no jōken*, 1956–1958) and Kobayashi Masaki's trilogy of films based on it (1959–1961) attempted to depict a new type of human (*ningen*) as opposed to the wartime man (*otoko*), who "is repeatedly connected to the crudest and cruelest of wartime excesses"

(126). The protagonist, Kaji, is a victim of the war and the men around him and of the Japanese state; Kobayashi himself thought of his film as a contrahistorical narrative of what Japanese men wished they had done during the war (Orr 128).[17] In the television drama and film *I Want to be a Shellfish* (*Watashi wa kai ni naritai*, 1958/1959), the protagonist has done what he is accused of—killing POWs—and his victimization comes at the hands of the Occupation that punishes him for following orders. To find him innocent one would have to believe in his complete lack of agency; the power of the narrative rests not only in its melodramatic quality, but also in its documentary-like feel (Toba 105–12).

We can provisionally call these narratives of emasculation, in the limited sense of "how Japanese men of the early postwar understood emasculation," with the proviso that there is a danger of reifying traditional gender roles and stereotypes and of preempting recognition of actual efforts to resist conformity by men and women alike. In such highly symbolic works, however, emasculation describes very specific circumstances: the loss of agency under the Occupation that was more acutely felt by men than women, given the abusive hypermasculinity of the wartime Japanese state, and a new postwar social order in which the perception—if not always reality—was that Japanese men were at the bottom. For Yasuoka, we can use the word with an equally circumscribed meaning: Just as Yasuoka's wartime characters struggle to grow up despite the restrictions placed on them, Yasuoka's postwar characters revert to childhood and find their agency challenged by the war's lingering presence.

In Yasuoka's first story to appear in a mass publication, "The Glass Slipper" ("Garasu no kutsu," 1950), the narrator is a night watchman at a hunting store. In making deliveries to US Lieutenant Colonel Craigow, he meets the Craigows' maid, Etsuko. The Craigows go away on vacation, and the intervening time for the couple is, as the title indicates, akin to Cinderella's night at the ball, made sweeter by its finiteness. They eat their way through the Craigows' food stockpiles and revert to childhood; while playing hide-and-go-seek and waiting for Etsuko to find him, the narrator inadvertently falls asleep in a water sack, a womb-like place where he is secure from the world outside. Etsuko herself is depicted as childlike, slow even. The narrator may be Cinderella, gaining temporary admission to a world of wealth he never imagined for himself, but Etsuko is no distaff Prince Charming; she isn't heir to the household, nor does she seek him out after the Craigows return and the magic is broken. Because of this, their inchoate romance never develops. The Americans represent the world of adults, but the narrator and Etsuko remain trapped in the childish world of a fairy-tale gloss on actual conditions in postwar Japan. Etsuko's work as a maid is a bowdlerization of the ways postwar prostitutes (*pan-pan*) and women with GI boyfriends (*onrii*,

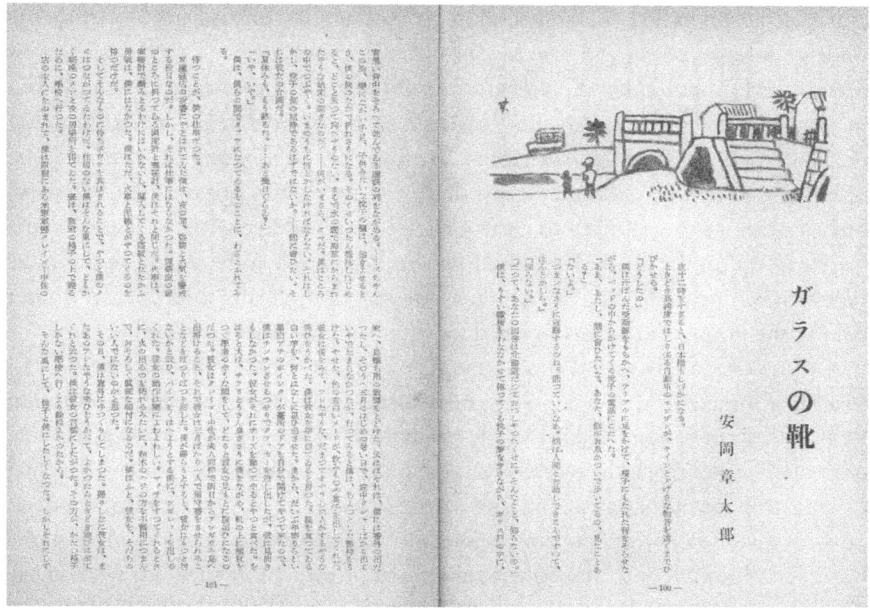

Opening pages of Yasuoka's first published story, "The Glass Slipper," in the June 1951 issue of the journal *Mita bungaku*.

from the English "only") were actually receiving money from Occupation forces, while the narrator's dependence on Etsuko for the lifestyle they lead emblemizes the collective displacement the men of the country were experiencing following the war defeat.

Clearly, "The Glass Slipper" could be read as a national allegory of defeat in that sense, as could a number of other early stories by Yasuoka set during the Occupation. In "The House Guard" ("Hausu gaado," 1953), the narrator is even more directly working at the whim of the Occupation forces. The Americans have requisitioned more houses than they need, under the assumption that, as Occupation personnel move in and out, a bit of leeway is needed in the system. They hire locals to guard the unused requisitioned houses for them, and the narrator finds himself in charge of a half-burned-down home requisitioned by GHQ that happens to be located next door to a house to which a Russian diplomat has been assigned. The narrator is sloth personified, and thus the root of his own troubles: Because there is no telephone in the house, he lives in constant fear that the GHQ inspector will pay a surprise visit and discover how unkempt the house is. In an echo of the games the young people played in "The Glass Slipper," the narrator here suggests that "being a house guard is just like hide-and-seek, and the person called the inspector is 'It' and shows up in a jeep"—with the understanding that he will lose his job if he is found loafing (YSS 1: 123). His fear drives him to constantly peer out the window whenever a car drives up, but invariably the car belongs to the Russian next door, who begins to suspect that the narrator is a spy for the Americans, so often does he look out the window. The narrator is told in no uncertain terms that he needs to stop agitating the Russians, but he cannot bring himself to clean up his house and live without fear of a surprise inspection. In the end it is the Russians who prove to be the more ominous threat; when he looks out the window one last time during a forbidden dinner date at the house, the Russian next door bursts in and pummels him.

Yasuoka actually served as a house guard during the Occupation, from 1947 to 1949 (Shimao Toshio et al. 419); he was still weak from his long, debilitating fight with spinal caries, and ironically he considered serving as a house guard one of the few things he could actually do. Again, however, it doesn't take much effort to read this somewhat autobiographical story as an allegory of national defeat: Japan is a ruined house that now belongs to the Americans, and the inhabitants have been brought into the American sphere of influence; they are seen as the Americans' running dogs by a wary Russia next door. The threat the Japanese government perceived in the Soviet Union in the last stages of the war was real; it was of particular concern to Yoshida Shigeru's clear-eyed faction as it sued the emperor in the spring of 1945 to commit to a brokered peace.[18] The Soviets' declaration of war on August 9, 1945, was a major factor in Japan's decision to surrender.[19] The fact that the narrator was hired by Americans and sees the Russians as a dangerous foreign presence indicates the degree to which the "Allied" Occupation was in fact an American one (Dower, *Embracing Defeat* 73). Like his country, the narrator finds that his desire to do the bidding of GHQ comes at the cost of unsettling the Russians.

In "The Medal" ("Kunshō," 1953), a triptych of anecdotes, access to tobacco is a measure of national power. In the first section, the author is scrounging for cigarette butts in Tokyo's burned-out streets; tobacco as a commodity represents all the other privations of war—the narrator even abandons his original mission to get rice for his extended family to look for precious filler for his *kiseru* pipe. In the second part, the narrator returns to Tokyo after two months on Mount Minobu following the end of the war. While he waits for a train, a young Korean approaches him and insists on giving him an American cigarette. He is suspicious of the man's motives, but accepts it, only to discover the unnerving truth behind the man's friendliness: "'Well, the world belongs to us now. Let's both make the most of it!' He jumped through the automatic door of his train as it closed, still under the impression that I was one of his countrymen" (YSS 1: 235). The people to whom the world belongs now are the Koreans (in the world of the story more than real life, it is probably safe to say). The Korean man's ability to procure a fresh pack of a cigarette brand the narrator has never before smoked is a marker of the way the Korean man's world is expanding even as the narrator's is closing in on him.

In the final section, the narrator gets a job as a janitor in GHQ itself, the former (and future) Daiichi Life Insurance building in central Tokyo. Again, he scavenges for smokes, but in a twist, he convinces an American officer to trade his pipe and five packets of tobacco for an army medal that belonged to the narrator's father. Soon after the trade is made, the cigarette market in Japan dries up, but not the pipe-tobacco market, leaving only those with pipes able to smoke. It is a small, thrilling victory for the narrator, and he gloats over the officer with the worthless medal in his desk drawer, but it is the only kind of victory left to the defeated: a childish, temporary one. The pipe has temporarily been rendered valuable in the absence of cigarettes as an alternative, but the medal's worthlessness is permanent; in handing over his father's army medal, the narrator has traded his patrimony, a once-premier symbol of Japanese masculine sovereignty, for something that will literally go up in smoke.

Flight and the Endless War

Narratives of an unbroken Shōwa can be constructed out of all these threads—displacement in time and space, a wartime conflation of sexual and political repression, and ongoing feelings of perpetual childishness and of being subsumed into the nation in the postwar. As literary tropes, they serve to suture wartime and postwar into a continuous linearity. There is still one piece missing from this schema, of course: Whither the war itself? Yasuoka went off to war in 1944 and spent a single miserable year in the Japanese puppet state of Manchukuo; his stint was cut short by a bout of pleurisy. He was discharged and released from the hospital in the summer of 1945, after the firebombing in the spring of that year had destroyed his family's home in Tokyo, and he was in the Tokyo area during the last weeks of the war. His time abroad, however, proved to be extraordinarily fertile ground for him, the subject of a small number of short stories and a single short novel, *Flight* (*Tonsō*, 1957). His war stories are generally comedic, savaging the absurdities of life in the Japanese Imperial Army.[20] On the whole, scholars of Japanese literature have generally been prejudiced against comedy in favor of socially committed, politically engaged literature.[21] This is all the more true of war literature. Narratives of the wartime Japanese army, including both those published during the war, such as Hino Ashihei's *Wheat and Soldiers*

(*Mugi to heitai*, 1938) and Ishikawa Tatsuzō's *Soldiers Alive* (*Ikite iru heitai*, 1938 [censored], 1945 [unabridged]), and those published afterward, such as Noma Hiroshi's *Zone of Emptiness* (*Shinkū chitai*, 1952) and Ōoka Shōhei's *Fires on the Plain* (*Nobi*, 1951), have in common the utter seriousness with which they treat the undeniably traumatic experiences of the soldiers. *Flight*, on the other hand, is a sardonic critique of the absurdity of war on the level of Günter Grass's *The Tin Drum* (1959) or Kurt Vonnegut's *Slaughterhouse-Five* (1969). At least one critic of *Flight* has argued that, with the passage of time, it has become Yasuoka's most important work (Komada 31). Katō Norihiro places Yasuoka's descriptions of his war experiences on par with two very different works by writers of roughly Yasuoka's age who survived the war in their own ways with their humor intact: J. D. Salinger's *The Catcher in the Rye* and Primo Levi's *The Truce* (Katō 785).

In *Flight*, the army is a madhouse: soldiers steal from one another, and officers and veterans beat newcomers, all for no apparent reason. The rules of the army, far from maintaining order within the ranks, seem deliberately designed to lower troop morale; Yasuoka's protagonist, Yasugi Kasuke, is perpetually hungry and surrounded by equally hungry men, but at one point he and another man are nevertheless sent to secretly dispose of rice so that the company's ration won't be decreased while some of their number are away on a mission. When Kasuke loses his rifle cap, he is told to search until he finds it, an awful situation to be in, considering that he knows it must have been stolen. He does a cursory look around the room and doesn't see it, which isn't enough for the veterans who tell him to look for it in earnest. "You think it's going to pop up when you just go through the motions like that?' [. . .] It was true, what Kasuke was doing was nothing more than performing the action of 'Looking.' And the crowd actually would appreciate a performance. But he couldn't just look to say he had looked—his performance had to have an aura of truthfulness to it" (YSS 5: 41).

Kasuke's performance bears a passing resemblance to that of the protagonist of "Gloomy Pleasures," who plays sicker than he really is in order to be sure he receives his disability pension. The demeaning life in the military and the suffering it causes in the postwar become games for Yasuoka's narrators, gloomy pleasures that nevertheless do not signal trauma or despair so much as black comedy. A sickly soldier is revealed to have been the one who stole Kasuke's rifle cap and other missing items, and he admits to having thrown all of the ill-gotten weaponry parts down the latrine; the brutal squad commander (*hanchō*), facing punishment himself for letting such things happen on his watch, goes down the hatch and sinks to his chest in excrement to feel around for contraband—a metaphor, it goes without saying, for Yasuoka's view of military life. The one

In his military unit in 1944 (Yasuoka, front row, second from left). Photograph courtesy of Yasuoka Haruko.

thing promised by the title—desertion—proves comically impossible. The ill soldier suddenly gains the energy to run away, but Kasuke remarks that the hostile landscape will force the ill soldier to return when he gets hungry. The flight of the title is an unexpected one: when the narrator falls ill himself and heads to the infirmary, his regiment leaves for the Philippines without him—he has regained his small parcel of freedom, but only because the *army* fled from *him*.

In multiple darkly comic stories set in the postwar, Yasuoka shows that the real trauma of the war comes long afterward, from its inescapability. In "War Song" ("Gunka," 1962), another story in which Yasuoka's alter ego is named Juntarō, Juntarō's mother is dead, and his father has come to live with Juntarō's family. Juntarō arrives home one evening to find his father sitting and drinking with two younger men, N. from the neighborhood and his friend B. His father badmouths Juntarō to the young men: "This guy here is my son, but I'm worried because he's such an idiot. He was coddled by his mother while I was out of Japan, so even one drink is too much for him. And since he's so stupid, he'll do whatever his wife tells him, it's awful," to which N. replies, "Yeah, there's nothing you can do about it—all of Japan has become a woman's country," effectively equating masculinity with wartime (YSS 3: 357). In fact, the young men want to sing an old military song, but Juntarō, the only one of the group who was in a military fighting force, doesn't know it. B. and N. were only in elementary school or middle school when the war ended, but N. engages in some historical revisionism:

> "Hey, pops, isn't it true that the Japanese army didn't really need to surrender? In China and Indochina and Java the army wasn't anywhere close to losing, right?"
>
> But Father's head was already just about down on the table. He had fallen asleep with his hand still clutching his sake cup. So N. turned on me. "You guys should have tried harder. It's your guys' fault that the enemy was allowed onto the mainland without spilling any blood. You're the ones who turned Japan into this filthy place. . . . All of the great men of your generation died in suicide attacks. If you guys had just managed to hold on a little bit longer, even another year or two, we younger guys would've been able to go to war." (358–59)

The implication is comic, not only because of the ludicrous aporia in young N.'s understanding of Japanese war losses, but also because N.'s entire speech is clearly bluster; when Juntarō punches the two young men in a flash of anger, N. begins crying because his mouth is bleeding. The supposed warmongers in the room are revealed to be two boys with no understanding of the tragedies of war and an old, broken drunk. Throughout the story, Juntarō thinks about those who did see action during the war, and the results were tragic: his friend K. was made to shoot himself in the head on Luzon to take responsibility for troop losses, while others died only days before the end of the war. Juntarō's first act of violence on behalf of the war effort is against B. and N., in the name of remembering the war as it actually happened. Juntarō then shoves Father into his room and holds the door shut. His father resists:

> "Come on, open it up. You're not going to open it?" As he grumbled, Father kicked against the door.
>
> "Nope. I'm not going to let you out until tomorrow morning, so you'd better just crawl into your bed."
>
> "What an ungrateful kid. You're an ingrate, you're disloyal, you're absolutely crazy!" As Father complained over and over, he continued to pound on and kick at the door. But his strength gradually ebbed. After a good ten minutes of this, the other side of the door abruptly fell absolutely still. (362)

Juntarō, forced by the others to play the role of the war generation again, responds with equal ferocity toward the war's innocents and officer class alike. His evening plays out as a sort of revenge fantasy against the older generation, holding them in check until they no longer have the strength to valorize or defend the war effort. The war that seemed absurd at the time reveals itself to have surprising power long after it has ended, its true meaning skewed by those who were young or old at the time.

In "Secret of the Trade" ("Shokugyō no himitsu," 1956), the war intrudes on everyday life even a decade after its end. The narrator tells us that insurance salesmen have never visited the narrator's house; he imagines it is all too clear that his family is too poor to provide a lucrative target for them, and the narrator is so sickly for years after the war that he likely wouldn't qualify for life insurance anyway. One day, an insurance salesman, Uchida, comes to the house to try his luck. Uchida recognizes a man in a photo in the narrator's house as Ono, the narrator's boyhood friend who went missing in the war. The narrator is momentarily stunned that Uchida knows his old friend—could Ono be alive somewhere?—but Uchida explains that Ono was in his regiment during the war.

Uchida has adroitly sensed the opening; his final sales pitch is likely not standard for him: "*I'm never, ever going off to war again. There's no way in hell I'll ever have to do boot camp again. . . .* When I put it that way, paying 2000 yen a month doesn't seem so bad, does it?" (YSS 2: 256). In one sense, the return of life-insurance policies can be seen as a return of the prewar everyday. Such insurance had been devastated by the social and physical toll of the war, as well as by the rampant inflation of the 1940s, only to rebound with the financial stability brought by the Korean War (Patrick 56). The life-insurance policies Uchida sells are structured to pay out at either retirement or age eighty; even after the bubble burst at the end of the 1980s, they continued to be a popular option for depositing household savings (Allison 201–2). As with mutual funds, life insurance's actuarial tables require a capitalist everyday to operate as a reasonable investment. Uchida mentions that an investment of 350 yen per month, for example, will pay out 200,000 yen in forty years. Life insurance is not simply a "peace dividend," a luxury on which to spend one's spare income. It is a belief system that precludes the reoccurrence of cataclysmic events such as another war.

Uchida had risen to be a captain (*taii*) in the army, while the narrator prides himself on never having risen above private (*nitōhei*). Had the war continued for another ten years on to the present, Uchida would be a lieutenant colonel (*chūsa*) or even colonel (*taisa*) by now, the narrator imagines (250). The narrator thought that he would educate Uchida in sales, but realizes it will be impossible when he senses Uchida taking on "the attitude of a company commander receiving an unimportant-yet-lengthy briefing from a non-com orderly" (252). The narrator, in turn, feels like a private all over again; he begins to think of the salesman as Lieutenant Colonel Uchida and feels acutely the other man's imposing physical presence. Time goes askew here: Although both men were born in 1920, a schism develops between them in the narrator's mind, in which the narrator himself is trapped in time as a lowly private while Uchida is granted a position in keeping with his current age. Even for Uchida, however, the role is one from a parallel universe, in which Japan was never demilitarized. The war's ability to disrupt the everyday continues on.

Dislocation and the Endless War: *A View of the Sea*

Marx's dictum that history repeats itself, first as tragedy, then as farce, is turned on its head in Yasuoka's works. The war and its chaotic aftermath, ludicrous and risible in nearly all of Yasuoka's short stories about the military, devolve into something tragic in his longer works set in the post-Occupation. The work that perhaps best symbolizes the endless war for Yasuoka and synthesizes all of these threads is the one generally considered to be his masterpiece, *A View of the Sea* (*Kaihen no kōkei*, 1959).[22] Yasuoka worked on it during the summer of 1959 at the publishing company Kōdansha's "Mountain House," a retreat in Karuizawa where writers could focus—or, from the publisher's viewpoint, be forced to focus—on their work. According to Yasuoka's editor at the time, Tokushima Takayoshi, Yasuoka's mother's illness during the time he was working on *The Angel of Mockery* (*Shitadashi tenshi*, 1958, discussed in Chapter Two), the trips he took to Kōchi Prefecture to visit her, and the funeral costs combined to bankrupt him (Tokushima 155). Now, two years later, he was ready to work through the fact of her death in his creative work. When Tokushima went to the retreat to check on Yasuoka's process, he often found paper scattered across the desk, and Yasuoka on his futon bedding, face down with his pillow under his chest, writing on the floor (Tokushima 155). For a novella that would bring Yasuoka back to the darkest moments of the still-young postwar, it seems appropriate that he continued to assume the very same position in which he wrote his earliest stories, when he was bedridden with spinal caries and could manage only two or three sentences at a time before needing to flop over and take a break.

In *A View of the Sea*, the protagonist, Hamaguchi Shintarō, and his father, Shinkichi, have committed Shintarō's mother, Chika, to an asylum in Kōchi Prefecture, and the novella fluidly moves backward and forward in time between various events: his father's return from the war; their eviction from property they rented from Shintarō's uncle and the subsequent separation of Shintarō and his parents, in which they move to his father's native Kōchi and Shintarō stays in Tokyo; the day a year before the "present" of the story when they deposit an increasingly erratic Mother into the asylum; and the present itself—the last nine days of his mother's life. Thematically, Kōchi represents a distant, dire past to Shintarō, removed from his own life in terms of time and place. He remembers his grandmother sending warnings to his father about the Tosa *inugamitsuki* spirits, which threaten them if they violate ancient directional taboos, and a Kōchi man in their neighborhood bringing his son to Kōchi once a year so that he doesn't "abandon the homeland (*kokyō*)" (YSS 5: 358). For Shintarō, both situations are suspect: the ancient spirits of Shikoku surely cannot dictate which directions Father can and cannot go in modern Tokyo, and the neighbor's obsession with providing his child with a Kōchi heritage regardless of reality leads Shintarō to think that "the 'homeland' is another imaginary concept" (358).

The notion that Kōchi is a different place (rural, distant) in a different time (backward, atavistic) plays a critical role in the novel. Kōchi is Shintarō's father's homeland, but his mother was born in Tokyo and raised in Osaka.[23] Her sequestering in Kōchi thus represents not only a physical pull away from Tokyo but also a movement away from the modernity it represents. Father went off to war, and Shintarō spent ten years alone with his mother in the modern metropolis. The principality of his position in Mother's life, and she in his, went unchallenged even after Father returned to the family. Father appeared half deranged on his return, and his unwillingness to look for work that would sustain the family turned Shintarō into the primary breadwinner. It is both a quintessential postwar narrative and an oedipal fantasy come true—Shintarō replacing his own father in his mother's affections and as a partner.

At one point during her final days, however, Mother speaks for the first time in a long while; she calls out in her pain for Shintarō's father, an act that stuns her son: "For Shintarō, it was as though he had lost something" (391). Has he reverted to childhood, unwillingly thrust back by the return of his father to his rightful place in the family? Etō Jun would have it exactly the reverse, in his attempt to delineate what has happened to the Hamaguchi family in his study of narratives by Third Generation writers, *Maturity and Loss: The Collapse of the Mother Figure* (*Seijuku to sōshitsu: "Haha" no hōkai*, 1978).[24] Using the research of psychologist Erik H. Erikson, Etō posits what at first glance is a broadbrush theory to explain differences between traditional transitions to adulthood in the United States and Japan: American children were forced out of the nest to go settle the frontier, while Japanese children generally stayed on their family land with their families. The most obvious problem such a comparison would pose to a study of contemporary fiction is that, by the time Yasuoka wrote *A View of the*

Sea, over sixty years had passed since Frederick Jackson Turner declared the end of the American frontier in 1893. Etō does not dwell on this, however, because he is more concerned with developing a frontier for Japan, one he locates in the Japanese educational system. To Etō, there is an antimony at work in the education-minded Mother figure in Yasuoka's works: She wants her son to go off to school, but success in this venture will send him far away from her. Shintarō acts toward his mother out of feelings of guilt, signified for Etō in Shintarō's empty act of shooing flies away from his mother's prone body. Etō argues that Yasuoka's generation is obsessed with the figure of the mother. They inevitably lose her, and maturity comes from recognition of that loss. Far from retrogression, for Etō it is the *past* that Shintarō loses in the moment.

It is possible to consider this a narrative of both casting off childhood *and* regressing to it, or perhaps of casting off one's childhood *through* regressing. What perhaps makes both of these readings possible is the slippage of time and space as they relate to the postwar in Yasuoka's writing. Shintarō's mother, of course, no longer knows how old she is or where she is, and to a certain point, Shintarō identifies with her. When he leaves her room to look out at the sea as evening sets in, the present blurs into the past:

> He imagined her face as she stood in the dusk, her arms at her chest. In that image were the countless faces he had become used to seeing since he was a child. Her face when they had climbed the long, stone staircase to his elementary-school teacher's house, to apologize together for his bad grades at school. Her face when she greeted her son who came home without warning from his school dorm during summer break. Her face when she dropped in to visit him at the army hospital, to tell him how their home had been destroyed in the firebombing. Her face the day before they would have to vacate the house on the coast at Kugenuma. And then her face on a summer evening last year at his aunt's in Y Village, when she moved back and forth from the gate to the entrance of the house for no good reason. It didn't take too much effort to recall these faces with this melancholy landscape as a background. But when he tried to get past them, to determine which part was linked to his mother's madness, he was at a loss. (368–69)

His mother is at once in the present and at various points in the past, and her faces at these times are overlaid onto her present visage; furthermore, all of these faces are set onto the view of the bay. This is the central symbol of *A View of the Sea*, for it is in seeing the sea that one maintains one's connection to one's memories, one's history, and to the past. The word for sea, or seashore, that

Yasuoka uses (海辺) is normally pronounced "umibe," but at some point along the way Yasuoka began referring to the novel using the less common pronunciation "kaihen"; the Shinchōsha paperback glosses the reading as such. Yasuoka, as befits someone for whom language has always been a conscious consideration, is fond of wordplay, and it doesn't seem impossible that 海辺 is a deliberate homophone for 改変 (*kaihen*, meaning "change"), which could refer to the changing of the tide, a change of rooms to the opposite side of the hospital, and to Shintarō's life hereafter.[25] When the family first brings the mother to the asylum, she is given a room facing the sea; patients who can enjoy such a view—those still connected to the world—are assigned to this side. Shintarō's mother is deprived of her room facing the sea when the doctors conclude that she is irretrievably lost, but Shintarō—still very much a part of this world—comes to look at the sea when he needs to reconnect the multiple pasts that make sense of the present.

It is obvious from all of these examples that in *A View of the Sea* the conception of time is inextricably linked with the conception of space; specifically, the progression of time—or lack thereof—can only be understood through the mediation of space, or landscape. The writer Sakagami Hiroshi, who considered Yasuoka something of a mentor, argues that the landscape itself becomes a character: "The [traditional] opposition between man and nature isn't applicable in terms of the reality of this novel. [...] It's the kind of world in which the view is inherently human" (Sakagami 37). To be sure, Shintarō watches patients "melting into the landscape" and is "determined to understand his mother from within this scene" (YSS 5: 368). At the same time, though, Shintarō's mother's time on this earth was marked in spatial terms as well. In the passage above, she appears on a staircase, in her home, at an army hospital, at their postwar house on the coast, and at his aunt's in Kōchi Prefecture. The passage of time in the war and postwar is inextricably tied to movement.

There is a double irony to putting Mother in a place with "a view of the sea." When they return to the institution a year later, they find her blind and relocated to a room on the mountain side of the building, with the other patients who are serious cases. Her new room receives the last light of the evening sun, implying that her original room was sunny in the morning. His mother thus has moved, symbolically, from morning to evening, and so, perhaps, has the postwar. As Mother's situation grows critical, a man who is both inmate and staffer advises Shintarō in the afternoon that he has time to catch some sleep, because people die at low tide, and the next one won't be until 11:00 p.m. that night. Shintarō wakes with a start at 2:00 a.m., thinking he is too late, but his mother is alive. She dies the following morning at 11:19, and when an emotionally drained Shintarō walks to the seaward side of the building, another element of the view becomes crucial.

Black stakes used in pearl cultivation are visible in the bay, indicating that Mother has indeed died at low tide—but one tide cycle later than the one Shintarō was anticipating. Etō Jun argues that in the moment Shintarō sees these stakes, he certainly thinks of the fact that his mother's last word was for his father and not him, and that "he must have been aware that he was not in the midst of nature but of society—in other words, that he would have to live on in the presence of other people" (Etō 33). This is undoubtedly true, but the final line of the work also points to an ironic, irreconcilable ambiguity: "As he looked out over the row of stakes, like the upright teeth of a comb, like grave markers, he saw with certainty that he grasped a single death in his own hands" (YSS 5: 451). Clearly these stakes represent "society" and "people," but it is a very particular subset—a lost society, and a deceased people. Within the cyclical flow of the tides, always a proxy for the ebb and flow of the fortunes of the living, is the iconography of an ending: As "grave markers" (*bohyō*), the stakes (*kui*) resemble nothing so much as *sotoba*—in their Japanese incarnation, wooden stakes that are left at graves on certain anniversaries of the death, the length of which measures the passage of time.

Like the young protagonist of "Homework" who feels most alive when he is by himself in the Aoyama cemetery, Shintarō finds a solitary peace facing—in his own mind, at least—a mass of graves. Here, it would be difficult to argue that these stakes-as-graves represent anything other than the dead of the war. In Kōchi, too, Allied firebombing had destroyed cities and military facilities alike; from January 1945 to the end of the war, Kōchi Prefecture had been attacked over three hundred times, with over six hundred dead, over four hundred of them in a single night's bombing, July 3–4, 1945, that effectively shut down Kōchi City (Ogi et al. 321–22). Although it has come years after the ostensible end of the war, Mother's death, while isolated and solitary, is not unique. The sudden difficulties of the postwar brought on her illness, the doctor determines, despite the many years that have passed and despite the fact that she was not ill until things began to get better for the family (YSS 5: 355). Yoshida Hiroo sees the novel through the lens of the family's slippage (*zure*), not from Yasuoka's family's actual history, but from the general sense that it is no longer the postwar:

> The "unconscious fiction" in *A View of the Sea* is perhaps the history of the way Hamaguchi Shintarō, his father Shinkichi, and his mother first lived after the war. It doesn't really matter whether this corresponds to the history of how the Yasuoka family lived. Facts are merely raw material; they can be changed to accord to a novel's greater truths. It is sufficient for us to pay attention to the fact that Yasuoka treats the history of the way the Hamaguchi family lives as a slippage. [...] As symbolized by the mother's mental breakdown, there

were people who, when the postwar came to an end and the system righted itself, were still confused and got on the bus too late. (Yoshida 136)

While Yoshida is correct to resist a biographical reading, the timeline of the novel does correspond to Yasuoka's own biography to the extent that we can say that Mother's death in the novel corresponds to Yasuoka's own mother's death in a Kōchi asylum in July 1957; the year that she was institutionalized roughly corresponded with the year following the July 1956 release of the economic white paper declaring that "it is no longer the postwar" (*mohaya sengo de wa nai*), a proclamation that quickly became part of the public parlance. Clearly this was not true of Yasuoka's family—he has referred to his mother's death as a belated war death—and clearly the individual narrative is at odds with the collective one.

And with itself: The final piece of evidence that compels the reader to consider this to be a war novel is the fact that it is rife with competing narratives about what exactly happened in this most personal of histories. Shintarō lies to Mother about where they are bringing her, and he questions whether he is lying even to himself about it (YSS 5: 332). In a flashback, he receives rival letters from Father and Mother each accusing the other of irrational behavior. Even those whose narratives should carry the weight of authority—the doctors themselves—are impossible for Shintarō to trust. Shintarō constantly has trouble determining who at the asylum is a doctor and who is a patient, but what seems to distinguish the doctors more than anything is the fact that the doctors *always* lie, while the patients show a surprising acumen for getting at the truth. This is in keeping with Yasuoka's already longstanding aversion to the official version of events, read: history. Shintarō fears that they have all been lying about his mother's sanity from the day they committed her a year earlier without telling her what they were doing:

> Maybe his mother had come to her senses and, knowing how things stood, was trying to resign herself to her fate? He should never have gone to the doctor for advice. (The previous day, Shintarō had asked the doctor at the hospital what the best way was of getting the patient to come here. The doctor suddenly had a bored look, and prevaricated, saying only, "Everyone has his own devices. There's something to be said for the expediency of lies.") (433)

The doctor has all but told him to lie to her. While the practice of withholding crucial information from the patient in serious cases had long been standard operating procedure in Japanese medicine, the doctor's unwillingness to take responsibility for the lies they are telling the patient is unnerving.

The doctors at the asylum are just as evasive with the family: They move Mother to the other side of the building without consulting the family. The doctor's assistant insists that he must feed Mother to keep her alive, but he dribbles too much liquid into her mouth, causing her to choke and die. Although Mother was clearly in the last hours of her life and Shintarō resolves not to hold anything against the attendant, it is this gaffe that allows the inmate-caretaker's prophecy—that she would die at low tide—to come true. In their disregard for human suffering and the dignity of life, the doctors have a lot in common with the wartime authorities.

The patients and ex-patients who approach the family in Mother's final days provide a counterhistory that brings Shintarō closer to the truth of his mother's existence in this place than the doctors' "official" narrative does. They, too, however, remind Shintarō of the war. A disheveled female patient who bums a cigarette from him reminds him of the men in the army who are nice to newcomers in return for favors later on, and the mystic patient who predicted Mother would die at low tide is bandaged around his neck and has "the face of a warrant officer in charge of recruits" (383, 387). A short nurse reveals herself to be a cured patient, and when she discovers Father was in the service, she mentions that her cousin died as an infantryman in the war. Father asks her where and when, but "the woman had already forgotten what she was talking about. And she probably didn't catch what Father was asking in his stuffy voice" (385). The deprivation and physical and spiritual wounds of the war are manifest in the patients as madness, and their efforts toward sanity mimic the efforts of postwar Japanese society to reclaim a semblance of order out of chaos. In each of the three encounters, the inmates look out at the sea as they talk. The stakes in the bay are a sign of death, but to face the sea—to reckon with the past in the light of day—is life giving. The past and present coexist, as do truth and lies, the faraway and the immediate, and memory and forgetting. The reader cannot help but feel that any narrative of Mother's death is a provisional one, and a constructed one, woven from the strands of competing storylines, much like the narration of the nation in war and postwar. The other inmates tell Shintarō that even at the end, when everything else was lost, she could still sing songs word for word. He remembers his mother's lullaby from his childhood, before the madness of war and postwar: "You were young and innocent, and when you cried I cradled you; have you forgotten the past?" (383). When she had forgotten everything else, what she remembered was a song that implored her son to remember her. The genius of *A View of the Sea* is that it serves as a reminder that narratives are also for the benefit of the teller; we construct narratives lest we ourselves forget.

2

The Generation of Deception

Canon and Archive in the Fiction of the Long Postwar

We have seen how the designation of Yasuoka Shōtarō as one of the so-called Third Generation of New Writers obscured the ways he grappled in his stories with national issues. Such an emphasis on literary generation creates other problems as well: It has served to overdetermine him as a writer of autobiographical "I-novels" (*shishōsetsu*), all evidence to the contrary that he was engaged in something more ambitious with his stories. It has also created a ready-made literary generation for him at the risk of submerging other generational identifications. Literary histories often conflate when writers first appeared on the literary scene with their chronological ages.[1] Although the Third Generation did indeed represent a group of friends and acquaintances of roughly similar ages, little differences meant a lot during wartime. The editor Ōkubo Fusao notes that there was a full eleven-year difference in age between the oldest and youngest of the Third Generation writers, Kojima Nobuo (1915–2006) and Miura Shumon (1926–2017), and that despite a supposed divide of two literary generations, Kojima was actually born the same year as Sengo-ha writer Noma Hiroshi (Ōkubo 129). The writers in the Third Generation with whom Yasuoka was closest, Yoshiyuki Junnosuke (1924–1994) and Endō Shūsaku (1923–1996), were significantly younger than he. Although they had suffered through some of the same difficulties as Yasuoka—both saw their education interrupted by the war, both were plagued by illness (in their case, tuberculosis) and ensuing periods of forced seclusion early in their writing careers—they never did go off to war. Endō was given a waiver for health reasons, and Yoshiyuki was provisionally accepted to the army but released almost immediately; they were still only in their first years at Keio University and Tokyo Imperial University, respectively, when the war ended.[2] Others were a few years older than Yasuoka. Kojima Nobuo and Shimao Toshio (1917–1986) were able to finish their university education before heading off to war in more privileged positions, as an English specialist and as a lieutenant in charge of two hundred men, respectively.[3]

Although the Third Generation writers were genuine friends, Yasuoka felt quite strongly that his experiences were not theirs, by virtue of his academic cohort:

> When the war became quite difficult, we were confronted with a strange fate, in which a difference of two or three months in when we were born became the thing that determined whether we lived or died. For us Japanese, the difference of an entire year or two became all the more pronounced, the equivalent of a difference of ten or twenty years in a time of peace. It goes without saying that normally we wouldn't expect there to be a difference in the way people think due to such a small gap in birthdate or age. And yet, [. . .] these gaps that you don't think much of begin to loom very large indeed. To be sure, the war and defeat are giant shared experiences, but when you break it down and try to talk about it with someone who wasn't exactly the same year in school as you, even though you were both members of the educated class raised in a time of war (*senchū-ha*), you find that your conversation doesn't line up, and you start to think, "What exactly is our shared experience here?" (BSS 1: 5)

The various theories of generation that have emerged since Karl Mannheim's "The Sociological Problem of Generations" ("Das problem der generationen," 1927) have mostly followed his lead: generations are important mainly because of their shared youths, when minds are most impressionable and life trajectories are set. Mannheim sees life experiences as dialectical, with one's memories of childhood forming the initial thesis: "All later experiences then tend to receive their meaning from this original set, whether they appear as that set's verification and fulfilment or as its negation and antithesis" (298). Generally speaking, one imagines a generation to be a cohort of twenty or thirty years, with arbitrary divisions between them, but even in Mannheim's early conception of the problem, he posited that "the transition from one generation to another takes place continuously" (301). Yasuoka's understanding of his cohort is completely different; he sees himself as being absolutely severed from those a few years, even a few months, older or younger. Although he was a central figure in the Third Generation, he always felt as though he lived life at a remove from them.

The Generation of Deception

The Third Generation of New Writers, Yasuoka's ostensible literary generation, at the Bunshun Club on November 21, 1958. Left to right: Yoshiyuki Junnosuke, Endō Shūsaku, Kondō Keitarō, Shōno Junzō, Yasuoka Shōtarō, Kojima Nobuo. Photograph courtesy of Bunshun / amanaimages / Minden Pictures.

The standard accounting of Yasuoka's place in literary history as a member of the Third Generation is only half of the story, and behind it lies a shadow history. There is another cohort to which Yasuoka belonged, one dispersed and nearly destroyed by the war. Yasuoka's writing was much more a product of his narrow-gauge, disrupted generation than of his friendships within the literary coterie known as the Third Generation. What appears to be an engagement with autobiography (as we would expect from a writer of "I-novels") is actually an engagement with narrative; and it is not truth to which Yasuoka aspires, but deceit, a bulwark against the pervasive force of grand narratives. The means of deception that Yasuoka used to survive in wartime are a function of his beleaguered generation, and the notion that one exorcises the war by casting away one's deceptions—and his own inability to do so—was a theme that dominated Yasuoka's writing into the 1970s.

Generation

Generational awareness has been a part of Japanese popular consciousness for nearly all of the modern nation-state's existence, ever since the generational shift that marked the Meiji Restoration, but never more acutely than during the fifteen years of war from 1931–1945. Yasuoka and his peers were always envious of those slightly older than they. Those who came of age between the end of the Russo-Japanese war in 1905 and the early 1930s would have been able to enjoy the freedoms of the "long Taishō era," coded then as now as a brief flowering of freedom and progressiveness before the descent into war.[4] Conversely, those who came of age after 1945 were still children when the war ended and were never subjected to the fear of being sent off to war. The term *yakeato sedai* (the generation of the ruins) came to refer to those who were still children when the war ended, who were evacuated from cities before the Allied firebombing, or who survived the firebombing to live on in the shells of the formerly great cities. In a more philosophical sense, it represents those who were the inheritors of the war, who were children when it ended and felt no personal sense of accountability for war or postwar. The term likely comes from Ishikawa Jun's classic short story "The Jesus of the Ruins" ("Yakeato no iesu," 1946), in which Ishikawa portrays a boy growing up in "the burnt-out shell of a metropolis" (Ishikawa 73). Nosaka Akiyuki (1930–2015) was one of those children; his autobiographical "Grave of the Fireflies" ("Hotaru no haka," 1967), written much later but set in the same period, would be another touchstone for the *yakeato sedai*. Today members of this younger cohort still identify as "Shōwa single-digits" (*Shōwa hitoketa*, i.e., those born between the first and ninth years of the Shōwa period, 1926 and 1934), shorthand for those who came of age in the deprivation following the war but who enjoyed Japan's extraordinary economic growth for nearly their entire working careers.[5] Yasuoka felt an extreme disconnect with the appearances on the literary stage of Ishihara Shintarō (born in 1932) and Ōe Kenzaburō (born in 1935), despite the fact that they came to prominence shortly after him, in the mid-1950s, because they had been children during the war, and in Yasuoka's mind, this simple fact allowed them to interact with larger ideologies in a way he always felt it necessary to refuse.

What, then, of Yasuoka's generation, the one that came between those of Taishō Democracy and the Generation of the Ruins? The literary theorist Hattori Tatsu defined those coming of age (*hatachi de atta*, literally "who were twenty") between 1936 and 1945, meaning, roughly, those born between 1916 and 1925, as a trapped generation. Of everyone associated with the Third Generation, Yasuoka felt the closest bond to Hattori, who was born in 1922 but was roughly his academic contemporary due to Yasuoka's delayed start in his higher education. Yasuoka appreciated Hattori because he, too, saw cohort in relation to the war as a central determiner in the formation of writers. In an article published in *Kindai bungaku* in January 1954, "The Writers of the New Generation" ("Shinsedai no sakka-tachi"), Hattori placed Yasuoka and himself late in a ten-year span:

The Generation of Deception

> We should conceive of the people who came of age between 1936 and 1945 as having developed spiritually during a time of war. All around them there was violence, and their souls grew up in the middle of this. People who were a little older had been given a span of time during which there was leeway to escape the violence outside and to create a separate world, however small, in one corner of it. The closer one gets to the younger side of the timeframe, the more likely it is that only those in special, privileged circumstances would have that option. Only those who had been ill, like Nakamura Shin'ichirō, or born to privilege, like Mishima Yukio, were able to acquire such a perspective. And yet, because any means of escape was closed off to them, that perspective was extremely abstract and formal [. . .] an aesthetic that was medieval, even Wildean in the way it went against the times. And everyone else was unavoidably taken up into the army in the middle of their formative period. (Hattori, "Shinsedai" 24; qtd in BSS 1: 123–24)

To Yasuoka, this was a pitch-perfect description of their generation. Clearly Yasuoka's academic holding pattern placed him all the more on the younger side of the generation, driven to desperation in the last years of the war:

> I didn't get to know Hattori Tatsu until after he had published these lines; I had neither met Hattori nor ever even been in the same room with him during the war, when we were students. Despite this, when I read the above it matched our experiences and the things we had thought down to the smallest details, such that it felt as though Hattori had been one of our number, or at least someone who had been close by the whole time. We surely had tried to "escape the violence outside and to create a separate world however small in one corner of it," but the time given to us to do so was already quite limited, and we weren't exactly blessed with family circumstances that allowed us to "acquire such a perspective." Even so, we needed to create a separate-world-in-a-corner as best we could—an air-raid shelter of the soul, if you will. The reason we decided to start living in rented rooms in the slums of areas that had such a romantic ring to their names—Tsukiji, Yanagibashi, Shinbashi—was because we really did dream of creating this other world. But the dream was all too fragile, and we were too easily awakened. (BSS 1: 124–25)

Those who did not have these experiences, Yasuoka felt, cannot truly be called his contemporaries.

To an extent greater than that in other places, there has always been a general feeling in modern Japan that those who share one's birth year will be the most sympathetic to one's view of the world. Socially, academic standing and workplace promotions have been fairly rigidly tied to age. Linguistically, conversations in Japanese among strangers suss out relative ages early on in order to establish the levels of discourse the various participants will employ. This tyranny of the cohort is visible in the cultural arena in various ways. For example, Ōoka Shōhei and Haniya Yutaka, both authors who wrote extensively about the war, both born in 1909, participated in a series of recorded conversations (*taidan*) entitled *Two Contemporaneous Histories* (*Futatsu no dōjidai-shi*) in which they spoke at length about the similarities they shared primarily because of their birthdates. The notion continues apace today: The February 2012 issue of *Bungei shunjū* was dominated by a series of articles under the banner "Oh, My Contemporaries" ("Aa, dōjidai"); "Born the same year—simple chance, and yet so important" (*takaga onaidoshi, saredo onaidoshi*), ran the tagline on the cover. One representative pairing was Empress Michiko and the singer and actor Ishihara Yūjirō, people with little in common other than the fact that they were both born in 1934; the article was written by a journalist and newscaster himself born in 1934, Tahara Sōichirō (Tahara 276–79).

World War II scrambled this sense of contemporaneity. The war claimed students in Japan in groups, as they enlisted, graduated, or—later in the war—as their deferments were cut off. A soldier could be forgiven for feeling that his generation was limited to those who were taken up into the army together. The age at which new recruits were taken pushed both younger and older as the exigencies of the war grew ever more dire, upending traditional age-based hierarchies; stories of middle-aged privates being bullied by ruthless young officers abound.[6] Yasuoka depicts his life in the late 1930s as a sort of sad-sack existence, perpetually unable to achieve his mother's dream of seeing her son ascend to one of the national higher schools that educated the elite of Japan at the time. Every era in modern Japanese history has had its *rōnin* (literally, "masterless samurai"), students who fail entrance exams and spend a year or more in the limbo of a preparatory school, biding their time until the following year's exams. For Yasuoka, it created an ersatz generation: In failing higher-school entrance exams three times running, Yasuoka was cast out of his age cohort and became friends in preparatory school with boys whose ages varied but who were going through the same experience at the same time. The image he projects of himself is as a hapless erstwhile student; in "Same Old, Same Old" ("Ai mo kawarazu," 1959), Yasuoka's protagonist spends the evening before an entrance exam throwing himself at a woman his friends have invited over for the night, and he worries about a rumor that the government will soon institute a three-year limit on deferments for *rōnin* (YSS 3: 102–6). It is a romantic self-mythology, one that creates a lens through which his short stories can be read as the autobiography of a lost soul in wartime. In reality, Yasuoka and his peers must have known that they were deliberately failing their entrance exams in order to stretch out their draft deferments as long as possible. In the self-mythology, he is always a loner at odds with his peers. In reality, he was one of a forgotten group of boys with literary ambitions who were wrenched out of place and thrown together by the war. Yasuoka became the sole canonical representative for them.

Canon and Archive and the Bad Company

If generation is destiny, it also determines who may serve as its representative figures. There is a limited number of works that can speak for a generation. The canon may have expanded to represent a wider readership and a more global concern, but the number of references that can linger in the collective consciousness at any given moment is finite. Aleida Assmann's conception of cultural memory first divides cultural production into two major categories, that which is remembered and that which is forgotten. The vast majority of human creation disappears into the void, and that which is remembered can be divided into things that are actively remembered, termed the canon, and those that are passively remembered, the realm of the archive (Erll and Nünning 97–107).

Assmann's elaboration of canon and archive is a universal framework that requires some finessing to apply to local conditions on the ground. Of course, just as there is no clear dividing line between generations, there is no clear line between canon and archive. What is canonical depends to a large extent on who is asking; it will vary according to national literature, but also according to region, political leaning, level of education, generation, and a host of other criteria. This is putting aside questions of media and genre; what is canonical to fans of science fiction and jazz is entirely different. Still, we can say, for a Japanese literary readership, although he has inevitably drifted from the center he once occupied, Yasuoka is surely a canonical figure in postwar Japanese literature. He is taught in college courses in Japan. He appears in significant collected works (*zenshū*) of modern Japanese literature. Yasuoka's "The Glass Slipper" appears in the most well-known collection of Occupation-period short stories (Kōno et al.). He has been treated at length by the most prominent Japanese literary scholars, including Etō Jun and Hasumi Shigehiko. Murakami Haruki has written admiringly of Yasuoka and the other members of the Third Generation in his collection of essays *A Guide to the Short Story for Young Readers* (*Wakai dokusha no tame no tanpen shōsetsu annai*,

1997), and a psychiatric hospital clearly inspired by Yasuoka's *A View of the Sea* is one of the main set pieces of Murakami's massive novel *1Q84* (2009–2010).

What we can propose is a more sophisticated model of canon and archive in which works are central or peripheral only in relation to other works, and in which "canonicity" does not simply draw from the archive (because neither category exists outside of the abstract), but relies on it for existence. It is impossible for a work to be "representative," after all, without something else to represent. Perhaps such a model better suits a world of coterie magazines, prize competitions offering entree to the literary establishment and tiers of prominence, and a community of writers in constant engagement with one another, all of which existed in Japan throughout the span of Yasuoka's career.[7] Yasuoka's career would not exist without his fellow strivers in his micro-generation of writers. Their shared stories surely inspired his writing, and the formation of his literary identity clearly relied on the closeness of the coterie. On a very practical level, it was one of them who introduced Yasuoka's work to the editor who published his first story, "The Glass Slipper."[8]

Yasuoka's years in the wilderness began when he graduated from middle school in March 1938; he failed the entrance exams for Matsuyama Higher School in 1938, for Kōchi Higher School in 1939, and for Yamagata Higher School and Waseda University First Higher School in 1940 (BSS 1: 75, 101, 106). In 1940, with a group of other young men who were also in a holding pattern in preparatory school, Yasuoka formed a literary coterie. Kurata Hiromitsu and Takayama Akira had been his classmates for two years, while another friend, Satō Morio, had been accepted to Waseda's science and technology division but continued to spend time with them. Another friend, Furuyama Komao, had entered the Third Higher School in Kyoto but joined them during school breaks. Furuyama would lead the other boys on tours of the red-light districts near Asakusa and in Tamanoi, and together the boys worked on a literary magazine, *Delinquent Club* (*Fūten kurabu*). Yasuoka's contribution was his first published story, "The Razor" ("Kamisori hanashi"), and he reports that the group worked through the night to bring the issue to completion; in the morning they could hear the anthem of the 2600th anniversary of the founding of the Imperial line blaring from the schoolyard next door, a symbol of the forces they were resisting, however passively (BSS 1: 119).

In 1941, giving up on public schools, Yasuoka was accepted to Keiō University's literature department, together with Kurata Hiromitsu. At about the same time, Furuyama gave up on higher school in Kyoto; he decided that he would write plays in Asakusa. Although Yasuoka was enrolled in classes, he was doing much the same thing as Furuyama: Instead of taking exams at the end of the first term in July, he holed up in the library at the Hiroshi campus and wrote a short story about his *bakumatsu* ancestor Kasuke (BSS 1: 159–60). With friends from his new college cohort—Ishiyama Kōichi, Kobori Nobujirō, and Koizumi Junsaku—he produced another coterie magazine. Originally titled *Freak* (*Kikei*), by the time it was released without the censors' permission in early 1942 it had been renamed *Conceptions of Youth* (*Seinen no kōsō*). The second issue of the magazine, renamed *Pale Horse* (*Aouma*),[9] caused Yasuoka to be brought before the Cabinet Information Bureau, his friend Satō Morio remembers (Satō 20).

These were the people about whom Yasuoka wrote most of his stories set during the war, the original "Bad Company" who would likely have been completely forgotten but for Yasuoka's fiction. Yasuoka lost touch with his school companions over the years, but he has commented time and again how only they could understand his relationship with the world. They were too young to enjoy the heady time of relative artistic and personal freedom known as Taishō Democracy, and their youths were spent watching the country tilt toward war and imperial ideology over the course of the 1930s. By the time the war started in earnest, however, they were too old to believe the military propaganda, and by the time Yasuoka's writing career took off, they had seen an American Occupation set a course, reverse it, and disappear. All of them disappeared from the literary scene except for Yasuoka's old friend and classmate Furuyama Komao (the model for the wild Fujii Komahiko in "Bad Company"). Even Furuyama has forevermore been displaced into the ranks of writers approaching the war from a distance because he took up editorial work after the war and didn't start publishing his own fiction until nearly a quarter century after the end of World War II; he won the Akutagawa Prize in 1970, and in literary collections, he is often grouped with younger writers who also debuted in the early 1970s with whom he has little in common. Yet Furuyama's war stories, including his own masterpiece, "Dawn in *Préau Huit*" (*Pureō yuitto no yoake* [Dawn in Prison Yard Eight], 1970), are of a kind with Yasuoka's: funny, sardonic.[10] As a writer of war stories, Furuyama perhaps shared with Yasuoka a belief that the war and postwar are contiguous and never-ending. What the war and occupation gave them as a theme was deception—both deceiving and being deceived by friend and nation.

Against Autobiography

The other members of Yasuoka's Bad Company are a forgotten generation of writers. Some died in the war. Others survive on the edge of the archive: In 1983, Satō Morio self-published *At a Crossroads* (*Magarikado de*), a memoir of his time with Yasuoka and Furuyama. Ishiyama Kōichi self-published his wartime diary covering roughly the same period, *Days with Friends Who Came of Age toward the End of the War* (*Senmatsu-ha seishun kōyū nikki*, 1992), in which the others appear regularly, as well as a collection based on his war experiences, *Go-Ahead-and-Die Stories* (*Shinyaa iin da yo monogatari*, 1988). Satō's memoir and Ishiyama's diary had print runs of three hundred copies each (Aoki 20, 46). Works such as these are available in a limited number of libraries, and sometimes only at the National Diet Library, Japan's equivalent of the Library of Congress. Practically speaking, they are untraceable except through the writings of peripheral figures in academia and the book trade. This marginalization led to a wedge between Yasuoka and his initial literary group in later years. Ishiyama wrote a somewhat critical essay about Yasuoka for the "tip-in" (*geppō*) that accompanied the volume in a series of contemporary Japanese literature in which Yasuoka appeared (Ishiyama, "Higurashi"); he later acknowledged that it may have led to the end of their friendship (Aoki 47).

Ishiyama Kōichi and Satō Morio gave up their writing careers after the war, and together with Furuyama they grew to resent Yasuoka for using their mutually shared escapades for his own stories. They all but disappeared from literary history until Aoki Masami, a bookseller in Tokyo's famous used-bookstore neighborhood, Jinbochō, found a copy of Satō's *At a Crossroads* in a pile of remaindered books. Aoki reports owning manuscripts of two unpublished novels, one by Yasuoka and one by Yasuoka's friend Satō Morio, written in the same hand; the one by Yasuoka, "Patterns and Adventures" ("Ishō to bōken"), had been dictated by Yasuoka and transcribed in its entirety by Satō Morio (Aoki 21). So close had the boys been that they made a practice of dictating their works to one another.[11] The Bad Company saw themselves in everything Yasuoka wrote about the time period.

Not only Yasuoka's closest friends from the war have read these stories as chiefly autobiographical; Yasuoka's early works are commonly classified as postwar "I-novels," or *shishōsetsu*. Beginning with Tayama Katai's *The Quilt* (*Futon*) in 1907, the vast majority of Japan's literary establishment (*bundan*) engaged full-time or part-time in writing about their (usually transgressive) experiences. For decades, the "I-novels" were considered largely autobiographical, and readers mined them for information about the writers' lives. Van Gessel treats the Third Generation as I-novelists, even while admitting that the "complete identification between author and protagonist has broken down" in their writing, owing to the fact that "there is a clear layer of irony separating the author from his storyteller" (Gessel 67). This irony was lost on some. In 1974 one literary critic, Kawashima Itaru, even took up the cause of Yasuoka's friends, who felt their personal histories had been mined, and wrote an essay entitled "The Scar Left by a Twisted Truth" ("Waikyoku sareta jijitsu no kizuato"). Among other grievances, Kawashima reports that Ishiyama Kōichi's cousin, who was the model for the "cow-faced" woman the protagonist spurns in Yasuoka's "The Wandering Minstrel" ("Gin'yū shijin," 1954, in YSS vol. 1), was humiliated to the point that she considered suicide after the story came out (Kawashima 16). Kawashima acknowledges that Yasuoka is part of a long lineage of confessional writers but maintains that he doesn't feel the pain of his predecessors:

> Yasuoka's way of distancing himself from his material, his capacity for cruelty, comes very close to that of the prewar I-novelists, but we must acknowledge an essential difference: for Yasuoka the novelist, there exists an absolutely inviolable sanctuary. [. . .] The reason the prewar I-novelists allowed themselves to discuss the events of their personal lives so freely is that they pursued lives of selflessness, not belonging to anything. They had made up their minds to live only in this special world called the *bundan*, separated from everyday society. There, an atmosphere of collegiality reigned, and the authors kept a careful watch on one another. [. . .] To have the purity of one who has cast away all safe-havens and renounced the world was an absolute prerequisite to becoming a member of the *bundan*. (36–37)

Kawashima's argument is contradictory in the extreme—because the prewar authors were writing autobiographical truths, he claims, they felt an obligation driven by "selflessness" to expose their own failings. Moreover, the literary establishment of the early twentieth century was a closed society, Kawashima writes, and those who entered into the *bundan* and began writing about one another did so with the understanding that they were doing so within a closed circuit, not in an era of mass publishing.

Kawashima presumes that Yasuoka is doing something aberrant within the very large corpus of twentieth-century Japanese confessional literature. He appears to see entry into the *bundan* as on par with taking ecclesiastical orders demanding self-flagellation, but more recent scholarship does not hold the prewar *bundan* in such high regard. Edward Fowler agrees that it was a world apart from society, but notes the way editors would willingly give a writer advances in an attempt to obligate him to produce; such "journalistic pressure frequently induced him to make 'confessions' he might not otherwise have penned and sometimes to commit bizarre acts that might not otherwise have occurred to him, in his desperate search for new material" (*The Rhetoric of Confession* 143). The "selflessness" of the golden-age *shishōsetsuka*, writers of I-novels, is debatable at best.

Over the past couple of decades, scholars have also forced a reevaluation of this notion of autobiography being at the center of these prewar writings. Irmela Hijiya-Kirschnereit finds the origins of the form in classical Japanese aesthetics. Edward Fowler, too, finds the rationale for *shishōsetsu* in the Japanese literary tradition, but also in the circumstances of the *bundan*, and more than anything else, in the nature of the Japanese language itself, which he claims encourages and even demands an absolute identification of narrator and protagonist. For Tomi Suzuki, the form is a construction-after-the-fact, in which the incorporation of Western literary models led to "a discursive field in which the corpus of the I-novel was retroactively created and defined and from which the standard literary histories emerged" (10). Disparate as these explanations may be, they overlap in their refutation of the long-held notion that *shishōsetsu* are faithful depictions of practitioners' private lives.

Furthermore, others have demonstrated that the prewar *bundan* was already operating in a mass society. Even while arguing that the Taishō-era *bundan* was an elitist, cloistered world limited to Tokyo and marked by coterie magazines with circulations in the hundreds, Fowler has nonetheless noted that Tayama Katai's ostensibly autobiographical *The Quilt* was popular enough with the general public that the model for the live-in pupil whom Katai's protagonist grows to love, Okada Michiyo, published an article of her own in 1915 stating that "his portrayal of a jealous teacher lusting after his pupil was a complete fabrication" (*The Rhetoric of Confession* 115).[12] Michael Bourdaghs has described a similar situation after the publication of Shimazaki Tōson's *New Life* (*Shinsei*, 1919): In May 1937 Tōson's niece, with whom readers presumed him to have had an affair, began publishing her own account of their relationship. Unlike Okada Michiyo, however, she denies only the shading of it: "What the novel records is almost entirely true. Yet whatever was inconvenient to my uncle was expunged" (qtd. in Bourdaghs 147). Yasuoka would appear to be in good company when he utilizes the exploits of his "bad company" to create stories that are, ultimately, fictional constructs.

An example can show exactly the degree to which Yasuoka drew from his archive, using a single autobiographical trope to different ends in different stories. There was one event more than any other that haunted the Bad Company. Yasuoka and another of the group, Kurata Hiromitsu, had a running rivalry in which each would try to deceive the other. It was playful at first, but in the spring of 1942, Yasuoka took the game to an unprecedented level. Yasuoka and Kurata had agreed to throw away their draft deferments and willingly enlist in the military, an ultimate gesture of despair at ever truly escaping the system. In the event, however, Yasuoka failed to go to his draft station, and only Kurata signed up. Kurata went off to war in 1942. He went missing in action and never returned (Aoki 22).

The Generation of Deception

The "Bad Company" (Warui nakama). Left to right: Yasuoka Shōtarō, Furuyama Komao, Kurata Hiromitsu. Photograph courtesy of Bunshun / amanaimages / Minden Pictures.

Yasuoka wrote about the betrayal in a number of stories, including "The King's Ears" ("Ōsama no mimi," 1954), "Same Old, Same Old" ("Ai mo kawarazu," 1959), and "Humid Morning" ("Mushiatsui asa," 1961). His fellow members of the Bad Company took these stories as a sign of regret and an admission of guilt on Yasuoka's part, but it would be difficult to see them as anything other than crafted fiction, if for no other reason than that they use the incident to tell completely different stories. In "The King's Ears," the narrator and his friend Toyota Fukumitsu (a play on Kurata Hiromitsu's name) play tricks on each other in an escalating war of deception. The two dream of running away to France and decide that the Japanese Imperial Army—which they have built up in their minds to resemble the French Foreign Legion—is the next best thing to it. The narrator doesn't get his application together in time for the deadline, and once Toyota realizes that he will be going off alone, he effects one last ruse to trick the narrator out of ten yen at what was supposed to be Toyota's sendoff party. Toyota is never heard from again, and the narrator grumbles that in this way Toyota had the last laugh on him, before sardonically admitting, "I imagine I was the one who killed him" (YSS 1: 318).

In "Same Old, Same Old," the protagonist Juntarō and his friend, here named Yamada, decide together to join the army. Yamada signs up early, alarming

Juntarō, but Juntarō agrees to meet Yamada at 9:00 a.m. one morning to cancel his draft deferment. In this iteration, Juntarō meets a woman the evening before the meeting and ends up drinking with her in Shinjuku and going home with her. In the morning, late for his meeting, he runs downstairs only to find his shoes missing; the woman tells him that he cannot leave without paying the person in charge. He realizes that she is a prostitute and that he is not going to make his meeting in time.

In the third variation, "Humid Morning," the central character is again named Juntarō. Although critics have taken Yasuoka's "Juntarō stories" to be part of the same reality, the story offers yet another conflicting explanation: Juntarō spends the night before his meeting with Yamada with his girlfriend Kazuko. A child in her boarding house is playing the drums, and Juntarō blames the drumming for changing his life: the noise puts Juntarō and Kazuko in the mood for love, and Kazuko becomes pregnant. Juntarō goes to a military base to have his draft deferment cancelled, but when the colonel in charge—a family friend—asks him why he wants to go to war before finishing his schooling, Juntarō cannot come up with an explanation and finally blurts out that what he really needs is a doctor willing to perform an abortion. The colonel scolds him in high military dudgeon—then promptly gives him the name of a hospital that will perform the procedure.

These are not stories about making amends; they mutually undermine one another's veracity, and they are told with a black humor the rhetorical logic of which deliberately resists any attempt at reading them as mere earnest "confessions." There is a keen irony in attempting to search for biographical truth in stories about lies. Rather, what makes them of particular interest is the way that the protagonist's deception is mirrored in the great national deception of the war. In "The King's Ears," lies about the army are a central part of the young men's mutual deception, because no conceivable future for them other than one in the military exists: "if we wanted to imagine a beautiful future ahead of us, even just a little, we had no other option but to make the army itself beautiful in our minds" (YSS 1: 312). In "Same Old, Same Old," the protagonist dissembles to all around him; he feigns interest in various hijinks out of a sense of "responsibility" to his friends, just as he takes the entrance exams year after year out of responsibility to his mother and just as he sits and answers the questions out of responsibility to the proctor (YSS 3: 106). The dedication to education that he is forced to affect is a ruse to avoid the army year after year. It is a passive resistance, masquerading as active complicity, and he notes that the self-sacrificial act of joining the army would represent the first thing he has actively done in his entire life (YSS 3: 126). In "Humid Morning," the colonel initially mistakes Juntarō's visit for nascent patriotism and tries to send him away with the reassurance, "I know exactly how you feel. [. . .] From here on out, young people need to be more like you" (YSS 3: 310). The colonel mistakes Juntarō's cowardice in not being able to ask for a recommendation to a good clinic for heroism; the irony is that postwar readers would reverse the criteria for those two categories, seeing resistance as the heroic option and enlistment as the passive, cowardly act. It would thus be impossible to write "truthful" stories even if one wanted to, because the truth would depend on who was telling it and in what year. One is reminded of the old detective Satō in Kurosawa Akira's 1949 classic film *Stray Dog* (*Norainu*); as Mitsuhiro Yoshimoto notes, Satō is proud that he has been putting criminals away for thirty years, a seemingly innocuous statement that turns frighteningly absent of any moral anchor when one considers how different the various authorities that Satō served would have been in the prewar, wartime, and postwar (Yoshimoto 172).

Stories about Stories

Placed in wider context, it is clear that this subversion of narrative is being put to greater use than simple self-protection. Studies of the Third Generation of New Writers have focused on their autobiographical work, but none of the writers in the group worked exclusively in that domain.[13] Yasuoka himself wrote a number of stories based on well-known Biblical narratives and fairy tales—through these, a clearer picture of his literary craftsmanship emerges. In nearly every story, the theme of deception runs deep; put another way, Yasuoka is particularly interested in stories that talk about storytelling. For example, he rewrote the story of Samson and Delilah in "The Woman Who Had Dreams" ("Yume miru onna," 1955), which takes as its epigraph Judges 16.4: "Some time later, he fell in love with a woman in the valley of Sorek whose name was Delilah" (NIV). The Biblical Delilah is a villain: She coaxes Samson into telling her the secret of his strength. He resists by lying to her three times, but on her fourth attempt he admits that his strength is in his long hair. Delilah quickly has a servant shave Samson's head and calls down the Philistines upon him. Samson is blinded and taken captive, but he prays to God for the strength to knock down the Philistine temple pillars during their religious ceremony. His wish for vengeance is granted, such that "he killed many more when he died than while he lived" (NIV, Judges 16.31).

"The Woman Who Had Dreams" is narrated by Delilah, humanizing her in the process. She complains that her lover always lies to her, in ways small ("there's a cat behind you") and large ("I killed a lion with my bare hands"). She worries that he is still involved with a former lover, a woman from Timnah. He insists that he only lies as a joke and has always been faithful to her, but she cannot be placated; she wishes there were a way to tie him up, constrain him. Men from a neighboring town tell her that they would like to beat her lover in wrestling just once; they wonder if there is a trick to what he does. She tries to get it out of him, but he lies to her over and over again. Finally, when he tells her the truth—"Cut my hair"—she does it, and he is led away through the Sorek Valley.

Delilah has suffered at the hands of Biblical scholars over the centuries; she is often taken as a prefiguration of Judas, willing to sell God's chosen one to his enemies for pieces of silver. In Yasuoka's hands, however, the line between deceiver and deceived is not as sharp. Delilah is genuinely anguished at rumors Samson is visiting other women elsewhere, including his former wife, a Philistine known only as the woman of Timnah: "Oh, if only I could tie this man up. If I were just able to do that, no matter how much he might still lie to me and deceive me, at least he couldn't go to see that woman from Timnah or any other women anymore" (YSS 1: 415). At the end of the story, she is as amazed as anyone else that she has sent him to his death.

Samson's supposed lies speak to the fundamentally unascertainable relationship between fiction and truth. Yasuoka has his Delilah refuse to believe a central feature of the Biblical narrative of Samson, the fact that he really did kill a lion with his bare hands: "The Spirit of the Lord came powerfully upon him so that he tore the lion apart with his bare hands as he might have torn a young goat" (NIV, Judges 14.6). In Judges, however, the lion represents a more complicated back story of deception for Samson: When he later passes the lion's carcass, he finds a swarm of bees making honey in it and conceives a riddle for his comrades: "Out of the eater, something to eat; / out of the strong, something sweet" (NIV, Judges 14.14). His friends convince his first wife to finagle the answer out of Samson, foreshadowing the later, more costly deception by Delilah. It is unknown why the first wife deceives Samson—perhaps because she is a Philistine, it doesn't require an explanation—but the larger question is why Samson falls for the same ruse when Delilah tries it. Just as Yasuoka's telling gives Delilah a rationale greater than that of simply making some money—she fears being betrayed—his version also makes Samson out to be more than a perennial patsy. The Samson of Yasuoka's story enjoys the game of deceiving and being deceived, and in fact shows affection for his wife by keeping their relationship in a constant state of play.

In "Bluebeard" ("Aohige," 1955), Yasuoka treats the legendary wife-killer made famous by the telling in Charles Perrault's *Contes* (1697). In that version, Bluebeard is a French aristocrat who leaves his new wife in charge of the manor while he conducts business in the provinces. He allows her full range of the house, except for one small room that he instructs her never to enter. Her curiosity gets the better of her, and she lets herself in to find the corpses of his seven previous wives hanging on the wall. Worse, in her shock she drops the key on the floor; it becomes stained with blood that will not wash off. When Bluebeard returns, he threatens to kill her with his scimitar, and only the timely arrival of her brothers saves her from the same fate as her predecessors. Perrault ends his version with two morals: first, that "Curiosity, with its many charms, / Can stir up serious regrets," and second, that "No longer are husbands so terrible" (Tatar, *Annotated* 157). A stretch though these may seem, Maria Tatar notes that scholars "have shown surprising interpretive confidence in reading Perrault's 'Bluebeard' as a story about a woman's failure to respond to the trust invested in her"; as for Perrault himself, she notes, his telling is full of "judgmental asides about the envy, greed, curiosity, and disobedience of Bluebeard's wife and her intimates, but he remains diffident about framing any sort of indictment of a man who has cut the throats of his wives" (Tatar, *Secrets* 20).

Yasuoka's Bluebeard is largely diminished. As the story opens, Aoki Shōkichi's wife is overcome with the same feeling of curiosity; she picks up a large envelope containing his diaries and letters from old girlfriends. Among them, she finds a letter addressed to one Isotani Miyoko, full of romantic phrases. She feels guilty for reading it, despite the fact that her husband said he wouldn't mind. She is susceptible to the power of suggestion: "If someone says something to me, it will inevitably come to pass. If I'm told 'You're going to fall,' I will tumble even if I have been running along as usual up until that very moment. If I'm told, 'You'll drop it,' I'll drop the dish I have been holding. If someone were to tell me, 'You're going to kill someone,' perhaps I would have to murder someone" (YSS 2: 48–49).

She asks Shōkichi what he would do if he were to catch her cheating, and he tells her he would cut her in half. But he is the one who needs to defend his trustworthiness; unlike his aristocratic predecessor, Shōkichi makes a point of telling his wife outlandish stories of his various indiscretions—in Paris, in Cairo, in Japan—that she regards as possibly true. They fight over Isotani, and when she threatens to go stay with another man, Shōkichi slaps her so hard that she grabs a knife and shouts "Murderer!" so loudly the police come and haul Shōkichi away. Three years later, she still feels the sting of his slap, and when she complains of it, she is surprised to hear that he slapped her not because she had insulted Isotani, as she had always thought, but out of jealousy that she was threatening to go to another man. He admits to her that his peccadillos were stories and nothing more. She ends up feeling sorry for Isotani, who had never been loved.

Unlike Bluebeard's wife, Shōkichi's wife gives as good as she gets. The scimitar that Bluebeard brandishes at his helpless wife appears here in the form of the newly stropped kitchen knife that Shōkichi's wife wields. The forbidden knowledge that Bluebeard incites his wife into seeking so that she may be punished—a violence that is being repeated for the eighth time in the fairy tale—is here freely offered by Shōkichi. It is a deception, but a painfully obvious one that Shōkichi's wife willingly accommodates; it doesn't require a great deal of skepticism to question how Shōkichi could have made his way to Paris and Cairo during the war or subsequent Occupation. At the same time, she deceives him herself: She appears to have no intention of going off with another man or of knifing her husband. The suspicion that Shōkichi engenders in his wife leads her to match him deception for deception.

A similar deceived woman appears in "Martha's Lament" ("Maruta no nageki," 1955), a story based on a passage from the book of Luke about Martha and Mary of Bethany, sisters of Lazarus:

> As Jesus and his disciples were on their way, he came to a village where a woman named Martha opened her home to him. She had a sister called Mary, who sat at the Lord's feet listening to what he said. But Martha was distracted by all the preparations that had to be made. She came to him and asked, "Lord, don't you care that my sister has left me to do the work by myself? Tell her to help me!" "Martha, Martha," the Lord answered, "you are worried and upset about many things, but few things are needed—or indeed only one. Mary has chosen what is better, and it will not be taken away from her." (NIV, Luke 10.38–42)

In John 12, when this same Mary anoints Jesus's feet and hair with ointment, she hears Judas make a similar complaint: "Why wasn't this perfume sold and the money given to the poor?" (NIV, John 12.5), to which Jesus replies: "Leave her alone [. . .] It was intended that she should save this perfume for the day of my burial. You will always have the poor among you, but you will not always have me" (NIV, John 12.7–8).

In "Martha's Lament," the narrator complains that her younger sister is a little off, but no one ever scolds her. As children, they heard the story of Cinderella in Hibiya Park, and she felt her situation to be quite similar to that of the stepsisters. Why, she wonders, was the storyteller so prejudiced against the older stepsisters? Men, she decides, even Jesus and Cinderella's Prince, are deceived; they don't see the younger sisters for what they really are (YSS 2: 73). Cinderella had as much envy and vanity as her sisters—why else would she lie to people and run out on them (74)? The narrator's husband used to work on a military base during the Occupation, where his old flame, Yajima Tomeko, was a waitress at the PX. Yajima, he claims, was from a wealthy family and resembled the American actress "J. F." They dated for seven years, until she went off to the hot springs with another man.

The Generation of Deception

The husband claims never to have truly been in love with Yajima, but he also admits that he crosses paths with her from time to time; for the narrator, something that she thought was in the past is in fact in the present (YSS 2: 77). How could he have been involved with this woman for seven years without the relationship progressing? She is driven to distraction after her husband tells her that Yajima resembles an American movie star, and when she finds herself in Yajima's neighborhood, she goes in search of the woman. The narrator learns that the Yajimas are the neighborhood fish vendors and that Yajima Tomeko decidedly does not resemble a Hollywood actress: she is a tall, loping woman, "like a giant eel," and a *panpan* prostitute to boot. The wife is disturbed to learn that her husband does not find this surprising in the least and finds it hard to believe he didn't know she wasn't from a wealthy family:

> "You never suspected what kind of family she came from?"
>
> "What reason would I have to suspect anything?"
>
> "All right . . . but you were thinking of marrying her, right? What would you have done if her lies had come out on your wedding day?"
>
> "It would have been all the more convenient. . . . Her family could have supplied the food."
>
> "But what was she thinking? Maybe she's vain down to the core, and she herself believes it even when she lies and says she comes from an old family or that they're landlords, so she isn't aware that it's a lie. . . . And she doesn't look a thing like J. F., does she? Maybe she believed that, too, from the moment she thought of it. You're really terrible. You were the first one to say that she looks like J. F."
>
> With that, my husband burst out laughing. "Saying that was the best present I could give her that didn't cost any money," he said. "Ahahaha, I really fooled her." (YSS 2: 86)

Again, the motif of deception rises to the forefront. The wife is disturbed by the husband's former relationship, which—like the couple in "Bluebeard"—is founded on willful, effortless lies. In the wife's eyes, Yajima is the Mary to the wife's Martha, a carefree younger woman able to captivate the men around her, who are incapable of seeing through her ruses. She may not look like the actress "J. F.," but there is reason to believe that she is being compared here to Joan Fontaine (1917–2013), winner of the 1941 Academy Award for Best Actress in Alfred Hitchcock's *Suspicion*. Yasuoka was a fan of Hitchcock, but Joan Fontaine as Mary of Bethany makes sense for another reason: she was the younger sister of two-time Academy Award-winner Olivia de Havilland (1916–). Although she was younger and far more ambivalent about the craft, Joan was the first to win Best Actress, an annoying development that de Havilland was rumored to have never quite forgiven, despite later winning twice herself. Both sisters were born and lived briefly in Tokyo.

The seven years that the protagonist's husband spent with Yajima resonate with Bluebeard's seven wives as well as with a host of other references throughout Western literature to the magical properties of the number seven. Of course, the seven-year relationship also bears some similarities to the Old Testament story of Jacob and his wives. Jacob agrees to work for Laban for seven years in exchange for the right to marry Laban's daughter Rachel, but Laban sends Rachel's older sister Leah instead:

> When morning came, there was Leah! So Jacob said to Laban, "What is this you have done to me? I served you for Rachel, didn't I? Why have you deceived me?"
>
> Laban replied, "It is not our custom here to give the younger daughter in marriage before the older one. Finish this daughter's bridal week; then we will give you the younger one also, in return for another seven years of work."
>
> And Jacob did so. (NIV, Genesis 29.25–27)

Jacob loves the younger sister more than the older one but is deceived into marrying Leah before Rachel. Jacob has given as good as he gets, however, having cheated his older brother Esau out of his birthright by deceiving their father Isaac in Genesis 27. This is true of the husband in "Martha's Lament" as well, as the wife notes: "'I really fooled her'? What is that supposed to mean? Wasn't he the one who had been fooled, for seven years?" (YSS 2: 86).

The husband here bears more than a passing resemblance to the autobiographical "I" whom Yasuoka has employed in other stories. The husband, like other Yasuoka protagonists, spent time at empty houses requisitioned by the American Occupation; in this story, such a house was one of the rendezvous sites of his youthful love with Yajima (YSS 2: 81). In Yasuoka's earlier stories involving relationships at unoccupied Occupation houses—"The Glass Slipper" and "The House Guard"—the male protagonist was the more deceived; he found love in the isolated, temporary escape from the greater world and just as quickly saw it slip away when the haven was invaded. Here the husband actively engages in lies of omission and commission. Perhaps one could read these stories of deception among lovers as a form of oblique confession, in which the protagonist who stands for Yasuoka has done something terrible. In literary terms, however, these stories demonstrate a preoccupation with deception as a narrative trope, a lens through which we must also read the later autobiographical novels of deception.

The We-Novel: *The Angel of Mockery*

On the evening of December 30, 1955, the literary critic Hattori Tatsu came to an important decision. He showed up at the house of fellow literary critic Shindō Junkō in the Kyōdō area of Tokyo's Setagaya-ku carrying a small duffle bag. It wasn't unusual for Hattori to stay over at the homes of friends and acquaintances; he often worked late in the city but lived some distance out from central Tokyo. As he left the following afternoon, Hattori abruptly asked Shindō's wife if she knew why great literature was impossible in Japan. "Because," he said, answering his own question, "the wives are faithful, and never for a minute fall in love" (Muramatsu 280). With that, he headed out, traveling by train via Shinjuku to Kobuchizawa, where he spent the night. On the first morning of 1956, he rode the Koumi Line to Kiyosato Station. He checked in to the Seisenryō Inn, where in one of the guest cottages he wrote a suicide note and letters to nine friends and colleagues. It is believed that at about 11:00 p.m., Hattori walked out of the cottage and into the wilds surrounding Mount Yatsugatake, never to return again.

Hattori and Shindō were critics affiliated with the Third Generation, and in Yasuoka's mind it was Hattori who best explained their works. Hattori, born in 1922, was roughly the same age as the Third Generation and thus wrote about those who had come of age in wartime from an inside perspective, but Yasuoka may have felt even closer to Hattori than the other writers. When Yasuoka writes that Hattori's comments "matched our experiences and the things we had thought down to the smallest details, such that it felt as though Hattori had been one of our number," he is talking about his wartime friends in the Bad Company, not the Third Generation of New Writers (BSS 1: 124).

Hattori was in the early stages of a promising career, and he intended to write a novel himself at some point; his suicide came as a shock to everyone around him. He had debts piling up, owing in part to expenses he had run up seeing A., a bar hostess in Ginza, on the side, but Hattori left word that she was not what had driven him to freeze himself to death on the slopes of Yatsugatake: "If it were only a question of my feelings for A., I would probably live on," he writes in his suicide note, published in the journal *Chisei* as "The Last Journal Entry" ("Saigo no nikki") (Hattori 278). Nor was it about the money: "I have a good amount of debt, but the debt collector doesn't go so far as to take your life" (278). Hattori points to something deeper, a "certain feeling of ennui and emptiness, lurking in the shadow of the players called Exhaustion and Pride" (279). He suggests that this ennui is not unique to himself: "Our lives are necessarily ones of boredom," he writes, and later in the note he adds, somewhat cryptically, "Healthy people are bored; it is possible that I am simply too bored" (279). Hattori is not quite able to express the real reason he is committing suicide, but his message is otherwise lucid and thoughtful, detailing what he did in the last hours of his life as well as the rationale behind his chosen means of suicide: "Owing to my sense of vanity, or perhaps my sense of aesthetics, I have no fondness for a method involving pouring my blood out or dirtying with my excrement a futon that belongs to someone else. The same goes for throwing myself in front of a train" (279). Hattori isn't sure that exposure to the elements will work in such a warm winter, nor that taking a bottleful of sleeping pills will do the trick, so he decides to combine the two: According to his note, he will take one hundred Brovarin, a Japanese-produced hypnotic and sedative, before walking toward Yatsugatake (279).

Hattori had tied his fortunes to the Third Generation, and he took their successes and failures to heart more than the writers themselves did. At the celebration following Endō's surprising Akutagawa Prize win in July 1955, the fourth of five for the group, Hattori announced to the assembled crowd, "The Third Generation are in full bloom!" (BSS 2: 167). It was a brief bloom indeed: In the July 1955 issue of *Bungakukai*, Ishihara Shintarō published *Season of the Sun* (*Taiyō no kisetsu*, translated as *Season of Violence*), a scandalous novella that threatened to overwhelm the collected accomplishments of the Third Generation. The one who most took Ishihara as a threat, surprisingly, was Hattori himself. Yasuoka didn't feel there was anything particularly new in Ishihara's story, but Hattori was less conciliatory: "That's it for me," he said to Yasuoka. "What I was trying to do has been done" (BSS 2: 172). There were rumors that Hattori was frequenting a Ginza bar that was above the means of a literary critic, and he seemed more and more distracted. "What was he thinking about? Women? Money? And yet, more than anything, the shadow of loneliness flitted across his face" (BSS 2: 174). For Yasuoka, Hattori's despair was of a more existential nature:

> The circumstances of the age had closed in and things had drastically changed—surely this is the reason he killed himself. [. . .] Hattori had been the first to proclaim the end of the postwar and the age of postwar democracy. Then journalism had seemed to bestow upon Hattori the role of starting pitcher of the ideology of the new era. Of course, Hattori was all too well aware of this. That said, however, I doubt whether he had prepared himself mentally for this, whether he had reserves sufficient to the task he was

undertaking. [. . .] At this moment when the postwar was at last at an end, Hattori must have turned his eye inward and recoiled at the sight: an infinite wasteland, so devastated that he could not touch it. And so, with nowhere else to turn, on December 31, he set off, stumbling toward Yatsugatake in the dead of night. (BSS 2: 180–82)

Hattori's literal stumble in the dark would begin the following night, in the new year, but the disorientation to which Yasuoka speaks is resonant with endings: of a year, of a postwar, of an ambition.

In *The Angel of Mockery* (*Shitadashi tenshi*, 1958), Yasuoka's first novel, he treats Hattori as yet another protagonist versed in the ways of deception: the narrator, known only by his surname, Okabe, is living a double life. He is ostensibly living with an older woman, Yoshida Kaneko, whom he met while working at a textile company when he was twenty-six and she was twenty-nine. Okabe invited Kaneko out to his house in K., a coastal city somewhat removed from Tokyo. He was initially looking for an ally at work, but from the moment Kaneko arrived, it was clear that she had larger plans: Kaneko began cleaning his apartment and cooking for him, and before long she had quit her job and was working in the K. area, teaching drawing to children and working on a nearby military base. Kaneko represents stasis to Okabe, whose desires, first and foremost, call for motion. What Okabe most wants is the freedom to come and go as he pleases, so he rents a room closer to central Tokyo, in Ōmori. His usual drinking route takes him through Shinbashi, Ginza, and Nihonbashi, and he meets a Ginza hostess, Chiba Yōko, among whose charms is the fact that, after work one night, she brings him to places in the city he has never been. Okabe and Yōko fall into bed together in a Shinagawa hotel, and Okabe is convinced that in Yōko he has found an "antidote" to Kaneko's suffocating ways:

> Yōko was a woman the polar opposite of Kaneko. While Yōko was impulsively direct, Kaneko was an iron fist in a velvet glove. Or perhaps I could call her the self-sacrificial type. But was true self-sacrifice really possible in human affairs? [. . .] For me, Yōko's directness was an antidote to Kaneko. For example, Yōko knew nothing about loving someone else; she was used to being loved. But if you're a woman who understands when you're really loved, you will respond in kind to that man's love—isn't that the same thing as knowing what it is to love? Kaneko was the exact reverse. Kaneko was always casting herself as a tragic heroine, and actually believed that, despite her earnest attempts at love, she was a woman betrayed. (YSS 5: 209)

Okabe begins seeing more and more of Yōko, but always when she is on the job and he is paying to do so. His debts start out small; he had cotranslated a work with his friend Okamura, and when he went to the publishing house to receive the fee, he signed for the total and soon spent Okamura's half. He receives money from his family for house repairs but spends a third of it on rent for his second home in Ōmori. Infatuated, he proposes marriage to Yōko; she, in turn, makes it clear to him that she herself would like a fur coat. Okabe's older brother has a solution: he works at a newspaper and has a connection who would like to have an English-language erotic novel titled *Helen and Desire* translated into Japanese.[14] His brother is as salacious as one would expect of a newspaperman in postwar Japan; he would probably even love to hear, Okabe muses, about his own deepest secret: that Okabe had slept with their sister-in-law, the wife of their older brother in Osaka. Okabe agrees to translate the novel.

Things begin to fall apart for Okabe, but as with his real-life counterpart Hattori, none of it overwhelms him: Kaneko finds out about his relationship with Yōko but tells him frankly: "All I care is that you come back to me" (249). Okabe thinks about his relationship with Yōko and thinks the same thing to himself: "All I care about is that you come back to me." In this sense, then, he is to Kaneko as Yōko is to him, with a crucial difference: Kaneko does not pursue him as he pursues Yōko. Meanwhile, the only truth for Yōko is money, he decides, and his money is mainly going for her enjoyment. As he dwells on this predicament, his brother contacts him with bad news: the publication of *Helen and Desire* has run afoul of the authorities, and Okabe's older brother informs him that it would be bad for the family were his name to be associated with the brewing scandal. Destroy the manuscript, his brother commands him, and return the translation fee to me.

Okabe goes to Osaka to beg his oldest brother for the money; they agree that he will receive the money as soon as he breaks things off with Yōko. As he leaves, he receives another shock: his sister-in-law has told the oldest brother about their brief affair so long ago: "The moment I heard my sister-in-law's hoarse, low voice whisper those words, absurd as it may be, the first thing that entered my mind was the realization, 'I've been betrayed'" (299). Within the world of the novel, it is a transformative moment in which his act of betrayal is undone when he himself is betrayed. He has come there to beg for money to pay back the fee for a forbidden translation; structurally, the deceptions in Okabe's personal life and those in the literature he translates are unmasked together. *Traduttore, traditore*—the translator's maxim, "to translate is to betray"—can apply just as well to the relationship of Yasuoka's life and this particular fiction. Although the more sensational elements of the story are taken from Hattori's own life—the debts, the affair with the hostess, the winter suicide—a number of the less pronounced ones resonate with Yasuoka's own experiences. Like Yasuoka (and his stand-in in numerous autobiographical stories), Okabe at various times lives on the "K Coast" and in Ōmori. He remembers always having summer homework to do as a child (281). He has a translation job at a company (180). He remembers at various points how he had hoped for peace during the war (181, 203). Has Yasuoka translated his own narrative into Hattori's?

It appears there is a confession hidden in the heart of this novel. If so, it is a confession that strives not to be understood, one written in code such that not even the parties involved recognized themselves in it. The name "Okabe" itself is an amalgamation of the second characters in the two friends' names, taking the "oka" of "Yasuoka" and the second character of "Hattori," here pronounced "be":

安岡　Yasuoka
服部　Hattori
岡部　Okabe

A confessional novel this may be, but the confession is cloaked in wordplay; it is hardly of a kind with the prewar *shishōsetsu* that gleefully revealed one's transgressions for the world to see. Rather, it is a discourse in which form follows function—the theme of deception in Okabe's life is echoed in the structure of the novel, which seeks to divert the reader's attention from the actual deception being performed, not by a character against his partner and friends, but by a narrative against its readers.

When the deceptions of the world were laid bare in the post-Occupation, they proved too much for Hattori, and his literary alter ego, Okabe, who follows roughly the same path as Hattori. Okabe writes a farewell letter to Yōko and leaves Shinjuku by train on the evening of December 31, 1956. He checks in at a rural hotel where he is the only guest, and on January 1 he walks into oblivion. There, in the wilderness, he sees Yōko in the distance; although they walk toward each other, he never gets any closer to her:

> Her figure seemed to melt into a white wall right in front of me. In that instant, I remembered what I had to say to her. "It was I who deceived you. The letter was a complete lie. Every last word of it. Why would I ever die over something like this?" Before I had finished saying it, however, the snow beneath my frozen feet began to give way without a sound. While I was wondering at the skin of snow that had ripped open right in front of me, small, hard crystals in an instant enveloped my body. (325)

It is Okabe's last desperate attempt to deceive without being deceived, to operate under the same terms he has always employed in a world that has moved beyond the strictures of the immediate postwar. As with other Yasuoka protagonists, Okabe's attempt to deceive someone to whom he is close blurs with his attempt to deceive himself.

At the same time, deceit is again revealed to be not only thematic but also structural: the "I" that readers presumed had literally lived to tell the tale speaks from beyond the grave in the final lines in which he depicts his own demise. If Fowler is correct that the Japanese language itself encourages one to conflate author and narrative voice, this ending represents a stunning splitting of the two. If Yasuoka were writing himself into Okabe, one would expect Okabe to survive as Yasuoka has done. The deception performed in the text, subsuming Yasuoka's own crypto-confession into that of his friend's, could be considered perhaps another in a string of betrayals by the author. But this ignores the craftedness of the novel, the way in which it serves not as a confession but as a commentary on confession. Okabe/Hattori's deceptions have been laid bare, and he has been lost along the way, but Okabe/Yasuoka has maintained the deception, has confessed without anyone realizing it, and has managed to survive the transition from immediate postwar to long postwar. As a work of art, the novel stands as a reminder that, in the postwar as well as the war, deception continues to be a means of survival.

Oneself in the Past: *After the Curtain Falls*

The publication of *After the Curtain Falls* (*Maku ga orite kara*) in 1967 was considered an act of confession by Yasuoka, but any such confession comes only in fits and starts over the course of the work. In the opening scene, the painter Nagano Kensuke is wary of a literal curtain fall: he is on stage in an amateur kabuki performance put on once a year by a small who's who of the Tokyo creative world.[15] Kensuke is dressed as a female character (an *onnagata*), and he is distracted; he has branched out into essay-writing and television appearances, and he worries that this role will add to his trivialization in the art scene. "When the curtain falls," one of his fellow performers tells him, "you have to be on your guard," as there are numerous accounts of actors and stagehands being crushed by the lead pipe that weights it down (YSS 7: 14). What exactly the curtain stands for is the subject of the novel.

If *The Angel of Mockery* was filled with a sense of foreboding, *After the Curtain Falls* is its counterpoint, a novel suffused with regret and visions of the past. From the stage, Kensuke sees Okuda Mutsuko sitting in the audience, and the memories he associates with her set the narrative on two parallel tracks, separated by five years. In the earlier story, set in the early 1950s, Kensuke and his parents are renting a house in K City from his uncle. Kensuke is an invalid, he can only crawl to get around, and his father is living a newly adopted agrarian lifestyle without any real skill at raising the myriad animals he brings to the property. Kensuke's mother trades on the black market, but it occurs to them that they can rent out part of the house—without Kensuke's uncle's knowledge—for five hundred yen a month, about ten times what they themselves are paying the uncle. The artist Okuda Kin'ichi and his wife Mutsuko thus move in. Kensuke is dismissive of Okuda as an artist at first, but as a growing crowd of fellow artists comes to visit the man, Kensuke comes to understand that Okuda has a certain prestige in the art world. When Kensuke's uncle shows up and intimates that he is considering selling the house, the balance of power in the household shifts: only the Okudas have the money to buy the house, and the only thing that seems to keep Okuda from doing so is the amount of compensation he would be obligated to give Kensuke's family in order to evict them. The two families go in three separate directions: the Okudas move elsewhere in the same neighborhood, Kensuke's parents head for Kōchi Prefecture, and Kensuke himself goes elsewhere in the Tokyo area.

In the other narrative, set five years later in the late 1950s, Kensuke wakes up the morning after the curtain falls on his kabuki premiere feeling out of sorts. On the one hand, life has changed, and he has changed with it. In the newspaper, he sees a reference to the growing consumer society's "three treasures of the household."[16] He reads about how students are losing their dining discounts and how black-market rice prices have equalized with above-ground prices, meaning that food supplies have returned to prewar levels. On a personal level, he has a wife, Teruko, he is healthy again, and he is progressing in his career. Kensuke's mother has passed away, and his father intends to come back to Tokyo to live with Kensuke and Teruko, an idea that Teruko finds unpalatable in the extreme. Kensuke sets off for the day, ostensibly to borrow money that will allow them to rent separate lodgings for his father.

The connection between this day in the late 1950s and the flashbacks to an earlier time would appear quite logical: the father's return triggers memories of the last time Kensuke lived with his parents. Problematically, however, Kensuke finds that it is a lack of certain memories that is tethering him to the past: "Ten years after the end of the war, it was perfectly natural that people's living situations should change; one couldn't go on forever living in the charred rubble of the post-firebombing. But . . . when Kensuke thought back to three or four years earlier, even if he tried to piece together how he had gotten to this point, something obstructed his memory" (66). Perhaps too many things had happened in the interim, he thinks, before reconsidering: "It wasn't only that there had been a surplus of incidents and occurrences, but also that something within him had changed in the meantime" (67). The change, whatever it consists of, has maintained this "surplus of incidents" within Kensuke; where there was once only one of him, there are now two: his present self and his past self who remains with him. When he looks at the first photo of himself to appear in a newspaper, he claims that he is not alone: "It was no longer only I who was looking at this newspaper, the color of dusty leaves; this man who had had his name emblazoned in the corner of the newspaper, he was looking alongside me" (67). However peaceful and stable the everyday has become for Kensuke in the late 1950s, the fog of the postwar continues to obscure the distance between the then and the now, and what appears to be a fragmented narrative is precisely the opposite: the past is too much with him in the present.

For Kensuke, the fear is that this inability to escape the past is similar to the way his parents fell victim not to the war, but to the postwar. A month after his mother dies, Kensuke's father comes to visit him and Teruko:

> Father, from where he had sat down in the chair in the sunny spot next to the window, looked here and there around the room with eyes crusted with sleep the color of glue. Kensuke tried to figure out what he was looking at by following where he was looking, but it was hopeless. . . . It had been exactly the same the year after the war ended, when Father, who had been imprisoned in Southeast Asia, suddenly returned home to the house in the town of K where Kensuke and his mother were living. (131)

Kensuke's father had somehow recovered, but at the same time his mother had begun her slow descent away from reality. From the beginning, Mother resented the Okudas for various reasons: Okuda is much older than his wife and "shamelessly" uses her as a model for his nudes, while Mutsuko speaks to the chickens in the yard using a mangled honorific language (*keigo*). Mother tells Kensuke that he needs to stop taking meals with the Okudas, because it gives them an excuse to steal food from Kensuke's family. Kensuke notes her paranoia, but it is only clearly connected to the past in the later narrative stream, when Teruko tells Kensuke that his father's drinking has inched up to the point that he is consuming more than a *shō* (about 1.8 liters) of sake a night, a problem that hadn't manifested itself since before the war began in earnest:

> It hadn't been unusual before the war for his father to drink in a single evening more sake than even the largest-size bottles hold; to be sure, once he had a little liquor in him he couldn't leave off, and no matter how much he

put into himself he would keep right on going. But after he had come to live with them in K after the war, his taste in food had changed—or perhaps it was better to say that his taste in food had disappeared—and what mattered to Father was shoving in as much of it as he could. He liked to smoke so much that he would stuff his pipe with butts he found on the ground, but he would exchange even the sake he received as part of their rations for food without the slightest sign of regret. He had pretty much quit drinking. (201)

Father's single-minded focus on food was not unusual for the postwar; getting enough food to survive was a daily challenge for the mass of people across Japan. Kensuke's mother's ongoing obsession with food long after the world had righted itself marked her as one stuck in the immediate postwar, while Kensuke's father's return to his old drinking habits was a sign of his own longing for happier times before the war turned sour, of his ability to move out of the postwar only by going backward. For Kensuke, the unshakable grip of the postwar is channeled through his parents, and thus linked to aging, madness, and death.

Kensuke's quest for money in the later narrative brings him to a newspaper office to try to get an advance on a story, and there he remembers a previous visit when the editor Wakabayashi had chastised a writer for bringing him a story that appeared too similar to one the writer had published in a different magazine the previous month. Kensuke wasn't convinced what the writer had done was wrong (234). The scene could be considered a commentary on Kensuke's own situation, as his life is full of incidents that could be considered retellings of the same story: his difficulties grasping the flow of time as echoes of what his father and mother once went through, his wife's scoldings as echoes of his mother's scoldings, his father's reappearance in Tokyo as an echo of the time his father came back from the war. As we have seen, Kensuke has claimed that there are two of him—is the Kensuke in the "present" of the story only a pretender, a mere imitation of what has gone before?

At the same time, it seems impossible not to read the editor's gripe as a meta-commentary on Yasuoka's own career, and on this very novel. Yasuoka wrote a number of stories in which the protagonist lives with his parents in a house borrowed from his aunt and uncle, and the family's harebrained attempts to make money are the driving force in any number of them: in "Prized Possessions" ("Aigan," 1952) the father is raising rabbits, in both *A View of the Sea* and "The Sword Dance" ("Kenbu," 1953) the father grows nausea-inducing tobacco, again in "The Sword Dance" the entire family engages in a racket making fake soy sauce, and so on. If Kensuke has read this story before, so have readers of Yasuoka.

One clear forerunner of the novel is "In a Neighborhood with Pine Trees" ("Matsu no ki no aru machi de," in YSS, vol. 2), published in *Bungei shunjū* in 1956. In this story, the "I" is an invalid living with his parents. People visit the house often hoping to rent the extra rooms, but the mother of the family explains that it really belongs to the uncle and that they don't have the right to rent it out. Mrs. Sakiyama, who is living across the way at A.'s place, begins to pay frequent visits to the protagonist; when he calls out in pain from a toothache one night, she comes and applies pressure to his face, explaining that she is a student of "homeopathy" and "telepathy," which should have been his first clue. He submits to moxibustion using her special recipe of garlic and miso, and eventually gets to the point at which he is able to move around on his own and wash his own face. What appears to be a burgeoning romance is diverted, however, when her husband stops by to ask the family if his wife can use their spare room as a massage parlor. Lured in at the thought of the extra money, the family agrees, and soon Mrs. Sakiyama's business is thriving. Her main competition is the polyglot blind masseur Muramoto, and to counter the worldly atmosphere of his parlor, she tries to convince the protagonist to sit around reading German books where people will see him. It turns out to be all for naught. A., from across the street, comes over one day to tell them that he is kicking the Sakiyamas out because of their constant fighting and, moreover, that Mrs. Sakiyama is a quack—everything she knows about massage she learned from listening to A.'s father's descriptions of the treatment he receives from an actual masseur. Soon thereafter, Mr. Sakiyama is outside their house destroying the sign his wife had posted advertising her services; she has run off with Muramoto, her blind competitor. The title "In a Neighborhood with Pine Trees" is ironic—the protagonist's father cuts down all of the trees early in the story, a metaphor for the various unexplainable transgressions the characters all commit, alerting readers to the very likely possibility that things will not end well for them.

We can also find predecessors to *After the Curtain Falls* in the aforementioned "The Fortune Teller" ("Uranaishi," 1954) and "The Pawnbroker's Wife" ("Shichiya no nyōbō," 1960), in both of which the protagonist is clearly enamored with an older, married woman. None of these stories, however, comes close to the extraordinary dual confession at the end of *After the Curtain Falls*. Spurned at the newspaper office, Kensuke turns toward the Okudas' new home, where, he tells himself, he will ask Okuda to take him under his patronage. Along the way he remembers how, toward the end of the time the two families were living together, Mutsuko started to touch him under the *kotatsu* heated table, even as they sat there with his mother. Mutsuko began to find reasons to be alone with him, and the two of them walked down to the river, where she continued to touch him:

The Generation of Deception

> Kensuke watched the sleek flow of the river, which lapped against the staked-off grassy shore and shimmered in the soft sunlight. As he did so, it became terribly, painfully clear that something inside him had gone missing. And whatever would replace what was missing? Next to him a pair of outstretched legs, in tight, worn slacks, matted down the yellowed, withered grass. It was ridiculous to think that *that* kind of thing would be useful in filling this void. –And yet, no sooner had Kensuke thought that than he was overcome with irritation. He pinned Mrs. Okuda's body down against the grass. (260–61)

The scene cuts off there, flashing forward to the next memory: Kensuke remembers how his mother forgot a bag at the house on the day they moved out. When he returned for it, only Mrs. Okuda was there: "For reasons unknown and unexplainable, he had come back to the house for the bag. In that instant, Kensuke was pierced, overwhelmed, by an anger mixed with desire, one that seemed to have just parched his entire mouth. He put his hands on Mrs. Okuda's rounded shoulders. He pulled her toward him, and they fell in a tangle to the freezing matting of the completely vacated room, banging together their front teeth, knees, bodies" (266–67).

Again, the narrative cuts off and is brought back to the present. Kensuke arrives at the Okudas' to speak to Okuda about his father's impending return to Tokyo, but it is Mrs. Okuda who answers the door:

> "Why don't you come in? Hurry in and close the door behind you; it's freezing when that wind blows in . . ." As she said this, Mrs. Okuda leaned against the wall behind her. She gave him a vague smile, as though hesitating for a moment about something. "Okuda went to Tokyo. I don't think he'll be back until late. . . ."
>
> Perhaps because the tension had dissipated, a sudden, gentle breeze flowed into his hollow, dry chest. Without a word, he began to take his shoes off. Mrs. Okuda's white, flaccid face drew near, and as it did so the space between her eyebrows flattened out. Her eyes narrowed a touch more than usual underneath their heavy lids, and Kensuke realized they were half-closed. (273–74)

For a third time, the scene cuts away, and because such a cut has been used twice before in the "past" narrative sequence to indicate a tryst, the rhetorical logic of the novel implies that the relationship has been consummated again. Not only has Kensuke had a relationship with a married woman, he has done so again now that he himself is married.

As with Shimao Toshio's autobiographical telling of his unfaithfulness to his wife and her subsequent mental collapse, *The Sting of Death* (*Shi no toge*, 1960–1976), those approaching the work in the I-novel tradition understand it as a confession on Yasuoka's part. However, the series of essays that critic Kawashima Itaru published from 1974 to 1977 on modern novelists and their mores, of which the aforementioned Yasuoka essay was the first, didn't treat Shimao. The Yasuoka essay was clearly the most personal to Kawashima and the most scandalous to the contemporary literati, but while "The Scar Left by a Twisted Truth" was apparently written out of duty to Yasuoka's old friends from his academic cohort, it mainly treats novels set long after his days with the Bad Company were over: *After the Curtain Falls* and its follow-up, *The Moon Is in the East* (*Tsuki wa higashi ni*, 1972).[17] In it, Kawashima uses his connections to people from Yasuoka's life, including the legendary Gunzō editor Ōkubo Fusao (known to Yasuoka as "the devil of literature," although Ōkubo saw himself as a contemporary and ally of the Third Generation [Ōkubo 138, 142–43]) and Yasuoka's friend from Keiō, Ishiyama Kōichi, to dig for information about Yasuoka's personal life. Kawashima notes that during the postwar Yasuoka's family took in a popular writer and his wife as boarders from September 1947 to February 1951. The writer took Yasuoka under his wing, much like an older brother would, Kawashima claims, but during this time, Yasuoka had an affair with the man's wife (Kawashima 11). With the man's permission, Kawashima reveals Yasuoka's real-life model for Okuda to have been the writer Imai Tatsuo (1904–1978), indicating that Imai naturally nursed a longstanding anger against Yasuoka because he had reneged on his promise never to write about the affair (14). But Kawashima also claims that Imai had to learn from Yasuoka's stories exactly what had happened—and that even after the sequence of novels was published, Imai did not want to believe there had been an affair—a problem which should not be glossed over.

Yasuoka wrote an appreciation of one of his literary idols, *On Shiga Naoya* (*Shiga Naoya ron*, 1968),[18] at about this time, and in it he noted the "transforming power" of the author's voice in autobiographical fiction, claiming that "The closer the contents of a story hew to one's own circumstances, the more this power will operate with actual force. There is nothing to be done about the fact that the 'I' in this will be inconvenienced, but that 'I,' the author, ultimately needs to take responsibility for the harm done to those around him" (qtd. in Kawashima 27). Despite making this observation, Yasuoka followed his work on Shiga with yet another confessional novel, *The Moon Is in the East*, proving to Kawashima's mind that Yasuoka's comments about taking responsibility are nothing more than lip service (28).

Kawashima argues that because Yasuoka builds a sanctuary (of fame, financial security, and literary success, presumably) around himself, he is able to confess his sins in these works. It would appear, however, that Kawashima has it exactly backward; this is not a narrative of confession but its polar opposite, deception. It is deception that brought people intellectually through the war and postwar and that threatens to destroy them. There is no sanctuary; as we have seen, the social circumstances of the early postwar continually, insistently force themselves on the "present" of the story. More to the point, there is no confession to be found in the text, only a narrative that repeatedly teases a revelation and cuts away each time.

It might be more fruitful to look at *After the Curtain Falls* through the lens of canon and archive. Here Yasuoka draws from a wider archive than simply the stories he shared with his generational cohort. The novel expects of its readers a working knowledge of the way that the "I-novel" canon traditionally functions. It also rewards those who know the Yasuoka archive well enough to recognize that his hallmark is as a deceptional writer, not a confessional one. The novel's constantly deferred confession makes a mockery of the form. In an even more dynamic sense, we can think of any given novel—including this one—as canonical by virtue of being the current object of attention, whether because we are now reading it or merely reading about it. In this conception of the text, the archive becomes the web of texts that supports this given work. The value of *After the Curtain Falls* is not in its author's decision to confess to a long-ago tryst but in its depiction of the deception that carried Yasuoka and others of his fractured generation through the postwar, at the cost of never being able to move forward. This happens on the level of the plot (Kensuke makes the same mistake with Mutsuko, years later), but also intertextually (Yasuoka draws from the archive of his own stories about the war and early postwar to describe the present).

At the end of the novel Kensuke has left Mrs. Okuda's house and is sitting in a café in a random part of Tokyo listening to a man try to convince his girlfriend to marry him. Kensuke understands the man's cravings: even though everything is at his fingertips, nothing quite satisfies him. The writer Nakaishi Takashi has referred to *After the Curtain Falls* as a "*Monsieur* Bovary" story, in which the male protagonist has affairs to escape the tedium that besets him (Nakaishi 249). The terrible violence and desperate circumstances of the war and postwar have been replaced by a placid everyday, but Kensuke's means of escape only leads him back to his past suffering. As he leaves the café, he sees himself in the glass door by the counter. The image is distorted, and he himself looks deformed. What better metaphor for an author to caution against autobiographical readings? It is also a flashback, of course, to the physical disability and inability to provide for his family that brought the Okudas to Kensuke's house as tenants in the first place. The curtain fall that Kensuke is told to beware in the opening of the novel, metaphorically speaking, appears to be the moment when one segment of life ends and the next begins. For Kensuke, trapped in an eternal postwar, the curtain never falls. He will forever be trapped between present and postwar.

The Past in Oneself: *The Moon Is in the East*

Yasuoka's final novel to take up the theme of deception and betrayal, *The Moon Is in the East* (*Tsuki wa higashi ni*, 1972), functions as a coda and a transition toward a new stage of Yasuoka's career. It begins on an airplane headed back to Japan from an unnamed country that is surely the United States: "The International Date Line is a strange thing. Just as you approach it, the dawn and sunset meet in the middle of the ocean; to the east, the sun that has just set rises again as the dawn, and to the west, what had been the morning blaze of sky becomes the darkening evening sky, brooding its way toward inevitable night. So it seemed, anyway" (YSS 7: 289).

The one watching the sunrise/sunset is Kasayama Sōtarō; he has been abroad on a fellowship, and now he is abruptly heading home early together with his wife. In the seat pocket in front of him is a watch advertisement, but he is suspicious of time, perhaps due to the advent of air travel: "Just because twenty-four hours have passed doesn't mean it's the next day" (290). Something has radically shifted; Sōtarō is a protagonist not trapped in the past, but floating completely outside of time.

Sōtarō is particularly worried about his friend Katagiri; will Katagiri come to meet them at the airport, and how will their reunion go? It soon becomes clear that Sōtarō has had an affair with Katagiri's wife, Fusae. Letters from Fusae and Katagiri, indicating that Katagiri knows about the affair, have prompted Sōtarō to cut his fellowship short and return to Japan early. At Haneda Airport, Sōtarō's cousin Tameko and Sōtarō's friend Hayakawa Shunsaku are waiting for them, and Sōtarō immediately starts evaluating their attitudes in an attempt to determine how much they know. Hayakawa has taken up with a woman who runs a hot-springs inn; although his estranged wife continually threatens to appear, Hayakawa is at peace with what he has done in a way that Sōtarō finds alarming. Sōtarō has returned to Japan, but not to the life he left; his relationship to the world is held in check by his paranoia: he is unable to determine who knows what, and as he himself says, it isn't the fear of being caught, it's not knowing when the confrontation will take place.

It becomes clear that everyone knows what has happened. Hayakawa knew—he was the one who broke the news to Katagiri—as does Tameko. When Sōtarō scolds Tameko for being out drinking while her husband Yoshio is out of town, she drunkenly turns on him: "You're looking out for me, hmm? Yoshio is going to be so moved when he hears that. But I've heard all about it, y'know, what you did with Katagiri's wife. Ten years later it all comes out. To have an affair and have it come out ten years later—I burst out laughing. That's just like our Sō" (413–14). When the two men finally meet face-to-face, Katagiri is initially enraged but then turns surprisingly philosophical; he tells Sōtarō that he is relieved it was Sōtarō and not someone else. Katagiri agrees to keep it a secret from Sōtarō's wife, Reiko, the only person who doesn't seem to know, but Katagiri breaks his promise and tells her while Sōtarō is away from home. When he returns, Reiko aggressively questions him and eventually pulls a knife on him.

At last, a protagonist reveals his crime in full detail, but his motivation for the acts is still rooted in the postwar. When Sōtarō writes to Katagiri to explain what happened, he lets the severity of the situation slip out little by little; later, when he tries to explain why the word "sex" hadn't appeared in his earlier missives, he claims, "For me, sex itself was something that produced an endless feeling of defeat, spiritually and physically" (389). "Defeat" (*haiboku*) and the opposition of things spiritual (*seishin teki*) and physical (*nikutai teki*) are conceptions rooted in the postwar. Like Kensuke in *After the Curtain Falls*, Sōtarō blames his indiscretions on the postwar: "The indecencies I committed with Katagiri's wife—everything about that time—was a result of the extreme stringencies of life then" (420). Isoda Kōichi argues that the postwar changed sexual habits in general, in particular the sharp division between the family and the parallel world of the entertainment districts:

> Even today [in the 1980s] half of the population middle-aged and above believes in what Itō Sei referred to as "the route that Japanese men have explored since the time of our ancestors." When the "household" was established to accompany the onetime solid hierarchy, the world of the geisha (*karyūkai*) was established as a parallel to it. The latter evolved in form—to cafes, bars, and so on—but the breakdown of the household that we see today inevitably crossed over to demolish by degrees the form of the countervailing world. These processes came to the surface starting in the 1960s, but to follow them back to their sources we are ineluctably pulled to the war defeat. (121–22)

Sōtarō is just enough of a public figure that his wife fears word of his affair getting out and the vicious cycle that will follow: "Pursuit and being pursued are directly connected to the essence of who we are. It isn't a question of why someone is chasing and someone is fleeing; if you are being pursued, you will run, and if someone runs, you will pursue him. For that alone, Reiko had good reason to fear the weekly magazines" (YSS 7: 435). The thrill of the chase—meaning, when the press is involved, of deceiving and being found out—is inescapable.

The closer these novels get to confession, the farther they move away from autobiographical verisimilitude; the process by which *The Moon Is in the East* was constructed is an amalgamative one. As with Okuda and his wife in *After the Curtain Falls*, Katagiri and his wife are clearly based on the Yasuokas' early postwar boarders. At the same time, however, the double deception between Sōtarō and Katagiri bears a resemblance to the stories based on the games between Yasuoka and Kurata Hiromitsu during the war. It would seem that Katagiri's deception (telling Reiko about the affair after promising he wouldn't) hardly represents justice for Sōtarō's deception (having a relationship with Katagiri's wife). Katagiri, however, is satisfied with Sōtarō's apology—in part because Sōtarō is earnestly regretful, but also because Sōtarō's deception has been turned around on him by his lover. "From my perspective, she betrayed you," Katagiri says (473). The deceiver has again been turned into the deceived.

Unlike *After the Curtain Falls*, in which the confusion of a specific timeframe in the early postwar overlays a present that exists in a later, more settled postwar, in *The Moon Is in the East*, all time collapses in on the narrator. Images of his life in America become entangled with his thoughts of Katagiri and Fusae: when Sōtarō's church-going friends accidentally bring him to see an avant-garde play with a nude scene, the actress's body reminds him of Fusae. When a young American student who is an aspiring writer asks him an innocent question about how he makes a living, it bears a striking similarity to Katagiri's accusatory one: "What do you really do?" versus "What did you really do?" (YSS 7: 387). At the end, he thinks again of the international date line; that moment of statis in which a day is magically erased. He wonders, could it also erase the past? In the last scene, with the sun at his back, Sōtarō marches forward onto his own shadow. He stomps on it as he goes—a symbolic attempt to destroy his own past—when he sees the moon in front of him and walks toward it.

Van Gessel has traced the title of the novel to a poem by Yosa Buson (1716–1783): "Flowers of the rapeseed / The moon is to the east / The sun is to the west" (Na no hana ya / Tsuki wa higashi ni / Hi wa nishi ni). Gessel notes that the sun and the moon here emphasize the expansiveness of the rapeseed field (122). At the same time, considering that this novel begins and ends with its protagonist hovering over the Pacific between Japan and the United States, the title offers a symbolism with real-world connotations of a postwar that does not end: The sun, the symbol of the Japanese Empire and the power located in the emperor, has moved to the west, across the ocean and toward the United States. What takes its place is the moon, a metaphor for post-empire Japan: not a source of light, but a reflection of a greater light. Nevertheless, Sōtarō moves eastward into the moon, hoping that the shadows the sun has laid before him will be effaced by the moonlight.

"It had been his shadow he was sporting with all along," Sōtarō realizes (YSS 7: 488). The game of deception had left him isolated from the world not because his crimes came to light, but because his obsession had been with himself the entire time; the effort of sustaining the deception—one that had preserved him for so long—had descended into self-absorption and narcissism. Again, the plight of the individual has been conflated with that of the nation. For the first time, however, an exit from the postwar appeared to present itself to Yasuoka. A visit to this unnamed country across the Pacific had made him aware of this possibility for the first time. The American South, home to a different postwar, represented a chance to change the future.

3

Local History, Global History, and the Triangulation of Memory

Yasuoka Shōtarō went to study at Vanderbilt University in Nashville, Tennessee, on a Rockefeller Foundation grant in November 1960, an out-of-place figure for any number of reasons. Obviously, he had come to a still-segregated South as a third party to what was a determinedly bifurcated society, making his memoir of his visit, *A Sentimental Journey to the United States* (*Amerika kanjō ryokō*, 1962), a rare first-hand, outside perspective on events.[1] He was forty years old at the time, too old to think of himself as an exchange student even though he was too youthful-looking to be taken seriously by the Vanderbilt English department faculty. Nashville in 1960 was itself between worlds; through a series of protests, rallies, and strategic boycotts by African Americans and their white allies, the entire American South was in the middle of a period of sweeping societal changes that had begun with the landmark 1954 Supreme Court decision against so-called separate-but-equal education in *Brown v. Board of Education* and the year-long 1955–1956 Montgomery, Alabama, bus boycott, and would culminate with the Civil Rights Act of 1964 and the Voting Rights Act of 1965. Nashville was a key flashpoint for the Civil Rights Movement in 1960 and 1961; it was where James Lawson and John Lewis, major figures in the movement, first became involved.[2]

Throughout his long career, Yasuoka reveled in the role of the contrarian, and in his very decision to go to Nashville when others of his generation headed to the North, we see an author whose personal displacement resonated with a city's, a region's, and a nation's. Yasuoka was the first postwar Japanese writer of his stature to spend significant time in the American South and write extensively

Third Generation writers seeing Yasuoka off at the airport on his way to Nashville on a Rockefeller grant, November 25, 1960. Left to right: Miura Shumon, Agawa Hiroyuki, Yasuoka Shōtarō, Yoshiyuki Junnosuke. Photograph courtesy of Yasuoka Haruko.

about the Civil Rights Movement. The Rockefeller Foundation, his sponsoring agency, had sent their previous selections to various places across the Northeast, Midwest, and West. Ōoka Shōhei had been at Yale in 1953–1954. Agawa Hiroyuki had spent a month in Hawai'i and five months in California before driving across the continental United States in a used car, in 1955–1956. Kojima Nobuo was in the United States from the spring of 1957 to the spring of 1958; he spent a few months in the South from November 1957 to March 1958, but most of his year in the United States was with families in the Iowa City area. Shōno Junzō was at Kenyon College from the fall of 1957 to the fall of 1958, and Ariyoshi Sawako spent most of the 1959–1960 American academic year at Sarah Lawrence College in New York.[3] Others had gone to the United States by other means. Oda Makoto was in residence at Harvard in 1958–1959 on a Fulbright scholarship and spent another year wandering the world. And, of course, the United States was not the only foreign country Japanese writers wanted to visit; Yasuoka's friend Endō Shūsaku was greatly admired for having headed to France in 1950, while Japan was still under Allied occupation.

Other Japanese writers toured the American South, but none engaged with the region as much as Yasuoka would. In the South, Yasuoka found multiple locations and multiple times intersecting. In *The Writing of History*, Michel de Certeau refers to "the place of history," "a complex that permits only one kind of production for it and prohibits others" (68). Certeau sees this place as the nexus of a physical location and an intellectual one not delineated by space or even time, a conflation to which Yasuoka would undoubtedly have been sympathetic. Yasuoka, together with the small community of Asian students and scholars he met in Nashville, found himself in an unusual relationship to the historical complex he found there, a confrontation between a white majority and a "colored" population, which—Yasuoka soon discovered—really meant only African Americans. He soon found that he had a valuable role to play as a witness to history. The organizers of the Civil Rights Movement saw national media attention as a crucial part of their strategy. While they may not have considered reportage from a Japanese writer-in-residence to be a primary audience, they were inspired by Mahatma Gandhi's non-violent resistance to British colonial rule in India, and the morality to which they appealed was a global one.

Aleida Assmann has identified four varieties of witness: the impartial legal witness; historical witnesses who have survived great tragedies, who often come as messengers to describe what they have seen; religious witnesses to martyrdom; and a new variety of witness that has appeared in the wake of the Holocaust, the "moral witness" (*Shadows* 66–73). As defined by Avishai Margalit, the "paradigmatic" moral witness has experienced traumatic events personally, as "one who is not just an observer but also a sufferer" (150); the physical bodies of moral witnesses vouch for the veracity of their testimony (Assmann, *Shadows* 71). What these moral witnesses require is an audience that will serve as secondary witnesses outside a legal framework, to which there is no recourse owing to the vastness of the crimes committed. The presumption is that the perpetrators will attempt "to efface historical traces and to defend themselves against guilt through denial and other evasive strategies" and that moral witnesses pursue a "mandate of truth" (72). Margalit opens the door to the possibility that observers, too, can qualify as moral witnesses, provided that they share in the suffering and observe for "a moral purpose" (151). Perhaps this is all the more true in a situation such as the Civil Rights Movement, in which deliberate witnessing played a crucial part. If so, there is a case to be made that Yasuoka served as a moral witness in both of these senses. As Vanderbilt and other institutions attempted to efface the reality of the Movement, Yasuoka both participated in the Movement and recorded his impressions in a memoir that carried the truth of the era to a Japanese readership; it has not gone out of print in Japan since it was first published in 1962.

At the same time, the American South played a role in helping Yasuoka determine a way out of the endless Japanese postwar. Yasuoka used his time in the

South to wrestle with fundamental questions regarding Japan and his place in it through a process of triangulation of his own devising: between postwar Japan, the American South, and late-Edo / Meiji Restoration-era Japan. How he managed to integrate these histories, using one postwar to make sense of another, is the subject of this chapter.

Predecessors

Yasuoka and other postwar writers were reconnecting with the world after two decades of dispiriting isolation. Japan left the League of Nations in 1933, and by the attack on Pearl Harbor in 1941, English and French were already considered enemy languages. During the 1945–1952 US Occupation of Japan, Japanese people were in a frenzy to learn English in order to communicate with the Americans who had effectively taken control of the country, but ordinary citizens were not permitted to go abroad, and in the vast majority of cases, they would not have had the money to do so anyway. In Agawa Naoyuki's two-volume study of Japanese intellectuals' writings on their experiences in the United States, *Did You Find America? (Amerika ga mitsukarimashita ka*, 1998), all eleven of the Japanese travelers in the prewar volume were dead by the end of the Occupation.[4] Agawa includes two scholars in the second volume who were in the United States in the late 1930s and early 1940s, but Yasuoka and the other postwar travelers represent a fundamental break from those who had gone before.[5] Although young Japanese students began to appear at universities across the United States in 1949 on US-funded Government Aid and Relief in Occupied Areas (GARIOA) scholarships, and later on Fulbright scholarships, major Japanese writers had been largely absent from the United States for nearly two decades when the Rockefeller Foundation exchanges began in 1953.

One of the few writers who escaped Japan during the Occupation was the novelist Endō Shūsaku (1923–1996). Endō was a Catholic, and he was permitted by the Occupation authorities to go to France in 1950 at the invitation of the Catholic Church. He studied at the University of Lyons for a couple of years and moved to Paris in 1952, where he contracted pleurisy, requiring him to return to Japan in 1953. After Endō and Yasuoka had both won the Akutagawa Prize and fallen in with each other as members of the Third Generation of New Writers, they grew very close, and Endō even persuaded Yasuoka to convert to Catholicism later in life. When they met in 1953, however, they knew each other only distantly from their shared time at Keiō University, from which they had both graduated in 1948. It was at Endō's homecoming party, by chance a day or two after Yasuoka had won the Akutagawa Prize, where they warily circled one another, each possessing something the other one wanted: Yasuoka had won the Akutagawa, but Endō had managed to go abroad, and to France, no less (BSS 2: 159–60).

Endō was aware of his good fortune, but he also felt pressure from the Catholic faithful who had brought him to France to study French Catholic writers. Endō grew up in a Japan in which France was the enemy, and his Catholicism made him feel all the more that the two nations were irreconcilable (Williams 59). In Endō's semi-autobiographical novel *Foreign Studies* (*Ryūgaku*, 1965), one character mourns the impossibility of grasping the long history, what he calls the "great flow," of France: "I just didn't want to be like so many Japanese students who come here to study and become architects just by stealing one tiny fragment of that great flow and using their natural talent to make imitations of it. I felt that, unless I as a Japanese could confront the actuality of that great flow, then my whole motivation for coming here would have been made meaningless" (120).

Endō's exchange students are reminded at all turns that they themselves are Japanese, living at a remove from the country they study. Douglas Slaymaker has argued that throughout the modern period "many Japanese intellectuals found in France a culture that, like their own, boasted a long literary heritage wherein the meaning of being 'French' or 'Japanese' proceeded from self-identification with that heritage" ("Yokomitsu" 120). For Endō's protagonists, France is France, and Japan is Japan, and efforts toward integration are futile.

For most of the Japanese writers who went to the United States in the 1950s, the fact of being in the United States—a country that had been an enemy state during their youths—was all the impetus they needed for their writing on it. Even more than the "great flow" of American culture, recent history kept them focused on their status as Japanese abroad at every turn, and their placement at elite private schools and major research universities meant that their encounters were largely with white America. Sometimes they extrapolated from their limited experiences. The American story for which Ariyoshi Sawako is best known, the novel *Not Because of Color* (*Hishoku*, 1963–1964), concerns a Japanese woman who marries an African American and settles down in the United States with him in a run-down neighborhood. According to Yoko McClain, however, while racial discrimination against black Americans was something that interested Ariyoshi, during her time at Sarah Lawrence she never went to Harlem (or, presumably, other majority-minority neighborhoods) and appears to have written the work largely from her imagination (215–16).

Kojima Nobuo had first-hand experience with the South but never turned it into a larger work. Kojima was assigned to the Iowa Writers' Workshop at the University of Iowa, which at that time was welcoming a number of international writers each year. Kojima did not want to spend his year attached to a college campus and was particularly dismissive of the mission of the Writers' Workshop; in his 1965 essay "Regarding Creative Writing Courses in the Academy" ("Daigakunai no sōsaku kōsu ni tsuite"), he expressed doubt that creative-writing programs were good for writing, although he admitted evidence to the contrary as well (Kojima, *Kojima Nobuo bungaku ronshū* 391–96). In Iowa, he quickly absconded from the university town in favor of Kalona, Iowa, home to Amish, Mennonite, and mainstream farming families. He returned to Iowa City in the fall to stay with a family connected to the university—a surprisingly different world from the one just a few miles down the road—and headed south to explore universities in Louisiana, Alabama, and Georgia. In March of 1958, he returned to Japan via Paris.

From 1958 to 1961, Kojima published in a number of literary magazines a series of six dialogue-heavy stories about his time in the United States that were eventually collected under the title *A Clown in a Foreign Land* (*Ikyō no dōkeshi*, 1970). Of the six stories, only one treats his time in the South, "On the Tragic Ground" ("Yogoreta tochi ni te"), and even taken together they provide only a cryptic account of his time in the United States. The clearest description Kojima offers of his US travels is in a series of letters written in English to Robert W. July at the Rockefeller Foundation during his stay.[6] Kojima wrote a few scattered articles for Japanese newspapers and magazines, but he is best remembered for stories of Japanese people encountering American culture as it came to Japan during the postwar, in the acclaimed short story "American School" and the masterful dark comedy *Embracing Family* (*Hōyō kazoku*, 1965).

Of the many different kinds of writing on American experiences that were produced by Japanese visitors, three memoirs that preceded Yasuoka's are of particular interest here, because they demonstrate how unusual his own experiences were. Shōno Junzō, Yasuoka's friend who convinced him to accept the funding from the Rockefeller Foundation that made his visit to Nashville possible, represents those who enjoyed a quiet sabbatical from their high-paced lives back in Japan, while Mickey Yasukawa and Oda Makoto saw discrimination firsthand in the United States but, although they visited the South, ultimately had other agendas.

Mickey Yasukawa

Shortly after the Treaty of San Francisco was signed in 1952, establishing the terms of peace between Japan and the Allied Powers and bringing an end to the Occupation, Yasukawa Minoru, a wandering young man who would later become the Japanese television personality Mickey Yasukawa, made his way to the United States. Between 1952 and 1956, Yasukawa was mainly in the American South, studying at a number of schools, including a couple of months in a fourth-grade classroom in Appalachian Tennessee as he ramped up his English skills, before advancing to high school and college. He wrote about his travels in his memoir *Vagabond Student* (*Furaibō ryūgakuki*, 1960).

On a Greyhound bus crossing the country, Yasukawa first encounters segregation at a stop in Houston. He doesn't know which bathroom to use, White or Colored, and consults with a black woman who appears to be a custodian:

> The woman stared at me for a long time, as if looking at a truly unusual object. "What are you?"
> "Japanese."
> "Japanese! Well, Japanese are yellow, so . . ."
> "So maybe I should use the Colored?"
> "You're really pale, though . . ." As though she were suddenly troubled, the woman clutched her head with both of her hands. While she agonized, it got to the point that I couldn't hold it anymore, and I made to dash for the Colored, which was closest to me.
> Before I could get in, a black man [. . .] came running toward me, waving his hands. "No, you're White!" And then a station attendant came trotting over. "This is only for black folks, so you can head on over there to the one marked White." (Yasukawa 22)

Back on the bus, although there are a number of open seats in the whites-only section up front, black passengers are not allowed to board. When he questions the bus driver about this, he is told that blacks are animals who don't mind waiting even four or five days for an open seat (24). Yasukawa is appalled, as he is later when a black coworker with whom he delivers floral arrangements is not allowed to enter customers' houses (140). His is often a narrative played for laughs, however; he ends up experiencing his fair share of fish-out-of-water encounters. On the whole, he pays far less attention to discrimination against blacks in the South than he does to the way that he himself is discriminated against by the white people around him. Although Yasukawa's book is largely forgotten today, and is perhaps less trustworthy as an historical document than other American memoirs, it represents a Japanese traveler's first-hand view of the South at this time and is a valuable record for that reason alone.

Shōno Junzō

Yasuoka's contemporary and friend Shōno Junzō had a perfectly pleasant year in the American Midwest. Shōno went to Kenyon College in Gambier, Ohio, on a

Local History, Global History, and the Triangulation of Memory 105

Rockefeller grant for the 1957–1958 academic year and wrote about the experience in *A Record of My Stay in Gambier* (*Ganbia taizaiki*, 1959). Shōno describes the town, its history, and its denizens in detail, much as Sherwood Anderson had done for another, imaginary town in the same state in *Winesburg, Ohio*. In that 1919 collection of stories, Anderson had hearkened back to a "simpler"—or at least, quieter—time in the state, before the "coming of industrialism, attended by all the roar and rattle of affairs, the shrill cries of millions of new voices that have come among us from over seas, the going and coming of trains, the growth of cities, the building of the interurban car lines that weave in and out of towns and past farmhouses, and now in these later days the coming of the automobiles" (Anderson 65). But in Shōno's account of late-1950s Gambier, aspects of the frontier still exist, even in this most civilized of small towns: Old Mr. Brown of Gambier's independent People's Bank was once kidnapped by armed bank robbers after they shot his pistol out of his hand (53); an epidemic referred to as the "Asian flu," which originated in China and spread across the world from 1956 to 1958, cancels the campus Halloween party (86); and the junior faculty take turns going to the larger town down the road, Mount Vernon, to pick up news from the outside world (in the form of the *New York Times*, the newspaper of choice for much of the faculty).

Shōno mentions the occasional difficulty he has with the English language: He encounters a creature that resembles the Japanese *tanuki* and buys a dictionary to confirm that it is a "raccoon"; on another occasion, he eavesdrops on a conversation at a local diner and cannot possibly imagine what sort of thing the women are talking about until he learns the words "cyclone" and "tornado" (28, 37). But the language barrier does not keep him from interacting with the campus community and the townspeople of Gambier. Shōno sits in on an introductory poetry class taught by John Crowe Ransom, a former member of the Southern Agrarian literary movement and the man who gave the New Criticism its name in a 1941 work. By the time Shōno meets him, his Southern, anti-industrial predilections have declined or even disappeared; Shōno mentions him often enough for it to be clear that their relationship was harmonious.

Part of what helps Shōno and his wife find their place in the community is its unexpected diversity. The Kenyon professors Shōno meets are from various places, including England and Poland, and the professor of Spanish is married to a Colombian woman. Shōno and his wife's closest friends at Kenyon are Minoo Adenwalla, an adjunct professor of political science originally from India, and his Illinoisan wife, June. They have a young daughter, Shireen, and Minoo's mother, Piroja Dinshaw (whom Shōno refers to throughout as "Dinshaw"), comes to visit over the winter.[7] Shōno and Minoo develop a friendship over their shared love of a good drink, especially sherry, and rarely does the fact that they are the two Asians in the community come to the surface of the narrative. When a professor mentions the Asian flu at a dinner party, it becomes a joke: "I laughed and said, 'I feel as though I'm responsible somehow,' to which Minoo, sitting next to me, replied, 'Not I. *We*. We're both Asian, after all.' When it was time to leave, our hostess said we should take an umbrella with us. Minoo clapped his hand on my shoulder and said, 'We Asian people are strong'" (97).

Ultimately, Shōno is occasionally made aware of his own race at Kenyon, but not to the point that he is compelled to confront issues of systemic racism in any significant way. Racism against African Americans was not limited to the South, of course, and Shōno, like Yasuoka and every other Japanese writer of the period, was not immune to the casual othering of African Americans that has been a mainstay of Japanese culture throughout its modern history. When Shōno goes with Minoo to pick up June at the train station one day, he casually records that "the waiting room was completely empty except for a couple of black people," before moving on with his narrative (130).

It is a peaceful, bucolic place, where Shōno idly wonders who is related to whom in the town and goes into detail about interesting rocks he discovers and a search for the perfect flower to pick. The worries they have seldom come to pass: the neighbors are pleasant and even friendly, snowfalls that could be crippling aren't, and Dinshaw visits unexpectedly not to bring bad news—as Minoo had feared—but simply because she received a free ticket.

Oda Makoto

If there is any Japanese author who set the gold standard for boldness abroad, it is surely Oda Makoto. *I'll See It All* (*Nan demo mite yarō*, 1961), Oda's memoir of his 1958–1960 tour of twenty-two countries around the world, is equal parts cultural criticism, how-to guide, and unapologetic braggadocio. In how-to mode, he generously shares tips for getting through a scholarship interview on bravado alone. A suspicious examiner corners him in the hallway: "'You've never spoken with an American in your life, have you?' When I answered, 'Can't you tell that just from listening to my English?' he nodded his head and answered, 'That's exactly right.' With that, I felt confident that I would pass. I was right" (17).

Confidence is the key to Oda's international success, and the book's title is his mantra; when confronted with the choice between doing something or not, he inevitably brings up his promise to himself that he would see it all. He makes a tour of gay bars and Beat hangouts in the New York area, argues with Edwin Reischauer at Harvard over Reischauer's conceptualization of Japan, and asks Nobel literature laureate Pearl S. Buck at a public lecture to describe where she was and how she felt when she heard that a nuclear bomb had been dropped on Japan. (She is gracious in her answer, although others in the audience are outraged, asking Oda where he was and how he felt when the Japanese attacked Pearl Harbor.) He accepts all offers of free meals and lodgings—including an all-expenses-paid summer at the MacDowell Colony for artists—and twice allows people in New York City to take up a collection to send him to Europe (the second time after the money from the original offering is stolen in a break-in).

The America that Oda encounters believes itself to be split between conformists and non-conformists. To a degree, Oda understands the Beats' frustrations; he too wants to flee the numbing sameness of the bus stations, Woolworth's, and A&Ps in the small towns (60). But when he visits a friend's family in Scarsdale, New York, he finds something worthwhile even in the "conformity" of greater America: "The conversation seldom strayed from what was in the pages of *Time* or *Life*, and because they generally said what I expected them to say next, it offered a good chance to practice my English expressions" (58–59). Moreover, Oda doesn't find the Beats all that different from mainstream society: "They all laugh in the same hysterical manner; they all dance like their heads have been lopped off. Everywhere you look, it's goatees, sweaters, and slacks. No matter where you go, you'll hear the same style of jazz, the sound of bongo drums" (54). Despite their claims to a greater freedom, the Beats operate in extremely confined sectors of a very large society. A woman in Chicago brings him to a hip coffee shop, and the next day a Beat poet takes him to the very same place. "In order to escape the 'smell of America,' the Beats head to this little piece of 'non-America.' They drink coffee while listening to awful poetry read aloud, and surrounded by people exactly like themselves, they are able to escape their feeling of loneliness by seeking out friends—or rather, duplicates of themselves" (62). To Oda, there is only one unique force at work in the America he visits: Oda himself. If Endō's characters were attempting to sublimate themselves into the "great flow" of European culture, Oda attempts to subjugate Americans desperate for something new into his own image.

He is traveling in the wake of a "Japan boom": Kurosawa Akira's *Rashōmon* and other Japanese films have appeared on the international art-house scene, and the world is rediscovering (read: creating) Japan. A decade before Roland Barthes claimed to "isolate somewhere in the world (faraway) a certain number of features (a term employed in linguistics), and out of these features deliberately form a system" that he called "Japan" in the opening of *Empire of Signs* (*L'Empire des signes*, 1970) (3), Japan was already being created in the United States and Europe. For the burgeoning counter-culture, Japanese culture represents an easy road to individuality. Oda mimics their thought process as they decide to connect themselves to Japan:

> *The fastest way to throw off one's conformism, or to affect the posture of doing so, is to throw oneself into the various appurtenances of another country. And we're not talking about the stingy French. China would be good, but we don't care much for their politics. And so, how about Japan. Japan is another grand, ancient country, and since we don't understand it very well, it appears to have a wonderful culture, and, according to my uncle who was there in the army, the scenery is beautiful and the people are warm, and that's not even mentioning the amazing women, and I think I'd like to study that Zen that everyone is talking about so much, and anyway there's probably something worthwhile over there . . .* Through this kind of ridiculous thought process, a "Japan boom" came about. (63)

Oda visits twenty-two countries, and in every one of them, he is asked whether he is Zen (130). He always takes advantage of their fascination; for better or worse, his family really *is* Zen Buddhist, and he buoyantly fulfills their stereotypes of Japan by saying so, especially if it could lead to a free meal or new experience (66). During one of his dalliances, he tells a woman that he likes her negligee. "What are you talking about?" she huffs. "This is a kimono!" (65–66). Although Reischauer keeps his distance from Oda at Harvard even after Oda promises not to write about him, Howard Hibbett is eager to spend time with him. Hibbett is translating Tanizaki Jun'ichirō's novel *The Key* (*Kagi*) and has any number of questions for Oda about the "erotic" elements (70). The only place where Oda's nationality has no currency is at McSorley's Old Ale House in New York City. For the patrons there, "it was as though World War II had never happened. There was even one old man who mumbled, 'Japan . . . hmm, weren't they an Allied country?'" (89). They are old men who don't speak English very well but have forgotten their native languages as well; Oda feels at home among them.

Oda purports to always feel out of place during his forays into Harlem to visit the Apollo and other sites; he dates an African American woman but can't understand her English, and when he brings a white date to a club in Harlem, he finds himself introduced by the MC as a mediator between blacks and whites. It is the first place he becomes aware of his own race, he claims (127). Perhaps this is because, although he has merrily cast himself as a Japanese *tabula rasa* onto which the people of the world are welcome to project their own images of "Japaneseness," the imaginary binary of black and white stifles him, makes him a bit player in a drama that doesn't concern him. Or, worse, makes him white; he crosses the American South on his way to Mexico and finds the experience painful:

> Many good things happened to me there. The people were kind. But with regard to the "White" and "Colored" signs, I have to say that it was a painful trip.

But on the other hand, perhaps it was just me. Even as I never stopped feeling anger about the discrimination, perhaps what I really found painful was the fact that I was safely ensconced in the world of whites.

Even in the South, I would walk through black neighborhoods, have a drink with them, go to see films in Colored movie theaters. But, to put it directly, it was with the eyes of a white person that I was always looking at them. (134)

Oda promises himself that he will fight for them for the rest of his life—a promise he made good on, if one takes "them" to mean the dispossessed in general, with his reporting on the Vietnam War and work on issues of discrimination within Japan. But before he delves too deeply into segregation in the South, the bus has carried him into Mexico, where he is on surer footing: the poverty of the place reminds him of postwar Japan (137). In such a brief visit, the South appears static to Oda; he isn't able to see that change is underway, despite the fact that, in the summer of 1959, he is arriving five years after the 1954 Brown v. Board of Education decision and two and a half years after the end of the 1955–1956 Montgomery bus boycott. A detailed examination of the South would have to wait for Yasuoka Shōtarō.

Dual Postwars in *A Sentimental Journey to the United States*

If Yasuoka is to be believed in *My Shōwa History*, he wasn't interested in going to the United States. He received an invitation to apply for a grant from the Rockefeller Foundation, and Shōno Junzō strongly encouraged him to accept the offer and take his place in line with Shōno and the other writers and critics who had gone to the United States on Rockefeller money. Yasuoka couldn't bring himself to refuse directly, so he concocted a scheme. Generally speaking, other Japanese writers and intellectuals had gone to college towns in the northern United States. While he might be sent to America's heartland, like Shōno, Yasuoka decided that given the unrest of the Civil Rights Movement it was very unlikely they would send him to the American South, what he called America's "shameland." And so, looking for a way out, he insisted that he could *only* go to the South, because he required a temperate climate for his health; to his alarm, the staff at the Rockefeller Foundation told him that the South was actually the perfect place for someone interested in contemporary American literature (BSS 2: 245).

The South that Yasuoka arrives in is a bastion of white privilege. Nashville had always prided itself on being a more moderate place than the Deep South, a

Yasuoka Shōtarō in Nashville, c. 1960–1961. Photograph courtesy of Yasuoka Haruko.

proposition that was put to the test several times in the 1950s, when it became clear that moderation in Nashville meant "a more or less genuine sympathy for black advancement undergirded by deeply felt assumptions of black inferiority and white superiority" (Houston 4). The *Brown v. Board of Education* Supreme Court ruling integrating schools across the country was handed down in 1954, but Nashville—like just about every other city in the South—slow-walked their plans for integration. When integration finally began, in 1957, only first-graders were allowed to cross the color line, and districts were drawn such that fewer than 10 percent of black students were eligible. On September 9, 1957, nineteen black first-graders bore the burden of integration on behalf of their elders and for future generations. In February 1960, having been trained in nonviolent resistance by James Lawson, a black Vanderbilt Divinity School student who had spent time in India studying Gandhian nonviolent resistance, a growing group of black Fisk and Tennessee State University students engaged in sit-ins at the lunch counters of the major downtown department stores. After months of resistance, and a bombing that galvanized public opinion in favor of the student protestors, the storeowners gave in, and the counters desegregated on May 10, 1960.

Textbook histories of the South during the Civil Rights Movement bifurcate the population between white and black, but the truth on the ground was naturally much more complicated, with tensions of class and religion straining both the white and black populations. In a deeply Protestant region, Catholic and Jewish minorities struggled to strike a balance between lending support to the Civil Rights Movement on the one hand and not raising the ire of the Protestant majority on the other (Houston 29, 49–50). Yasuoka had expected that he might be marginalized because of his inability to speak English and his Japanese nationality, but, to a good degree, Yasuoka was marginalized because he could not be categorized. Segregation in the South was made possible by creating a duality between White and Colored, meaning that hybridity was legally and practically disallowed; "one drop of blood" rules defined everyone with any black ancestry as black, so that there were two sets of bathrooms, waiting rooms, restaurants, and cinemas, obligating everyone to self-identify at the door, including Yasuoka. What is a visitor from Japan to do?

Yasuoka knew which side of the color line he stood on even before he arrived in town and needed to use the facilities, putting him a step ahead of Mickey Yasukawa: "Having envisioned the bathroom problem before I left Japan, I obediently went into the one marked 'White'" (Yasuoka, *Amerika* 24). "Colored," Yasuoka discovers on the ground, is essentially determined visually, and applies only to those who appear to be African American—he mentions Indian students who wear turbans and saris when they go out in Nashville so that they may enter restaurants and cinemas, and a pair of Indonesian exchange students who enter a restaurant, only to have one refused service while his lighter-skinned friend is served (86).[8]

Despite everything he believed before his arrival in Nashville, Yasuoka also encounters a small number of Japanese exchange students. There is an entire population of people of Asian ancestry with a spectrum of skin tones giving the lie to the entire proposition that segregation is even possible. Yasuoka scorns the binary, refusing to identify fully with either side. In doing so, he also rejects the notion that one can easily create common ground among the wider community of people of color who could potentially consider themselves "Colored." Yasuoka meets another Japanese traveler who "proudly recounts" having used "Colored" bathrooms across the South in a show of solidarity with the black community. Yasuoka strongly questions his motives: "Practically speaking, what he did was meaningless. Doing that kind of thing doesn't really draw the ire of whites, nor does it endear him to blacks. The only thing he's doing when he says, 'I use the "Colored" bathrooms,' is feeling a vain sense of superiority and self-satisfaction" (87). For a visitor already alienated from both whites and blacks, rejecting the actions of one side will not automatically lead to common ground with the other.

Integration had not made many inroads at Yasuoka's host institution, either. As a private institution, Vanderbilt at the time had taken the position that there was no need for it to integrate its undergraduate school, as there were several black undergraduate institutions in the area, but that it would provide an opportunity for blacks to enroll in any Vanderbilt graduate program for which there was not a black equivalent in the state of Tennessee. There were limits to its "progressiveness," however, and Vanderbilt had a standing policy at the school that any students caught participating in the protest movement would be expelled for conduct unbecoming a Vanderbilt man or woman.

Yasuoka arrives in the aftermath of an uproar: in the spring of 1960, James Lawson was arrested for his role in the sit-ins and expelled. After a lull occasioned by the long summer vacation—because so much of the Civil Rights Movement's energy and membership came from the ranks of undergraduates in Nashville—the demonstrators had moved from lunch counters to movie theaters for the 1960–1961 academic year. Despite the prohibition, Yasuoka goes to a rally at Fisk University with a couple of Vanderbilt students, and later they take a camera to the stand-ins at downtown cinemas (Yasuoka, *Amerika* 105, 126). When Robin, the son of Yasuoka's tutor, "Mrs. P.," is assaulted and visibly injured while participating in a demonstration, the P. family fears that the university will find out and expel Robin.[9] A friend of Yasuoka's, meanwhile, comes to him with bad news: "You went to the black demonstration downtown yesterday, didn't you? There's a huge photo of you in today's newspaper. [. . .] It says that you're a Communist" (131). Before Yasuoka can process this, the friend suddenly breaks out laughing and tells Yasuoka he's only kidding. The friend is not pulling the supposed slur out of thin air; participants in the Civil Rights Movement, and particularly Martin Luther King, Jr., were often thought to have Communist tendencies, and W. E. B. Du Bois even applied for Communist Party membership toward the end of his life, in 1961 (Branch 563). But the implication is clear: while white students such as Robin risk being expelled for taking sides in the struggle, the thought that Yasuoka would be anything but invisible is laughable.

An examination of local newspapers from the time Yasuoka spent at Vanderbilt reveals just how invisible he was. There appears to have been no announcement of his arrival or departure, no human-interest story about him, no acknowledgement in either the campus or city press that a prominent writer is visiting Vanderbilt. Articles from the student newspaper, the *Vanderbilt Hustler*, from the 1960–1961 academic year reveal how provincial and stifling the campus atmosphere was at this point in its history. A program in "Oriental Studies," including Chinese classes, was returning to campus after a fifty-year hiatus, an article announced, right next to another article about the student senate voting

Local History, Global History, and the Triangulation of Memory   113

down a proposal to support the Civil Rights sit-in movement—future US Senator Lamar Alexander cast the tie-breaking vote (February 24, 1961). "I don't see why they are fouling up the good deserts of Nevada when they could hold the A-Bomb tests on the Vanderbilt campus," one student wrote to the editor on March 3, 1961. The Vanderbilt Foreign Student Association, representing Vanderbilt's 110 international (mostly graduate) students, felt obligated to deny to the *Hustler* that any of them were participating in the stand-ins around town (March 17, 1961). A later editorial bemoaned the state of international relations on campus: "Rarely is there any real friendship, understanding, communication, between the Vanderbilt American student and the Vanderbilt foreign student" (April 28, 1961). This is the milieu into which Yasuoka was quietly placed.

When Yasuoka arrives in Nashville, the professors of the English department at Vanderbilt are pro-Southern and conservative, the remnants and intellectual heirs of the Fugitive and Agrarian literary movements that had flourished there in the 1920s and 1930s, counting among their numbers John Crowe Ransom, Donald Davidson, Allen Tate, and Robert Penn Warren. Of the four, only the reactionary Davidson remains, assiduously lending an intellectual veneer to an increasingly indefensible pro-segregation movement.[10] At a department reception Yasuoka finds the current faculty dismissive of his career: "The professors clearly thought that I was just another exchange student from the Orient. When they asked me what I did in Japan, I told them that I was a writer. 'Ho ho!' one of the professors chortled in surprise. 'Have you published anything?' 'About ten books,' I replied, and then thinking about it, 'No, maybe fifteen. I would have to count'" (Yasuoka, *Amerika* 29). They are certain that nothing of importance could be written outside their own tradition, and this is the beginning and end of any meaningful contact between Yasuoka and his host department.

For his part, Yasuoka was hardly a paragon of international networking; he was shy, and his hosts complained to the Rockefeller Foundation about his refusal to engage with the community (Kim 237). In one sense, his aloofness was rooted in the disconnect he felt from the world, as a Japanese visitor to the United States at this particular point in history. For people who had taken the grant just a few years ahead of him, there were economic considerations; time spent in the United States was time not having to worry about making ends meet in the difficult situation of postwar Japan. That era had passed, but not the feeling for Yasuoka that Japan was still a "closed country":

> Of course, we had never known the era before the war when one could travel abroad freely, so while the country may have been closed we weren't necessarily cognizant of it being a "closed country," and we imagined things

would go on this way for the foreseeable future. In that sense, we were living in an era just like the one at the end of the Edo period, when people wondered if the ports would really open up or not. (BSS 2: 241)

Early in the Edo period (1603–1868), Japan "closed" to the West. This seclusion was never as complete as the common conception has it; the ruling shogunate's awareness of the outside world was filtered through the East Asian continent on one side and the Dutch trading post of Dejima in Nagasaki on the other, which supplied the Japanese authorities with a fair understanding—with extraordinary gaps—of what was happening in the outside world. When Commodore Matthew Perry of the United States sailed into Edo Bay in 1853, it served to accelerate a political process that was already underway, resulting in the collapse of the shogunate and the establishment of the modern nation-state of Japan in 1868. Perry served notice to the shogunate that the country would need to open up, and he returned the following year for an answer. The Convention of Kanagawa was signed between Japan and the United States in 1854. It was the first of the so-called unequal treaties, soon followed by agreements with the United Kingdom, Russia, and France. Under the terms of the Kanagawa Treaty, the ports of Hakodate and Shimoda were opened to foreign sailors, and the first American Consul General, Townsend Harris, was named in 1856. The 1858 Treaty of Amity and Commerce that Harris negotiated opened up another handful of ports, including present-day Yokohama, Nagasaki, and Kōbe.

Eight years after the end of the Allied Occupation following World War II, the Japan of 1960 still struggled to open up to the outside world, and—like the Japan of the 1850s and 1860s—found its connection to the wider world mediated by the United States. For Yasuoka, even the "expel the barbarians" (*jōi*) movement that furiously resisted the opening of the treaty ports and foreign concessions appeared to rear its head again in the 1960 resistance to the renewal of the Security Treaty Between the United States and Japan (*anzen hoshō jōyaku*), a struggle commonly known in Japan as Anpo after the abbreviated name of the document itself. The tumult over the treaty would abruptly end with its renewal in June 1960, shortly before Yasuoka ventured to the United States, its meaning to a number of Japanese cultural arenas not yet clear.[11] Yasuoka thought that he was fleeing a closed country struggling to open itself up to the world when he went to Nashville in 1960–1961, not realizing he was headed for a place in surprisingly similar circumstances.

All protestations to the contrary, Yasuoka's time in the South was not entirely the product of a bluff gone awry. He admits in various writings that he wanted to go to the South because other Japanese writers hadn't gone there, and that he had

Local History, Global History, and the Triangulation of Memory 115

great admiration for William Faulkner's writing. In *My Shōwa History*, Yasuoka mentions that Faulkner had once said the South and Japan had both lost wars to the Yankees, and they perhaps had something in common that way (BSS 2: 254). He was perhaps thinking of Faulkner's "To the Youth of Japan," composed for a 1955 visit to Nagano, Japan, in which Faulkner writes about the devastation of the South and claims, "Americans from my part of America at least can understand the feeling of the Japanese young people of today" (Faulkner 82). On that same visit, Faulkner had been asked to compare Japan and the South, two places with an "old tradition," and his response had traced a similar line: "We had at one time a tradition of an aristocracy something like the Japanese *samurai*, and also a peasantry which was somewhat like the Japanese peasantry, that was the connection I saw between our two peoples to make us understand one another possibly" (Jelliffe 85–86). In *A Sentimental Journey*, Yasuoka appears to expand Faulkner's sentiment:

> It isn't as though I had a great deal of knowledge about the South before I got there. But here and there I had heard various things about the South. In this region that had lost a war, the Civil War, a landowning class that had relied on a slave system for its agriculture had collapsed. It had shifted from an agricultural economy to a commercial and industrial one, and from a structure that emphasized families to one that emphasized the individual. Even while struggling to shed its old ways it was still being forced to change all the more under pressure from the North (the Yankees). I knew enough about it to think, *if that's how it is there, isn't it just like the current situation in my own country?* (*Amerika* 20)

Fifteen years after the end of World War II, Yasuoka felt that the Japanese postwar went on, and ninety-five years after the end of the Civil War, the South could be said to still be in a postwar mode. It is not simply a question of unreconciled political and economic facts, such as Japan's failure to make amends with other East Asian powers, or the South's continuing lower standard of living as compared to the North (both of these "long postwar" issues, it goes without saying, have now continued well into the twenty-first century). Rather, it is as though, in coming to this place, time and history have conflated for him, making possible an immediate and conjoined experience of both postwars.

In part, World War II resurfaces because Yasuoka's trip to the United States naturally evokes memories of the War in the Pacific and its aftermath for both Yasuoka and the people he meets, but the American experience is not a universal one; in the North that Yasuoka encounters there is a sense that the past is the past. During a brief stay in New York City, a taxi driver tells Yasuoka that his brother had been to Okinawa and had married a Japanese woman, but that he has been dead for two years (64). At a lonely diner in Delaware on Christmas Day, Yasuoka suddenly realizes that the manager has put on a record of Japanese music for him, which conjures up the memory of another Christmas present:

> I pictured the face of an American G.I. handing out chewing gum to children on the corner right after the war. I remember the G.I., wandering the bombed-out streets, handing me a stick of gum with a "Merry Christmas!" [. . .] At the time, all I could feel was that I was a demobilized soldier, and he a soldier from the victorious country. But this man standing here now [. . .] was just a man, nothing more. I had no way of knowing whether he had been a soldier, whether he had been to Japan. (75–76)

It is no longer the postwar in the North, neither of the Civil War nor of World War II.

In Nashville, however, World War II is no longer a receding memory. The view from the ninth floor of the Andrew Jackson Hotel reminds him of Northern Manchuria (18). When he goes to the Ringling Brothers' Circus, he is set upon and interviewed by a radio reporter and feels that "it was just as though I had become a sideshow pony given the title 'Hirohito's Horse,' that people could look at for ten cents" (150). The husband of the secretary to US Senator Estes Kefauver takes advantage of the rare opportunity to talk to a Japanese person by asking Yasuoka whether or not he feels Truman is "responsible" for dropping the bomb. Yasuoka demurs, but the man prods him, asking, "Is he responsible, or not?" (162).

Moreover, Japan post-World War II is conflated with the American South post-Civil War. A writer who has read the English translation of Dazai Osamu's *The Setting Sun* (Shayō), which depicts the Japanese upper class in decline under the American Occupation, tells him that "only we Southerners could understand that work" (121–22). The comment is reminiscent of Yasuoka's earlier comparison of the two postwars: "After the Civil War, there was a period of seven years (1865–1872) in which the Yankees drove the Southerners out of public office. This is coincidentally the same length of time that General MacArthur displaced our own statesmen [1945–1952]" (89). The relationship between the two postwars is a haunting one: if the South is unable to shake itself free of the postwar moment ninety-five years after the end of the Civil War, what hope is there for Japan fifteen years out from World War II?

This, of course, is the white perspective, the yearning for the Lost Cause that took shape in Reconstruction and endured through Jim Crow into the era

Local History, Global History, and the Triangulation of Memory   117

of the Civil Rights Movement. It can hardly compare to the stasis felt by blacks in the South. Yasuoka wants to take a small trip to see "Tent City," a temporary community outside of Brownsville, Tennessee, that is comprised of black sharecroppers who have been evicted from their land by their white landlords for demanding voting rights. His tutor, Mrs. P., is particularly interested in sending him there, saying, "When you get to Brownsville, go with your eyes wide open, and take a good look at the misery of the black people. You're a foreigner who can't speak English very well, so use that to your advantage. Ask whatever you want, offensive or not; ask the things we can't. And maybe you can go places we can't, too" (185). The outsider who observes America, seeing what people within the system cannot see, has been valorized in the United States at least since Alexis de Tocqueville's *Democracy in America* was published in 1835. Yasuoka could not have any direct effect on the system as it stood, but he could observe, and there was value in the witnessing. In Brownsville, the mayor is flummoxed when Yasuoka asks to visit Tent City. This is one of two towns in Tennessee that doesn't allow blacks to vote, he tells Yasuoka. When Yasuoka asks him why—asking the questions others can't—the mayor's response is stunningly blunt:

> Why? What a strange thing for someone to ask. Because they don't have the capacity to do such a thing, that's why. Now, needless to say, we're concerned about that. We need to do whatever we can to educate them and get them moved to other cities. In other words, our whole plan is to disperse them. But even though we go to all this trouble to send them off to factories in the North, within half a year they come right on back here. And why would that be? Because they don't have any capabilities. Around here at least they know they ain't going to starve to death, whereas up north they really do die that way. We think an awful lot about what's best for black folks. (188–89)

The mayor declines to show Yasuoka Tent City and instead brings him to meet Mamie, his former servant whom the mayor's wife taught to read and write. Mamie is supposed to be a success story, but she lives in unimaginable squalor, with not a single possession in her dilapidated, clapboard house. Then they go to the high school the mayor has founded for the black population. The school's black principal was once one of the mayor's hired hands and performs a role expected of him:

> "The Lord made my people different from black people, don't you think?" the mayor asked the principal for my benefit.
>
> "Oh, yes. We are different peoples. And that's why it is only right that we should live separately from white folks," the principal agreed unequivocally.

[. . .]
> "It wouldn't be good for black people to get the right to vote. Don't you agree?" Mayor C pressed on.
> "Oh, I do. It would be terrible for black folks to get the right to vote."
> (193)

Yasuoka admits that he, too, has had his doubts about elections and the democratic process in general, but he is floored by this absurd performance. He wonders, what possible response can there be to this?

His answer is contained within the terms of the Civil Rights Movement itself. On the one hand, the act of providing witness or testimony of traumatic events appears to have deeply affected Yasuoka, such that their suffering appears to be his. That which Yasuoka has witnessed without intending to do so—the abject poverty forced on blacks in the South, the seemingly intractable refusal of those with political power to do anything but make token changes to the system that governs their lives—leaves him speechless and despairing, what Shoshana Felman has called "an anxiety of fragmentation" produced by the act of witnessing something traumatic, a deep feeling of disconnection (Felman and Laub 49). In these moments of helpless despair, Yasuoka is disconnected from the violence that has risen to the surface in the South, just as he is disconnected from his own national past. He is a witness simply in being.

At the same time, however, he serves in support of Margalit's "paradigmatic moral witnesses" as a principled observer of travesties that their perpetrators would just as soon see buried. During the protests, people allied with those practicing civil disobedience were always on hand as observers, both to lend moral support and because of the importance of having people uninvolved with the demonstrations directly witness what was happening to discourage violence. During one sit-in, an angry crowd was kept at bay by a single elderly white woman, who asked them to think how they would feel if it were their family being attacked (Houston 97). When the lunch counters finally integrated, each gathering of black diners was accompanied by observers from the Unitarian group United Church Women (118). In this sense, Yasuoka's decision to ask what others cannot ask, see what others cannot see, and leave a written record of it, is a profoundly optimistic act—that this outsider's record, written in Japanese and thus inaccessible to the vast majority of the American South, will be of interest to people back in Japan who might also believe, together with Dr. King, that injustice anywhere is a threat to justice everywhere. The hopefulness of this act aligns with that of the moral witnesses: "that in another place or another time there exists, or will exist, a moral community that will listen to their testimony" (Margalit 155).

Local History, Global History, and the Triangulation of Memory 119

The way forward for Yasuoka lies in the connection of these two conceptions of moral witnessing via his liminal existence in Nashville, a synthesis that offers both him and society a pathway out. By the South's definition, he is not "colored," and he feels it would be emotionally dishonest to claim solidarity with the Civil Rights activists; while many of the white people he meets don't accept him as one of their own, he cannot bring himself to feel particularly victimized by them, either. But the American South opens up a historical place of memory in a new light—one where he is both central figure and sympathetic observer. Yasuoka triangulates from postwar Japan, via the American South, to late-Edo Japan, framing the American experience of the 1860s and 1870s in terms of the coeval period in Japan, the *bakumatsu* and the beginning of Meiji:

> In the end, rather than saying that the South resembles contemporary Japan, it would probably be better to say that the South was a place that had directly received the influence of 18th-century Britain, and it was the Southern patrician class that modeled themselves body and spirit after the lifestyles of the rural landowners of that period. And it has a certain similarity in spirit to the landowning class that was in our country until about the Meiji Period. (*Amerika* 124)

He visits the Hermitage, Andrew Jackson's plantation, and is struck by its similarities to his ancestral home in Kōchi (114). Jackson was a slave owner, while Yasuoka's family were *gōshi*, or "country samurai" who had been allowed to purchase their samurai status and profit from the labor others performed on their land. Yasuoka's ancestors during Jackson's time, often portrayed as second-class citizens by history, nevertheless enjoyed relatively high status, and whatever advantages Yasuoka received early in his life were surely a bequest of the Japanese class system. At the same time, he makes it clear that the binaries the Southerners around him envision—of black and white, of victim and victimizer—are constructs that he can transcend. His very presence in Nashville, and the very fact that he is the one telling the story, make it so, a sentiment that his tutor, Mrs. P., appears to share. When he compares the South to the postwar Japan he himself has known, the connection is obvious: both have been defeated/occupied/victimized by the Yankees. When he compares the South of Andrew Jackson to his family's high status at the time the South lost the Civil War, however, he sees the privileges that have been passed down to him. By moving past the fragmentation of Japan's and his own wartime and postwar experiences, Yasuoka is able to return to the *bakumatsu* and Meiji, an era of great despair for his own ancestors, their grievances handed down through the generations, and for the first time see that he can redeem them through narrative—and thereby save himself in the process (the subject of Chapter Five).

Yasuoka realizes that he has, right in front of him in Nashville, a model for turning to the past as a way of overcoming postwar myopia. Mrs. P. spent most of her early life as part of a missionary family. Toward the end of his Nashville stay, Mrs. P. lets slip what happened to the family in Fujian Province, where they worked as missionaries: the Japanese army invaded, and they were forced to flee toward the interior. The family presumably left everything they owned behind, and Mrs. P.'s daughter Gail was infected with chicken pox and measles along the way.[12] Mrs. P. never said anything about this to the Yasuokas, and she refused to accept money from the Rockefeller Foundation for the hours she spent tutoring Yasuoka in English (208–10). "You couldn't say that we were completely unrelated to her past trauma," Yasuoka acknowledges (209). In the same way that the sit-in protesters trained themselves to respond to brutality with love, Mrs. P. has apparently determined to do the same with the Japanese visitors to Nashville in 1960. The spirit of nonviolent resistance, which moved from the convictions of Leo Tolstoy in Russia to Gandhi in India to James Lawson and Martin Luther King, Jr. (Branch 85–87), to the people of Nashville and Mrs. P., has been transmitted from Mrs. P. to Yasuoka, who will convey it from the American Southland back to Japan.

Intertwined Pasts in *A Sentimental Journey to the Soviet Union*

The power of Nashville to serve as a point of triangulation for Yasuoka—as a waystation en route to his own personal and national past—is even more apparent when we compare it to the record of a subsequent foreign journey. In 1963, Yasuoka visited the Soviet Union with a delegation invited by the international PEN Club's Soviet chapter, and the following year he published a memoir of his time there, a follow-up of sorts to *A Sentimental Journey to the United States*, entitled *A Sentimental Journey to the Soviet Union* (*Sobieto kanjō ryokō*, 1964). One could read these as companion texts. Again, there is the sense that Yasuoka is late on the scene; he mentions getting advice for the trip from those who have been members of previous delegations: Kaikō Takeshi, Hotta Yoshie, and Ōoka Shōhei among them. He feels as put-upon in the USSR as he had in the United States: he is scolded for taking photos of empty countryside from a moving train, even though no one had minded in the least when he had taken photos of the rather-more-strategic port facilities through which they had entered the country (YSZ 7: 298).

The parallels end there, however. The tour of the Soviet Union is mediated through an ever-present guide and lasts only two months. Yasuoka has intellectual traveling companions for this journey, the scholar of Russian literature

Local History, Global History, and the Triangulation of Memory

Yasuoka (second from right) in Kiev on a tour of the Soviet Bloc, July 1963, posing with hosts and the Japanese critics Kobayashi Hideo (far left) and Sasaki Kiichi (center). Photograph courtesy of Yasuoka Haruko.

Kuroda Tatsuo and literary critics Kobayashi Hideo (1902–1983) and Sasaki Kiichi (1914–1993), who was the brother-in-law of Hiroshima writer Hara Tamiki. A tour guide captures their attention with a description of the Siege of Leningrad, in which the Russians held off the German army in World War II for eighteen months, at the cost of six hundred thousand lives. But when the guide attempts to establish an emotional connection with the Japanese visitors, he fails:

> "In other words, we are connected to you through this tragedy. Leningrad, Hiroshima—these are exactly the same tragedy."
> [. . .] How were Hiroshima and Leningrad connected? I didn't take kindly to Hiroshima being treated in such general terms.
> "Hiroshima and Leningrad are different," I said. "The people of Leningrad died after putting up a valiant defense. But the people of Hiroshima didn't do anything; they were simply killed." (373)

Yasuoka's sense that postwar Japan had an affinity with the American South was developed not in spite of, but actually because of, the triangulation required to make such a leap. By the same token, it is clear that the Soviet Union cannot serve as a double for Japan precisely because the two countries have shared too much recent history. Yasuoka feels it from the moment he steps off the boat from Japan in the port city of Nakhodka:

> The only image that comes to mind when I hear the name "Nakhodka" is of ships repatriating troops after the defeat in the war. For me, the song "Hills of a Foreign Land," which I heard many times on amateur-hour radio programs, carries with it all kinds of gloomy memories—of homemade bread made with flour from corn used to feed American army horses, of living in a house without electricity—and "Nakhodka" taps into the same bitter feelings. (290)

"Hills of a Foreign Land" ("Ikoku no oka") had been written by songwriting great Yoshida Tadashi while he was in a Soviet internment camp, where hundreds of thousands of former Japanese soldiers were used by the Soviets as slave laborers for, in most cases, years after the war had ended. The song was released on Victor Records in 1948, and became famous when another returnee from Siberia, Nakamura Kōzō, sang it on NHK's amateur-hour program *Proud of My Voice* (*Nodo jiman*). It was the basis for a film released by Tōhō in 1949, directed by Watanabe Kunio and starring Uehara Ken. The song was part of Yasuoka's own postwar experience, and for him, the deprivations of the internees in Siberia were interwoven with his own domestic deprivations in Japan. He himself had intimate knowledge of songs sung in the field, and even of the hills of this particular land:

> When I remember how, under a sky that would never get dark, we would be made to practice military songs, it seems like a dream that I am sitting here on a bench at a little station in Siberia. At that training center, every time I saw the train heading north, I would have the strange feeling of imagining myself as a deserter. The train, which chuffed up white smoke and looked like a toy as it disappeared into the distance, was called the "international train"; from Heihe it crossed the border and probably connected to the Siberian railroad. . . . What we saw before us now, needless to say, was not the same train as the one I had gazed down on from a hill on our training grounds. But I could at least say that the empty dream I had had twenty years earlier had now become a reality in a completely unexpected way. I had made it to the area on the other side of the national border that it had been forbidden to cross into for many years. (294–95)

Had Yasuoka's dreams of escaping into Siberia come true during the war, his fate would have been far worse. The irony of the situation—that the very thing he most longed for during the war would have resulted in either his death or long-term imprisonment—is not lost on him. The Soviet Union, for all of its ideological constraints, represents a moral morass to Yasuoka. Calling this a "sentimental journey" would appear to be an even more ironic gesture in the Soviet Union than it was in the American South.

Even more than its ideology, the physical space of the Soviet Union feels hopelessly stuck in the past even by the time of Yasuoka's 1963 visit: hotels are functional, service is dispirited and slow, department stores are virtually empty. The past in which they are stuck, metaphorically speaking, is that of the immediate Japanese postwar. As in the Japanese postwar, American influence is the dominant paradigm that everything must either resist or risk being subsumed into. At a restaurant in Moscow, "When the Saints Go Marching In," "My Blue Heaven," "Mack the Knife," and other American jazz standards of a previous era are playing, free-flowing signifiers in time and space that appear to have a following even in Cold War Russia:

> Every time one of these strange songs started playing, the people dancing came to life, and even the people sitting down clapped their hands and stomped their feet on the floor. . . . I had a memory of seeing a scene like this somewhere before. A vision came to life as though I were seeing it right now, of the faces of a group of people in 1947 or 1948, dancing in a hall renovated after having been bombed out; their hair shined with machine oil, and they wore things like jumpers made from mended army uniforms. (314)

The "overearnestness" with which the Muscovites approach the American art form rivals that which Yasuoka saw in the faces of the Japanese people who danced in the postwar (314). Not even the most monumental, iconic locations in the Soviet Union can escape the association with postwar Japan: "My first impression of Red Square, in front of the Kremlin, was that it resembled the row of stalls lining the street along the way from Shibuya to Dōgenzaka. [. . .] I felt I was strolling the stalls right after the war ended, when everything had burned down and only the paving stones remained" (349). The mortar buildings "change color as they are weathered by wind and rain, and in the places where they are starting to crumble, they invite comparison to the architecture of early-Shōwa cafes and coffee shops" (350). Like postwar Japan, the Soviet Union struggles to define itself vis-à-vis East and West, but Yasuoka finds only a way to the past there.

The City Anew: *My Alt Heidelberg*

Yasuoka saw the history of modern Japan as a lost epoch, a terrible turn toward great-nation status that ended up obliterating his youth and his generation. The signs that he saw in Nashville in 1960–1961, nearly a century after the Civil War, made him despair that anything resembling normality would return in his own lifetime. A subsequent trip to Nashville would leave him elated at what had been achieved. Even Yasuoka could not help but be buoyed by a sense of optimism that things can change.

Yasuoka went to Nashville again in 1968, a trip he recorded in *My Alt Heidelberg* (*Waga Aruto-Heideruberuhi*, 1969, in YSZ, vol. 7).[13] The world was falling apart, and so much work remained to be done, but for Yasuoka—who knew only what he had seen eight years prior and was comparing his journey to that moment in time—the Civil Rights Era had been a stunning success. He is amazed to find that, in eight years, everything he knew about the city has changed—generally for the better. The flight from New York that took eight hours in 1960 could now be done in half the time. The red-light district has been torn down, replaced by a nursery school. The buildings are a little taller. The change that has made the city most unrecognizable, however, is in the people themselves: he sees black people and white people sitting together on a bus-stop bench, and he sees a black man being served at a snack stand. It is hard for him to believe there were ever stand-ins and protests here. Perhaps a larger change is visible in the attitudes among the young black people he sees on the street:

> The postures of the blacks and whites of eight years earlier had been completely reversed. The black people I had seen here before had walked with slumped shoulders, their heads downcast, while the whites, with their curt, cosmopolitan faces, had strode boldly, dispassionately forward. To put it more simply, as the blacks' sense of themselves had risen, the whites perhaps inevitably became more reserved and adopted a low profile. Something very similar had happened in Japan: As the student strikes spread, teachers would adopt that very same posture when they walked by students. (YSZ 7: 238)

Yasuoka doesn't take the empowered attitude the black citizens of Nashville display when they walk down the street to mean that everything is better. As with the boxer Cassius Clay (who had become Muhammad Ali since Yasuoka had last visited the United States, Yasuoka points out), Yasuoka senses a performance at work, a show of pride that is deliberately outrageous because it is in fact a demand for acknowledgement of the overwhelming gap in the circumstances between white and black living conditions in America (245–46). Nevertheless, an extraordinary change has come to Nashville in an extraordinarily short time, and it has had an effect on Yasuoka as well; whereas he had been in a postwar state of mind during his 1960 trip, the changes wrought on Nashville in the interim have had the effect of bringing him into the present.

Unlikely political change has come to the white residents of Nashville as well. Yasuoka calls his old tutor Mrs. P.'s phone number, and soon he is reunited with Mrs. P. and her friend, Mrs. S. Yasuoka had always thought that Mrs. P. was more progressive than Mrs. S., but in another sign that Nashville has gone topsy-turvy, they have reversed positions due to the Vietnam War: Mrs. P. supports the war, while Mrs. S. is set against it. Mrs. P.'s openness to Yasuoka was in alignment with her pre-Civil Rights Era Republicanism. It was also a result of her longstanding connection to East Asia; she grew up in China as the child of missionaries, only leaving when the Japanese Army invaded. Despite her extremely liberal views toward racial reconciliation in the South and elsewhere, however, she supports the Vietnam War. Mrs. P.'s political stance keeps her in the mainstream of the shifting Republican Party. Yasuoka reveals a rather keen understanding of the changes that had happened in American politics with the passage of the Civil Rights Act of 1964 and Lyndon Johnson's apocryphal comment at the signing of the bill, "We have lost the South for a generation": "The Republican Party that Mrs. P.'s family had supported for generations was no longer a party that represented the opinions of the anti-slavery Free Soilers; it had already come to be supported by the conservatives that pushed for discrimination against blacks in the Southern states. It wasn't that the nature of the Republican Party had changed; it was that the South, along with the situation of blacks within it, had changed" (275). Given her background in prewar China, Mrs. P.'s newfound conservativeness likely sees the war as a necessary form of resistance to communist China. Meanwhile, Mrs. S., who had been very much against the Civil Rights protests eight years earlier, stands firmly on the side of the resistance to the escalation of the Vietnam conflict; her Harvard-educated son ripped up his draft card and went to Mexico, where he was now teaching. The South has fundamentally changed, showing a way forward for Yasuoka.

The *Asahi Journal* Roundtables and Multidirectional Memory

In *Multidirectional Memory*, Michael Rothberg resituates Holocaust memory in terms of global decolonization, generally considered to be a completely different political arena. Rothberg resists the "logic of scarcity" that concludes that Holocaust memory has shoved everything else to the side, demonstrating that "far from blocking other historical memories from view in a competitive struggle for recognition, the emergence of Holocaust memory on a global scale has contributed to the articulation of other histories" (6). Memory is always "multidirectional," "subject to ongoing negotiation, cross-referencing, and borrowing" (3). In terms of the hierarchy of memory places, Rothberg's is a discussion of center and periphery. The connections that Yasuoka was able to draw show, however, that multidirectional memory is possible even for two peripheral, asynchronous arenas.

Such histories can be mutually generative, opening up new understandings through their juxtaposition. One example operates in the background of Yasuoka's first journey to Nashville: The South and Japan see their experiences in insular terms, but they are connected in more ways than Yasuoka's hosts realize. The United States had already had treaty relations with Japan for seven years by the time the South attacked Fort Sumter in 1861 to begin the Civil War. American attitudes toward people of African descent very likely influenced Japanese attitudes from the very first significant interaction between the two countries, the Tokugawa government's 1860 mission to the United States. Masao Miyoshi has noted that the mission was in Washington, DC, on the day Abraham Lincoln secured the Republican presidential nomination (61). Miyoshi notes the contempt with which almost all members of the Japanese delegation viewed black Americans and the reason why: "In their identification with the white Americans, they were prepared to reject any people the white Americans scorned. Thus American racism did not bother them much, nor did white supremacy, since the Japanese would be like the whites some day" (64). When someone in the Vanderbilt English department asks Yasuoka who founded his alma mater, Keiō, and what the person is doing now, Yasuoka replies, "I don't know; he died a hundred years ago" (29–30), but this is a bit of an exaggeration; Keiō's founder, Fukuzawa Yukichi, was alive and well and participating in this 1860 mission to the United States exactly a century before Yasuoka's visit to Nashville. The prejudices the Japanese delegation developed on that trip reverberate over the course of a century of exchange with the United States and are surely visible in the depiction of African Americans in all of the postwar texts treated here.

Multidirectional memory is also at work in Yasuoka's own life, in a more positive vein: Nashville had an outsized effect on Yasuoka's career, because it gave him the imprimatur of someone with something to say on issues of social justice. In addition to the Soviet Union record, other travelogues would follow, including one of a trip to Africa to observe primates in the wild, *When Monkeys Came Down from the Trees* (*Saru ga ki kara oriru toki*, 1970) and one of a subsequent 1976 trip to the United States and Canada, *American Blood and Temperament* (*Amerika-jin no chi to kishitsu*, 1977), but no other place would figure as prominently in his

Local History, Global History, and the Triangulation of Memory 127

thinking and writing as Nashville. Over time, the victimization and circularity omnipresent in Yasuoka's earlier writings would give way to a concern with social-justice issues. At times, Yasuoka is forward-leaning about this: Yasuoka was one of the co-translators of the Japanese version of Alex Haley's 1976 juggernaut *Roots*, published in Japanese in 1977. But as often as not, his reputation moves ahead of the man himself. He served as a unit director on sequences involving African and African American athletes for Ichikawa Kon's 1965 documentary of the Tokyo Olympics, a demonstration of the sense of social justice he felt for people elsewhere in the world, but it is not clear that he sought out such a role (see Chapter Four). And he was an unlikely regular in a public discussion of issues of discrimination in Japan. His is not a clarion call for justice, nor does he always evince easily discerned passion for the cause. Instead, he provides a voice all the more convincing for its introspective doubt.

In 1976 and 1977, the *Asahi Journal* published a series of *zadankai* roundtable discussions involving Yasuoka, Noma Hiroshi (1915–1991), and a revolving third member: writers Mizukami Tsutomu (1919–2004),[14] Sugiura Minpei (1913–2001), Ōoka Shōhei (1909–1988), and Nakagami Kenji (1946–1992); *zainichi* poet Kim Shi-jong (Kimu Shijon, 1929–); folklorist Miyamoto Tsuneichi (1907–1981); cultural historian Takatori Masao (1926–1981); and the jurist Aoki Eigorō (1909–1981). The series was occasioned by Noma's extensive research into the Sayama Incident, which he began publishing in the journal *Sekai* in February 1975; the series would continue until the January 1991 issue, shortly before Noma's death.

In 1963, in Sayama, Saitama Prefecture, a sixteen-year-old girl was abducted on her way home from school. Her parents received a ransom note with orders not to inform the police; nevertheless, police were sent to surround the drop-off site. The abducted girl's older sister brought money to the abductor at the appointed time, but despite a cordon of forty officers, the suspect slipped away. Embarrassed by their botched attempt, the police arrested a young man in the area, Ishikawa Kazuo, and forced a confession out of him. Ishikawa was sentenced to death, which was subsequently reduced to life imprisonment by the Tokyo High Court. The Sayama Incident, as it came to be known, became a cause célèbre in which the court was accused of discrimination because of Ishikawa's *hisabetsu burakumin* background. The *burakumin*, Japan's largest minority group, have long been discriminated against based on their family background as "outcasts" in the premodern caste system. The system was abolished at the beginning of the Meiji period, but discrimination continues, despite the fact that such discrimination can only be carried out through a form of detective work involving family histories and historical addresses, among other things. For Noma, the Sayama Incident would

At home with the writer Nakagami Kenji in 1982. Photograph courtesy of Yasuoka Haruko.

become his "lifework" (Noma 10). The discussion series is perhaps most famous as the setting for Nakagami Kenji's carefully edited intimations that he himself is a *burakumin*, what Anne McKnight has called his "crypto-confessions" (72).

Nakagami later complained to the editor of the *Asahi Journal* that Noma and Yasuoka had been "half-hearted" in their roundtable with him (McKnight 104). This is somewhat ironic considering that the complaint comes in the context of Nakagami writing a new bit of reportage for the *Asahi Journal* based on the global success of Alex Haley's *Roots*, for which Yasuoka was one of the co-translators. At the same time, one can understand Nakagami's complaints. Yasuoka changes the subject, he digresses, he tells stories about his youth. But this playfulness is a seriousness of another sort. For Yasuoka, the danger is in thinking that one is too enlightened to discriminate:

> Discrimination isn't always overtly cruel. When I hear that someone is a *hisabetsu burakumin*, I might feel sympathy for them even while harboring cold feelings toward them. This is a simplification, I'm sure, but everyone feels the urge to discriminate.
>
> Of course, I understand intellectually that these people against whom we have discriminated for generations are people just like us. What kind

of response should we have to that? I think we can sense the fissure in the bottoms of our hearts. It's frightening to peer too closely into it, but at the same time we have this titillating curiosity. That's when we can see how ugly we really are. (Noma and Yasuoka 22)

More than Noma or Nakagami, Yasuoka was always more interested in oppression in general than the specific *burakumin* discussions. The *Asahi Journal* roundtables were also a chance for Yasuoka to conceive of discrimination in a broad sense. From the beginning of their discussions, Yasuoka focused on his Kōchi ancestors, who were lower-ranking samurai oppressed by their social superiors. The Tokugawa-allied Yamauchi Clan ousted the former rulers of Tosa, the Chōsogabe, and brought their own retainers in from their former stronghold in present-day Shizuoka. For two hundred fifty years of Yamauchi rule (Yasuoka calls it three hundred), those retainers' descendants occupied nearly exclusively the top echelons of the domain hierarchy; it was a form of systemic discrimination, Yasuoka argues (Noma and Yasuoka 11). In 1976, Yasuoka was beginning his own massive project dedicated to this family history at the same time he was translating Alex Haley's *Roots* (see Chapter Five). As a scion of the lower-upper-class, Yasuoka couldn't possibly consider himself in the same abject position as the *hisabetsu burakumin* or African Americans, and it is clear he was not intending to claim there was any sort of equivalency. But his own ancestors, privileged and oppressed all at the same time, offered Yasuoka the opportunity to thread the needle again, to occupy a liminal space as a representative of those who have been wronged, but one with the ability to reclaim the anonymous dead and make them visible to posterity through his writing. From his experiences in the American South, where solidarity was developed in the least likely ways, Yasuoka found a model for turning to the past to liberate the present, giving new meaning to William Faulkner's description of the allure—and terror—of the South: "The past is never dead. It's not even past."

4

Long Shots in *Tokyo Olympiad*

It is a truism that the 1964 Tokyo Olympics represented Japan's symbolic return to the community of nations, an event that normalized Japan in the eyes of the world and—with its bullet trains, world-class facilities, and star architecture—served as a harbinger of a new image for Japan as a high-tech wonderland. Andrew Gordon notes that while the number of foreign visitors was lower than expected, it was an event made for television that produced a "media-induced surge of national pride" (*Modern History* 264). The 1964 Olympics became sacred space; as Oda Makoto pointed out at the time, only in the Japanese language does the "Olympic torch" become a "sacred flame" (*seika*) (Ishii 56). At the same time, it was contested ground, a knot of competing narrative threads, to a degree of complication perhaps only Hiroshima's "narratives of national collectivities" combined with a "universal referentiality" can rival (Yoneyama 15). Igarashi Yoshikuni has demonstrated how the 1964 Olympics also "conjured up memories of war and destruction" (Igarashi 143). More than usual, national narratives of the Tokyo Olympics butted up against the more universal ambitions of the Olympics agenda. A particular city's attempt to leave its mark on an individual iteration of the Olympics always runs against the fabula of the Olympics as sporting event—the World and Olympic Records, personal bests, medal counts, and other familiar tropes that exist irrespective of location. We can say, for example, that at one and the same time, the 1964 Olympic marathon was of importance to people living in Tokyo for the particular route it took through the metropolis; to the Japanese Olympic Committee because a Japanese athlete won bronze, the only track and field medal of the Olympics for Japan; to fans around the world because Ethiopia's Abebe Bikila became the first marathoner to successfully defend a gold medal; to posterity because of the times the various runners posted; and to the documentarians because of the opportunities it provided to portray aesthetically the limits of human endurance.

When the Japanese Olympic Committee (JOC) commissioned Ichikawa Kon to direct the official film documentary of the 1964 Tokyo Olympics, *Tokyo Olympiad* (*Tokyo Orinpikku*, 1965), they were primarily interested in producing a document that narrated the Olympics along the party line, as an event that Jordan Sand has called "the monumental expression of a supposedly reborn Japan" (3). Although this is the narrative that has survived in the collective memory, it most assuredly was not the one represented in the film itself. What Ichikawa and his crew of 561 produced was an embarrassment to the JOC: a film that captured jowls at the shot put, scowls in ceremonies and even at the finish line, and trysts under the bleachers during the opening ceremony. Denounced by the government bureaucracy and in the Japanese Diet, *Tokyo Olympiad* was nevertheless released as scheduled in March 1965 and went on to become the highest-grossing film in history to that point in Japan.

At stake in the struggle for control of the narrative of the 1964 Tokyo Olympics is nothing less than memory itself. Mnemotechnics, the art of memory, has its origins in Cicero's account of Simonides, who happens to leave a banquet just before the building collapses, burying everyone inside. Simonides is able to give a full account of the dead by remembering where each person was sitting, establishing the relationship between memory and spatiality. This tradition survives and gives rise to the memory palaces of medieval and Renaissance Europe, where prodigious feats of memory are always made possible through placing information in various rooms in the mind. In her remarkable history *The Art of Memory*, Frances Yates shows how it survives even into the age of the printing press (127–28). Aleida Assmann refers to this as memory as art (*ars*), as opposed to memory as a vital force (*vis*). Memory as *ars* is a form of storage—rememberers' journey through the memory palace allows them to access memories exactly as they left them in their various rooms (Aleida Assmann, *Cultural Memory*, 18–19). The JOC believed documentary film to be a means of storing memory, preferably showcasing Japanese gold-medal performances "as they happened" for posterity, in the service of the nation-state. Memory as *vis*, on the other hand, reverses the formula: We start by remembering, and try to work our way "from the word back to the image, then back to myth" (22). It is "a driving force that follows its own rules," one that strategically deploys forgetting, "the enemy of storage and the ally of memory" (20). From script to film to legend, we will see how *Tokyo Olympiad* forgets what it has been tasked to remember for the sake of remembering a greater truth.

Tokyo Olympiad is a documentary on the cusp of what Assmann considers another great shift in the progress of memory, the digital revolution, the greatest transformation since the printing press "opened up new areas of memory because print broke the monopoly of the Church and the court over memory, thus facilitating new modes of access to the past" (40). Hovering over the Olympic stadium is the in-house symbol of technical progress: a mammoth digital Seiko scoreboard. It appears at multiple points in the film—to share the Olympic motto, to report athletes' times, to say farewell—as a constant reminder of all that has changed in what Assmann calls an age of "overwriting": "After the extended dominance of the print age, the governing principle in the era of electronic writing is now the permanent overwriting and reconstruction of memory. Through information technology and new research into the structure of the brain, we are now experiencing a change of paradigm, by which the concept of a lasting written record is being replaced by the principle of continuous rewritings" (11).

This change of paradigm brought about by the digital age extends to the film itself. We are interested here not only in what new media make possible, but also in their particular limitations. Memory is possible only with limitations on it; even the mnemotechnics of Simonides, after all, allows memories to survive only by placing them within the confines of an architectural structure. Ichikawa and his crew worked under physical constraints that made a different kind of remembering possible and always with the possibility that their efforts would be overwritten and erased: by auteurists who would treat this as an "Ichikawa" film, by an Olympic narrative that focuses on stars and medal counts, and by an Olympic committee that would call for a more nationalist cut of the film.

Yasuoka Shōtarō was an unlikely participant in this project. In a roundtable conducted for the April 1965 issue of *Bessatsu kinema junpō* devoted to Ichikawa's *Tokyo Olympiad*, while the film was still being edited, the somewhat incredulous moderator asked Yasuoka what his qualifications were for being made one of about a dozen unit directors on the film. "I happen to like film," Yasuoka replied ("Orinpikku eiga shindan" 177). Yasuoka loved cameras, and he had always been an avid moviegoer. But he was being too modest. In the lead-up to the Olympics, Yasuoka had published a series of essays on foreign and domestic films, from Charlie Chaplin's movies to Kurosawa Akira's *The Seven Samurai*, in the journal *Sekai*; the essays appeared from October 1963 to September 1964 and were collected in book form that same month—right before the Olympics—as *A Sentimental Education in Film* (*Eiga no kanjō kyōiku*).

Among other segments in *Tokyo Olympiad*, Yasuoka was involved with the lone narrative sequence at the heart of the film, about a track-and-field athlete from Chad, and was a key figure in the execution of the film's design as a point

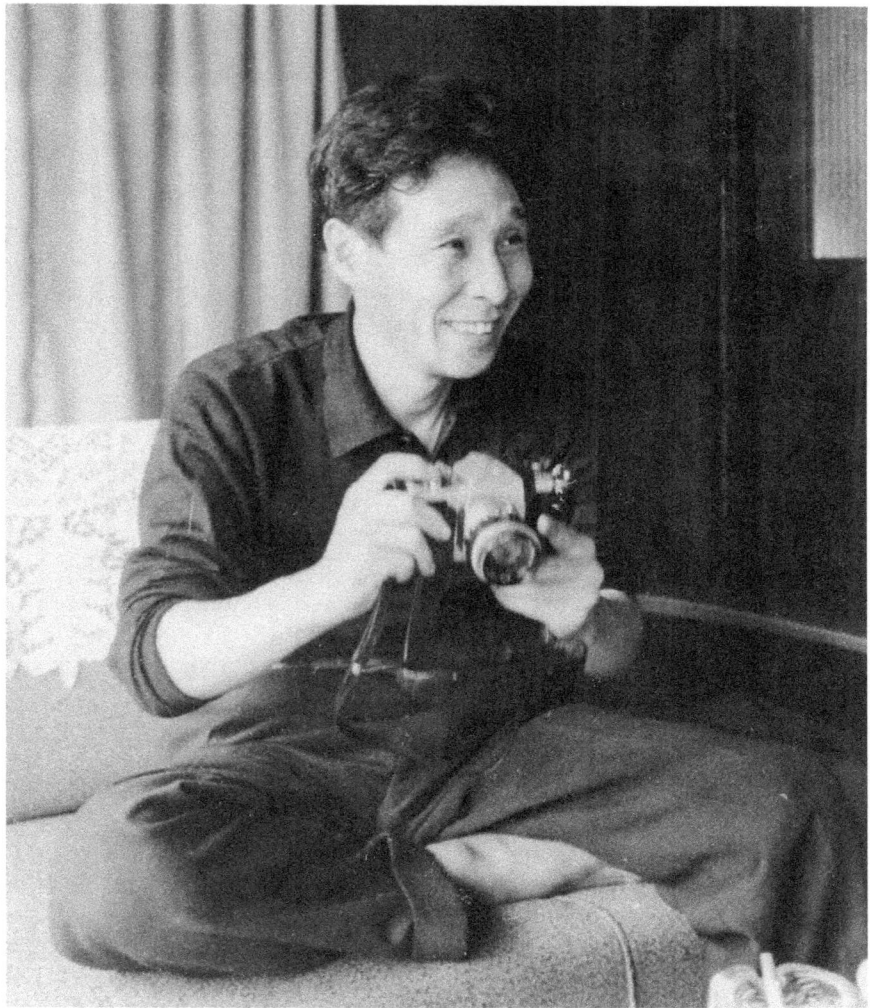

Yasuoka, photography fanatic, with his camera. He was particularly fond of Leicas. Photograph courtesy of Yasuoka Haruko.

of resistance to established sports narratives, particularly Leni Riefenstahl's documentary of the 1936 Berlin Games. At the same time, the wiliness of *Tokyo Olympiad* was hardly *sui generis*. The Japanese literary community was both critical of and captivated by the Olympics, writing reportage for newspapers and magazines during the lead-up to the Games and fanning out to nearly every event during the Games themselves. We will look at Yasuoka's lifelong relationship to film and selected literary responses to the 1964 Olympics before turning to the creation of *Tokyo Olympiad* itself.

Filmic Memory

Yasuoka was indeed a lifelong film fan. His memory throughout his early life is anchored in film. He titled one of his books *My Twentieth Century* (*Watashi no nijū-seiki*, 1999), "even though it is almost entirely about film. [. . .] but in one sense, I saw a great deal of the twentieth-century through film" (9). It's no wonder that a young man who found his own countrymen so incomprehensible and uncomprehending would find meaning in a visual context. As a teenager he was crazy about the cinema; he would go to school with film magazines instead of his schoolbooks in his backpack. With the advent of talkies, he developed personal favorites among directors: René Clair, Jacques Feyder, Julien Duvivier, and Jean Renoir representing French films; John Ford, William Wyler, and Alfred Hitchcock for English-language films; and Uchida Tomu, Mizoguchi Kenji, Kumagai Hisatora, and Yamanaka Sadao among domestic directors. It is a testament to the power of the moving image that one of the central writers in postwar Japanese literature would say that it was film that got him started reading novels: Gorky's *The Lower Depths* thanks to Jean Renoir's 1936 *Les bas-fonds*; Dostoyevsky's *Crime and Punishment* thanks to Pierre Chenal's 1935 *Crime et chatiment*. Through seeing films based on their works, he learned the Japanese writers of a previous generation: Ishikawa Tatsuzō, Ishizaka Yōjirō, Ozaki Shirō, and Ozaki Kazuo (BSS 1: 41). It was Shima Kōji's film *Rosy Glasses* (*Nonki megane*, 1940), based on Ozaki Kazuo's story of the same name, that made him want to become a writer, he claims. Ozaki had won the fifth Akutagawa Prize in 1937 for "Rosy Glasses," and Yasuoka's friend and fellow writer inchoate Furuyama Komao told him after they saw the film version of "Rosy Glasses," "If you can win the Akutagawa Prize, you can make your living as a writer. Actually, even if you don't win and you're just nominated for the Akutagawa, it's enough. Both Takami Jun and Dazai Osamu were only nominated for the prize, and they're able to make good livings as writers" (BSS 1: 116). In the event, neither needed to test this theory: Yasuoka won the Akutagawa Prize in 1953 and Furuyama in 1970, both toward the beginning of their respective writing careers.

As is apparent from Yasuoka's international taste in film, moviegoing was a cosmopolitan endeavor for Yasuoka and his friends. It was part of an upper-class lifestyle that included trips to the kabuki theaters, travel to Kansai and elsewhere in Japan, outings to the red-light district, and visits to a favorite coffee shop of coffee connoisseur Yasuoka, where, his friend Ishiyama Kōichi reports in his wartime diary, they were greeted in French (Ishiyama, *Senmatsu-ha seishun kōyū nikki* 21). We do not have a record of Yasuoka's wartime movements, but Ishiyama's diary reveals that Ishiyama and Yasuoka spent a fair amount of time together, probably even on days Yasuoka isn't specifically mentioned. Ishiyama was going to see French films whenever they screened in Tokyo, often years after their original run in France. On June 24, 1941, he saw *À nous la liberté*, a 1931 French film by René Clair. On August 7 in Shinjuku, he saw another film from 1931, German director Géza von Bolváry's *The Theft of the Mona Lisa* (*Der raub der Mona Lisa*), and on September 9, another film by René Clair, this one from 1930, *Under the Roofs of Paris* (*Sous les toits de Paris*). Yasuoka saw many of the same films, likely together with Ishiyama on occasion, and certainly discussing them regularly with him.

This love of film was so serious that it was a film that made Yasuoka turn against the Axis. Yasuoka admits that he didn't question Japan's increasingly militaristic tendencies until the Japanese premiere of Jean Renoir's 1937 *Grand Illusion* (*La Grande Illusion*) was cancelled after the film was criticized by Joseph Goebbels: "I liked Germany, and I didn't dislike Hitler or the Nazis. [. . .] Had I not been a film buff, surely I would have continued to feel this way for a long time. But because I wasn't allowed to see a film that had been talked about all over the place as being Jean Renoir's immortal masterpiece, I despised Goebbels, and at the same time I suddenly hated the Nazis, and Hitler, and Germany" (BSS 1: 67). It was a lasting grudge, apparently: according to Ishiyama's diary, on November 10, 1941, annoyed at their professor's discussion of *Mein Kampf*, Ishiyama and Yasuoka stormed out of the classroom (20).

As an adult, Yasuoka viewed the potential shortcomings of film as a depiction of reality. "These days, whenever you see a film or a television drama about a student going off to war, unfailingly there is a lovely girl in a school uniform or a fiancée standing behind him. Perhaps this is an unavoidable fiction for the purposes of the drama. But for me and for everyone I knew, there was no such vision of beauty there" (BSS 1: 209). Yasuoka is actually understating the case here; the "love interrupted by war" motif has a long tradition that goes back to the postwar melodramas: Gosho Heinosuke's *Once More* (*Ima hitotabi no*, 1947), Imai Tadashi's *Until the Day We Meet Again* (*Mata au hi made*, 1950), Ōba Hideo's six-hour, three-part *What Is Your Name?* (*Kimi no na wa*, 1953–1954), and Kinoshita Keisuke's *Immortal Love* (*Eien no hito*, 1961), to name a few. The first three use the same plot device: would-be lovers, torn apart by the war and other bad luck, agree to meet at a certain spot at a certain time but keep missing the appointments. In *What Is Your Name?*, the would-be lovers meet on a bridge during a bombing and agree to meet there again six months later. It seems like a ludicrous set-up, yet Yasuoka made a similar pact just before he went into the army in 1944, years before these films and their source texts were made. Isolde Standish has noted that the melodramatic-encounters-on-bridges genre was probably inspired by *Waterloo Bridge* (1940), starring Vivien Leigh and Robert Taylor (195). *Waterloo Bridge* wasn't released in Japan until after the war, but the basic plot may have been known to Yasuoka and his friends. It wasn't with a potential lover that Yasuoka made his pact, however, but with his friends, all of them aspiring to careers in literature. They wondered how long the war could possibly last and settled on a surefire place and date: They would meet on the Pont des Arts, a bridge in Paris, on July 14 (Bastille Day), 1950 (BSS 1: 212). They correctly guessed that the war would be over by 1950, but failed to anticipate that they would not be able to travel out of the country by then, or that some of their number would be dead.

When Yasuoka finally arrives in Paris in the summer of 1963, he stays in a hotel that Rilke had once stayed in and is amazed to find a bidet in the center of the room. The bidet is something of a panopticon to Yasuoka; no matter where he goes in the room, the bidet is visible in all of its splendor and vulgarity, somehow making Yasuoka exposed to it in all of *his* splendor and vulgarity. Something physical, if not moral, is at stake. He wonders that Rilke never mentioned it in his memoirs, and he is even more disappointed to find that of all of the films that he watched with his friends, that had made them dream of Paris—René Clair's *Under the Roofs of Paris* and *Bastille Day* (*Quatorze juillet*, 1933), Julien Duvivier's *Under the Paris Sky* (*Sous le ciel de Paris*, 1951), and Marcel Carné's *Hôtel du nord* (1938)—not one of them showed a bidet on screen (BSS 3: 78–80). Clearly, film's central position as an arbiter of a communal sense of reality and as a repository of collective memory has been attenuated, even undermined, in an age of world travel.

After the war, Yasuoka finally did see *Grand Illusion*, the film whose suppression had made him hate Hitler and the war effort, but he ended up not liking it very much, because he now knew too much: "The age and the environment had changed too much from the time when I was looking forward to seeing the film and the time I actually saw it; I finally had to turn away from the screen." Watching a film set on the eve of World War II, in a cinema that still bore scars from the bombing, was "like finally meeting a lover one has been separated from for many years but finding that you don't really connect anymore" (BSS 1: 70).

Criticism of the Tokyo Olympics

For Japan, as elsewhere, the Olympics have always been a nationalist endeavor, beginning with the first time the country competed, in the 1912 Stockholm Games.

Toeda Hirokazu has shown how the writer Yokomitsu Riichi, puffed up by his publisher and fans alike as "the god of literature," wrote about the 1936 Berlin Olympics "with the rhetoric of war," as did many other articles in the *Tokyo nichinichi* newspaper where he published his account: "For readers who received war news primarily from the newspaper, the repetition of such expressions fostered a sensibility in which the Olympics and the war were conflated" (181). It was a small part of the collaboration for which Yokomitsu was denounced by critic Odagiri Hideo, filmmaker Kamei Fumio, and others in the early postwar.

Perhaps aware of this history, writers at first approached the 1964 Tokyo Olympics with suspicion.[1] A year before the Olympics, in *Gekkan asahi sonorama*, the Naoki Prize winner Yamaguchi Hitomi ridiculed Pierre de Coubertin's famous take on the Olympic spirit—"The most important thing in the Olympic Games is not to win but to take part, just as the most important thing in life is not the triumph but the struggle"—because Yamaguchi hoped for victory from his countrymen: "Students study for entrance exams with the intention of being accepted. If you don't have any hopes of succeeding from the start, maybe you should just quit, because you're wasting the money you're spending on the examination fees. The Olympics work the same way. If you're participating with the mindset that you're going to lose and disappoint all of us, just quit now. For starters, you're wasting our taxes" (Ishii 46). And this is one of the more positive takes. On the whole, the literati were inclined to tweak their noses at, if not outright ridicule, the Olympic effort. The community of writers who were, as Endō Shūsaku put it, "pressed into service like the press corps during the war," were largely suspicious of Olympic ideals, if not the entire Olympic effort (Ishii 170).

In the leadup to the Olympics, the focus was on corruption, both financial and of the flesh. The Olympics make a brief appearance in Abe Kōbō's novel *Woman in the Dunes* (*Suna no onna*, 1962) as one dark news item among many: "Mother Strangles Two Children: Takes Poison. Do Frequent Auto Thefts Mean New Mode of Life Breeds New Crime? Unknown Girl Brings Flowers to Police Box for Three Years. Tokyo Olympics Budget Trouble. Phantom Stabs Two Girls Again Today" (93). In his essay, Yamaguchi points to corruption in ticket distribution; although tickets go on sale in Japan first, somehow a year before the Games even start the best seats have already made their way to the hands of American businessmen (Ishii 45). The mystery writer Matsumoto Seichō, no fan of sports, wishes the entire thing would just be cancelled. Who is happy the Olympics are coming to Japan, he asks. "Hotel operators, Nikkō, and the monks of Nara and Kyoto, that's all. Have no doubt, there are going to be cases where innocent bystanders are bothered by overbearing Americans," he warns (Ishii 47).

Maruya Sai'ichi addresses wild concerns regarding language difficulties in the October 1964 issue of *Fujin kōron* with an article titled, "The Dangers of English" ("Abunai eigo"). He poses a few scenarios with mock seriousness: How is a young Japanese woman to properly respond to the athlete who says, in a hotel or in the athletes' village, "Won't you come up to my room?" If she responds to this question according to the rules of Japanese grammar, she might soon find herself in trouble when she says, "Yes," meaning, "Yes, that is correct, I won't go up to your room," not realizing that an English speaker would understand this to mean, "Yes, I *will* go up to your room." And what if one accidentally expresses interest in increased "intercourse" with foreigners without realizing that Americans primarily use the word to mean "sex" (Ishii 48)? Maruya raises all of these concerns only so that he can dismiss them as ridiculous, but the fact that such fears can be used as article fodder offers a reminder that to some segment of the population, perhaps not a small one, the Olympics represented nothing so much as the largest sudden incursion of foreigners onto Japanese soil since the end of the war. One can imagine a readership not so willing to dismiss Maruya's worst-case scenarios, still burdened by the memory of widespread end-of-war fears of young women being violated by Allied Occupation forces.[2]

Once the Olympics were underway, however, the critical distrust of the Games dissolved in the excitement of the moment. In "From Rome to Tokyo" ("Rōma kara Tokyo e"), an essay published in the *Mainichi shinbun* on the opening day of the Games, October 10, 1964, Inoue Yasushi refers to de Coubertin's emphasis on "not the triumph but the struggle" in a much more sympathetic mood than Yamaguchi had a year earlier. That day, de Coubertin's statement would appear on the digital scoreboard during the opening ceremony, and Inoue writes with a sentiment worthy of an opening day that he looks forward to the "beautiful struggle" of the Japanese competitors (Ishii 43). Writers of all political stripes went into martial mode. They fanned out across the venues over the span of the Tokyo Games, October 10 to 24, making the Olympics a virtual Rorschach test of their anxieties and desires. Mishima Yukio, covering the first day of boxing (of course), at first focuses on the physicality of the athletes, then on the political situations in their home countries against which their performances must necessarily be read. He ends where he began, with their immediate circumstances: The first pairing, randomly drawn, have the great good fortune not to have to wait their turn, an ordeal for any athlete. What Mishima feels is envy of these boxers; he is reminded of a poem by the French poet Charles Vildrac after World War I: "I would like to have been / the first soldier to fall / on the first day of the war" (Ishii 65; French original: Vildrac 22). This quick equivalency of sports with personal annihilation is particular to Mishima, perhaps, but he is not alone in his enthusiasm. Ariyoshi Sawako, in an article for the *Asahi shinbun* titled "The Witches Won" (Majo wa katta"), about the women's volleyball gold-medal match, in which the Japanese "witches of the Orient" defeated the Soviet Union, is breathless even by sportswriter standards:

> They won.
> It was a great match. And they did it in straight sets.
> Even for those who had faith that Japan would win, did they ever imagine it would be this much of a blowout? It was so wonderful that it is fair to say that the Japanese team's performance was perfection itself. (Ishii 86)

When the Olympics were over, the warmth quickly faded for many. Endō Shūsaku felt the malaise of the morning after. In an essay published in the *Asahi shinbun* on October 24, the last day of the Olympics, he wondered what would come of the massive infrastructure Japan had poured into the Olympics: "When I stand in the center of Tokyo, and look at the faint light of the autumn afternoon land on the new roads and hotels we built just for this, I feel a certain emptiness. And I am sure I am not the only one wondering what that emptiness will feel like next year" (Ishii 171). On the same day, Oda Makoto wrote a story for Kyōdō News, decrying the public funding for the Enoshima yacht harbor that was destined to end up as a private club. Oda managed to interview Olympic head Avery Brundage, famous for his commitment to amateurism in sport. Oda tells him to his face that in light of how much money is in the Games, amateurism is a fantasy (Ishii 173).

The novelist Sono Ayako—known later in life for her right-wing politics, including advocating apartheid for immigrants to Japan—perhaps showed some early xenophobic tendencies in an essay published in the *Yomiuri shinbun* three days after the end of the Olympics, titled "The 'Great Expectations' of the Tokyo Olympics" ("Tokyo Gorin no 'Ōinaru isan'"), referencing the Dickens novel. She blames the visiting athletes for rising vegetable prices during the Olympics and notes that housewives are being forced to make do with *moyashi* bean sprouts, having been priced out of the lettuce and cucumber markets: "Perhaps when they hear the smarmy athletes at their all-you-can-eat cafeterias exclaiming 'Very nice!' and 'I don't ever want to go home!' the Olympic committee takes it at face value and thinks the Games have been a great success, but the fires of the cooking pots of the people have become very wispy indeed" (Ishii 175).

The Japanese Olympic Committee's final report counts 5151 athletes from ninety-three countries; it seems unlikely that they had much of an effect on the supermarkets of a nation of close to one hundred million people.[3] More to the point, with the phrase "cooking pots of the people" Sono here evokes the mythical origins of Imperial Japan. Semi-legendary Emperor Nintoku was supposed to have gauged the welfare of the people by going up to the roof and observing their cooking fires. The story is related in both of the major foundational texts of Japan, the *Kojiki* (Philippi 303–4) and the *Nihon Shoki*, or *Nihongi* (Aston 1, 278–80), as well as *Shinkokinshū* poem 707, purportedly by Nintoku himself:

> climbing the highest
> tower I gaze about me
>   and see the thick smoke
> rising from the cook stoves of
> my people   what happiness
> (Rodd 1: 291)

The phrase is also evocative of the deprivations of the not-yet-so-distant war. Again, it is impossible for a writer to treat the Olympic Games without hearkening back to wartime Japan and the notion that the outside world is treating Japan unfairly.[4]

Hirabayashi Taiko wrote a companion article with a similar spirit. She could not bear to watch the open-weight judo gold-medal match in which Kaminaga Akio lost to Anton Geesink of the Netherlands, calling it "as gruesome as a medieval death match" (Ishii 181). The women's volleyball gold-medal match, however, gave her no such trouble. The disparity, it appears, lay in the meaning of the particular sport to the nation:

> The difference in my two moods reveals the double awareness that permeates the Olympic Games. It's not that we don't care if we lose in either judo or volleyball, of course; the Japanese volleyball team burst into tears when they won gold, so hard had they worked for it. But with volleyball, it's easy enough to throw around words such as "the Japanese national anthem" (*kimigayo*), or "rising-sun flag" (*nisshōki*), or "gold medal"—we can simply treat the sport as nothing more than a sport. With judo, however, isn't something bigger at stake, something that can't be represented merely by a single playing of the national anthem or a single gold medal?
>
> For judo, this "something bigger" goes beyond the life's work of a particular young man, or the fundamental authority obtaining to a particular organization. I don't mean to say that it is directly linked to the rising tide of nationalism that is even now creeping up on the sports world. But [. . .] I felt acutely while watching the judo that sports is something that can lend itself very easily to other antagonisms. (Ishii 181–82)

Judo originated in Japan and was making its Olympic debut at the 1964 Tokyo Games. Japan won gold in all classifications except for the open weight. Judo is, needless to say, informed by traditional Japanese culture and conducted with a Japanese vocabulary. And it is a martial art, a competition in which the skills of the battlefield have been defanged by sports culture. As nation-states poured their nationalistic feelings into the proxy of sports competition, those who lived through the war may have felt something greater at stake with judo—as well as an uncomfortableness with that feeling, simmering just beneath the surface.

As the Olympics end, Ishihara Shintarō, who decades later as the governor of Tokyo will spearhead the drive that eventually brings the Olympics back to Tokyo for 2020, writes of the "sacred flame" that it "doesn't go out; it simply moves elsewhere" (*Tokyo Orinpikku: Bungakusha*, 217). He claims that the athletes who won medals for Japan remembered what it meant to give everything; that reminder, Ishihara argues, made the expense of the Olympics worth it (218). Can there be any doubt that the sacred flame of which he is speaking is one that moves from the battlefield to the sporting venue? Each in her or his own way, the writers demonstrated not how far the country had come since the war, but rather how much of a presence the isolation of war and Occupation continued to evince. The breezy popular narrative of the 1964 Olympic Games as a marker of Japan's return to the world stage conceals as much as it reveals. The unease, even antagonism, that many writers and artists felt for that official narrative of the 1964 Tokyo Olympics has disappeared from public consciousness with time. The sole reminder of it, it seems, is the documentary film *Tokyo Olympiad*.

Tokyo Olympiad and the Space of the Games

For a long time, the circumstances surrounding the making of Ichikawa Kon's masterpiece have been considered the stuff of screen legend, as compelling and idiosyncratic as the film itself: Commissioned by the Japanese Olympic Committee, the film was turned over to Ichikawa after Kurosawa Akira left the project over control and budget issues in the spring of 1964 (Galbraith 360). Ichikawa was chosen for the very reason that he was deemed a reliable filmmaker who could be trusted to work under the artistic constraints of the project. They weren't completely wrong; in many ways, it was because of these constraints that Ichikawa produced the work he did, as we will see.

Artistically, scholars have read *Tokyo Olympiad* as Ichikawa's response to Leni Riefenstahl's alternately-praised-and-maligned masterpiece *Olympia*, the documentary of the 1936 Berlin Olympics; by this auteurist measure, Ichikawa's Olympic documentary is history repeating itself as farce, the whimsical, cheery counterpoint to Riefenstahl's mass ornament-ization of the athletic body.[5] Riefenstahl's opening sequence is perhaps one of the most famous in documentary film: among the (soundstage) ruins of Greece, a camera lovingly pans across a collection of posed statuary; each statue dissolves into a human being moving through a range of motion captured by the statue—throwing javelins, dancing, and so on. It is at once a connection to the past as well as an advertisement for the power of documentary film: the "single frame" of a statue frozen in time is liberated by the flicker of the moving image, and the representation of humanity expressed by the statue gives way to a medium, film, that purports to be a record of reality. Compare this to Ichikawa's film, which opens with a shot of the rising sun, centered on the wide screen and of perfect proportion to the background to evoke the Japanese flag. This graphically matches to a wrecking ball mid-swing, smashing into an old building in Tokyo. If Riefenstahl's film is about preserving a classical mythos, this film will be about demolishing at least two spurious pasts at the same time: those of the Nazis and the Japanese Empire. The emphasis here will be not on the mythical, but on the real: the sequence of shots of buildings being destroyed to clear room for the Olympic facilities, the creation of actual ruins, contrasts to Riefenstahl's manufactured ones, just as Ichikawa's shots of the actual torch relay across Europe and Asia correspond to Riefenstahl's staged ones.

To an incredible degree, Riefenstahl had control over the Berlin Games: her biographer Steven Bach reports that "cameras flew overhead in dirigibles, light planes, and free-floating balloons when the games opened on August 1. [. . .] Trenches were [. . .] dug for low-angle views; steel towers [. . .] erected for high" (151). Ernst Jäger, press chief for the film, reported that the crowd threw beer bottles at the filmmakers, so much did they get in the way (Graham 84). In the same way, Riefenstahl had singular control over her film crew. She flew to Greece to personally oversee the shots of the beginning of the torch relay, and one report from the time details the degree of oversight she had on every aspect of her film: on the third day of the Games, she "discussed five different takes with each of 34 cameramen," and talked "to each of them for an extra ten minutes about material, filters and apertures" (Bach 155).

In interviews with Mori Yūki, Ichikawa took pains to describe Riefenstahl as an influence, but not as someone to whom he felt the need to stand in opposition (Ichikawa and Mori 302). That being said, their conceptions of the limits of documentary are at odds with each other. In a discussion with the essayist Sawaki Kōtarō, author of a book on Leni Riefenstahl's film called *Olympia: In the Realm of the Nazis* (*Orinpia: Nachisu no mori de*, 1998), Ichikawa mentioned that he had seen *Olympia* when it was first released in Japan in 1940 but hadn't given it much thought at the time. When he watched Riefenstahl's film again

Long Shots in *Tokyo Olympiad*

as he was preparing to make his own Olympic film, however, her techniques struck him for the first time. It was obvious to him how many of the shots were reconstructed, filmed after the initial event and silently inserted as though they had been taken in the actual moment of competition. "When I was selected to direct *Tokyo Olympiad*, I decided that I would simply not reshoot scenes the way Riefenstahl had done," Ichikawa told Sawaki (Ishii 139).

To Ichikawa, these staged shots are the defining aspect of Riefenstahl's work. In his conversation with Mori, Ichikawa points to the famous pole-vault sequence, in which the American Earle Meadows outlasts two Japanese competitors to gain the gold. The end of the sequence makes use of a re-enactment conducted specifically for the film, because the event itself lasted well into the evening, after it became too dark to shoot—not surprisingly, the Japanese runners-up participated in the reshoot of their loss only reluctantly (Ichikawa and Mori 301–2). Sawaki Kotarō's book, incorporating interviews conducted over a span of two decades, includes a description of the reshoot by pole-vault silver medalist Nishida Shūhei and triple-jump gold medalist Tajima Naoto, who served as interpreter for the two Japanese pole vaulters at the reshoot (pole vault bronze medalist Ōe Sueo died in battle in 1941). Riefenstahl explained her desires to Tajima, who relayed them to the two Japanese participants: "Snag the bar right there," or "This time, make the jump beautiful" (Sawaki 115). The reshoot was held at a practice field attached to the athletes' village. For the sake of logistics, Riefenstahl wanted the bar set at 3.50 meters, even though the two Japanese competitors had been stymied at the 4.35-meter level. Nishida complained that if the director wanted a realistic reenactment, she needed to give them similar conditions: "Even though you want us to miss, if the bar isn't set at a certain height, we won't be able to jump smoothly" (115). They compromised at about 4 meters (115).

The resistance we find in the aesthetics of *Tokyo Olympiad* are a reflection of the circumstances of its production. If Riefenstahl had an iron grip on every aspect of her film, Ichikawa relied more on serendipity and collaboration. Ichikawa did not micromanage his own film. He went to only a limited number of events, and in the Mori interview he credits many of the small touches that critics have viewed as "Ichikawaesque"—close-ups on shoes, a sea of umbrellas popping open in the rain—to the "unity of spirit" among the crew (Ichikawa and Mori 306). Ichikawa claims that he offered up the job of following the torch relays to anyone on the crew who wanted to go (he recalls having had several takers) (309). Some of this is Ichikawa's working style, but the abbreviated timeline also forced him to delegate responsibility: Kurosawa had eaten up too much time in preparation for this film, starting with the 1960 Rome Olympics, before bowing out. Ichikawa didn't take over the helm of the film until April 1964, a mere six months before the Olympics. He walked into a bare office and found three staff members, all of whom were patiently waiting for instructions from the new director before beginning any work on the film (296).

The first stage of Ichikawa's monumental task, then, was to staff the film. The cinematographer Miyagawa Kazuo agreed to make *Tokyo Olympiad* his seventh film in eight years with Ichikawa, a run that had started with *Enjō* (*Conflagration*, 1958). In his memoir, *A Cameraman's Life* (*Kyameraman ichidai*, 1985), Miyagawa recalls learning the hard way the most important rule of documentary: "You never hear, 'Take two!'" (Miyagawa 109). He notes that of the 164 cameramen on *Tokyo Olympiad*, he was the only one coming from fiction films, as opposed to newsreels and other media, but he overlooks a number of people Ichikawa hired as assistant directors and writers despite a complete lack of *any* major film experience, among them the photographers Hosoe Eikō and Tōmatsu Shōmei, the poet Tanikawa Shuntarō, and Yasuoka Shōtarō. Hosoe and Tōmatsu had at least worked on small, experimental films, but Tanikawa was well outside his normal milieu—he wrote at the time that he was also "willfully ignorant" of sports, that he had never even seen a baseball game (Tanikawa 170).

Ichikawa was also in no position to demand control of the Olympic event, as Riefenstahl did and as Kurosawa reportedly had: no trenches or camera-bearing dirigibles for him. Without the permission Riefenstahl had to privilege her filming over anyone else's experience of the Olympics, the Japanese crew used several kinds of innovative zoom lenses to capture the action from far away. It was hard to focus on people from far away, several members of the film crew have noted in various recollections; at that distance, once the subject was lost, there was simply no finding it again. As an example, Miyagawa points out that there isn't a close-up shot of the Olympic torch entering the stadium because the runner strayed a little from the mark set in rehearsal, and they could not find him with the telephoto lens (Miyagawa, 111–12). Making a virtue of this limitation, the camera crews turned their attention to the felicitous everyday life at the margins of the event. The zoom lens, designed to capture the events on the field from far away, deliberately misses its mark and captures life around the periphery.

Yasuoka Shōtarō and Furuyama Komao had also seen Riefenstahl's documentary when it was first released in Japan. It had been the talk of the town; when the first half of it opened in Japan in the fall of 1940, it was so eagerly anticipated that two thousand people showed up for the first screening at the Tokyo Gekijō theater, mainly because they knew it included the performances of several Japanese athletes at the 1936 Games (Sawaki 10). In his memoir-cum-history *My Shōwa History*, Yasuoka recalls seeing an ad for *Olympia* at the time, and thinking, "But for the war, the Olympics would be here now" (BSS 3: 108–9). The only remnant in Tokyo of the cancelled 1940 Olympics, Yasuoka notes, was a chain restaurant that had been named The Olympic in the hopes of capitalizing on the event; it went from selling beef to deer meat to no meat at all before closing down. Satō Morio remembers Yasuoka and Furuyama discussing *Olympia*. Furuyama was opposed to anything with Hitler involved, while Yasuoka felt that the aesthetics of the film made it worthwhile (10).

Perhaps this is why Yasuoka jumped at the chance to participate in the 1964 Olympic film. In *My Shōwa History*, when Yasuoka meets Ichikawa Kon at a film premiere in 1964 and the director invites him to take part in the Olympic documentary, Yasuoka tells Ichikawa he knows nothing about sports, to which Ichikawa replies, "I'm useless when it comes to sports. But I think it's *because* we know nothing that we can come up with some interesting visuals" (BSS 3: 110). And Yasuoka sees an opportunity to at last take part in the making of a film.

Ichikawa and his crew had produced one of the more unusual scripts in Japanese film history: a narrative of the 1964 Summer Olympics completely written before the start of the Olympics, given over not only to the Japanese Olympic Committee, but also to the film magazine *Kinema junpō*, which published it in its special summer issue in July 1964.[6] One can see in the script a number of things that would have appealed to the Olympic committee: coverage of the torch relay, speeches, major events, and modern facilities. Other aspects are more puzzling: The script indicates that extended coverage will be given to women's volleyball (Wada, Shirasaka, et al., 28–29), in which Japan was known to be strong (the gold-medal victory in 1964 didn't come out of the blue), but covers judo, another perennial (quadrennial) source of pride for Japan, in a mere eight sentences (29–30). Some elements of the film that may have given the JOC pause were right there in the original script, such as a line of narration in which the 1940 and 1944 Olympics are said to have been cancelled "due to the war" (10), albeit without mention that Japan unilaterally cancelled on the world in 1940, and scenes of the torch proceeding through locales that bore the brunt of World War II—Manila, Hong Kong, Taipei, Okinawa, and Hiroshima (7).

The script gave special attention to the men's one hundred meters (15); after the appearance of Jesse Owens in Riefenstahl's film, this was not only acknowledging the longstanding preeminence of the event, it was also presumably an homage to the earlier Olympic film. In the film itself, Ichikawa and crew are clearly using the men's one hundred meters to tweak their collective nose at Riefenstahl. The winner of the 1964 outing, another African American, Bob Hayes, manages to run the race in ten seconds flat, a noteworthy event. And yet, Bob Hayes was not competing under the disapproving eye of Hitler, nor was his victory deemed to be "snatched away" from the host country. Even while saluting his achievement, the filmmakers acknowledge that Bob Hayes is not Jesse Owens by placing a Jesse Owens-type figure in *Tokyo Olympiad*'s one hundred meters sequence—namely, Jesse Owens himself; he actually appears in the scene. Hayes's gold-medal run is captured in slow motion, using the aforementioned zoom-lens technology to capture him from start to finish in a medium-long shot. After Hayes wins the medal, the scene cuts to a series of close-ups on faces in the crowd: a stunned Japanese man, a Caucasian man taking a photo, and finally, Jesse Owens, shaking his head in good-humored wonder at Hayes's speed. On the surface, Owens appears as the final figure in a multicultural triptych of anonymous fandom and is not identified in the film. For those in the know, however, his presence also serves to undercut Hayes's own: Whatever singular achievement Hayes has accomplished today, he, too, will one day take his place among the nameless crowd.

The original script—really, a series of gestures toward what the film might become—contained the genesis of what would become the film's actual response to Riefenstahl's Jesse Owens. The filmmakers wanted to portray an anonymous athlete from a minor country with no chances of winning a medal:

> Close up on a single (male) athlete.
> Perhaps someone who has traveled around the world to get here. He's not very tall, he's skinny. He could be dark-complexioned, or Asian.
> From the time he lands at Haneda Airport he's alone. The only thing he's carrying is a canvas bag. He comes down the gangplank from the plane, following a large contingent from another country swarming out in their matching suits. We get the impression he is a nice fellow from the way he smiles at the bustling reception at the airport; he observes the scene as though he isn't part of it. He walks down a smart little lane in the athlete's village, canvas bag dangling in his hand, looking for his own lodgings. (Wada, Shirasaka, et al., 30)

From there, the script has him hounded by a Japanese boy seeking an autograph, practicing alone, eating alone. For an unknown figure they were hoping to find, the script is surprisingly specific about his story: He is twenty-two, the oldest of eight children, and has to return to his country the day after his competition because he works as an auto mechanic and appears to be out of vacation days. Even better, they have decided that their anonymous star will be an athlete in the Olympic walk; their intention is clearly to valorize this anonymous footsoldier of the Olympic movement and demean him for a few laughs at the same time, which isn't out of keeping with many of the other moments in the film that make Olympic competitors seem like obsessive-compulsive types. From the

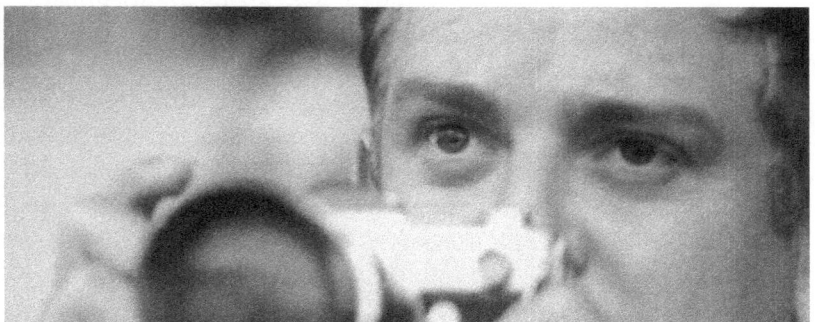

A triptych of spectators react to the results of the men's 100m in Ichikawa Kon's documentary of the 1964 Tokyo Summer Olympics, *Tokyo Olympiad*. The last spectator is Jesse Owens, gold medalist in the 1936 Berlin Olympics.

script: "Competitive walking is simply a ridiculous event. Even though they are in a hurry, they are walking, and the way they walk is quite particular: they shake their hips and waddle down the street" (31). (By chance, Cary Grant's last film, the 1966 comedy *Walk, Don't Run*, was set in Tokyo during the 1964 Olympics and featured race walking to similar comedic effect.)

Yasuoka's job was to turn this fictional script into non-fiction reality. In an article published in the December 1964 issue of *Fūjin kōron*, "A Record of the Olympic Film Struggles" ("Orinpikku eiga-zukuri funsenki"), Yasuoka notes that his crew scoured the lists of the race-walk events for the type of person they were looking for, but no one fitting the idealized description was on the roster. Instead, they went to Haneda Airport and found a single runner from the country of Chad, Ahamed Isa. At first, they filmed him from a distance using the same zoom lenses they were relying on to shoot the sporting events. They felt he had the look they were going for, so they continued to shoot him from a distance and slowly approached him to learn more about him (*Tokyo Orinpikku: Bungakusha*, 330–31).

The crew makes plans to depict the three men from Chad (two athletes and an official), but they know very little about the country. André Gide had visited Chad on his tour of North Africa (in 1926-1927), but all Yasuoka can remember from Gide's account is that cannibals still existed there. They plan to have one of the athletes write his name in "Chadese," a task made difficult by the fact that such a language does not exist (BSS 3: 112–13). When the athletes do arrive, however, they are far from the savages the crew has been expecting. One even knows all about the Meiji Restoration and the Russo-Japanese War; he read about Japanese history in his school textbook, written, of course, in French (BSS 3: 122). Sharalyn Orbaugh has convincingly demonstrated that *Tokyo Olympiad* was guilty of "elision" with regard to race, just as Riefenstahl's *Olympia* had been before it ("Raced Bodies," 307–9), but at least in Yasuoka we have a participant in the filming who sees the absurdity brought about by the crew's near-total ignorance of their subjects' country.

Yasuoka spends the two weeks of the Olympics running from place to place, from competition sites to practice sites to athlete lodgings. He gives up carrying the film camera after a single day, which frees his hands to take still shots of various events. For a few days in October 1964, Tokyo is the center of the world's attention and, thanks to those lenses, at the cutting edge of technological sophistication. On October 15, however, the Chinese conduct a successful nuclear test that demands the world's attention. Yasuoka reports feeling that "the state-of-the-art Japanese-made lenses suddenly came to seem insignificant" (BSS 3: 120). What is more, their Chadian guests also unwittingly demean Tokyo's

Still photos of Opening Ceremony, track and field event taken by Yasuoka at the 1964 Summer Olympics. Photographs courtesy of Yasuoka Haruko.

technical prowess. Yasuoka brings them to Shibuya and Harajuku, where the athletes are amazed at the sight of the Tokyoites: "Everyone runs everywhere," they point out. "They work in the evening when they should be resting" (BSS 3: 122). In the minds of the Chadian athletes, the world-class transportation and the bright lights of the city, far from easing life for its inhabitants, have intensified and spoiled it.

Someone decides that the Chad delegation may be interested in seeing film of the previous year's National Sports Festival (*Kokumin Taiiku Taikai*, or *Kokutai*). The 1963 edition had been held in Yamaguchi prefecture. When Yasuoka's crew shows the Chadians the film, however, their response is unexpected:

> When the athletic stadium appeared on the screen, they asked, "And is *this* stadium in Tokyo as well? You didn't show it to us on the tour yesterday . . ."
>
> "No," somebody explained to them after the film, bringing out a map, "it's not Tokyo. This is an athletic meet that was held in a provincial city on the far western tip of Honshu. It's an annual event that rotates from prefecture to prefecture in Japan."
>
> In an instant, they were so stunned that their dark faces seemed to drain of color. (BSS 3: 124)

What amazes them is that these sports facilities look as though they could just as well be Olympic venues. "Not only in Chad, but in each of the former colonies of Africa, one or two cities had become modern metropolises, looking just like European capitals that had been taken apart and rebuilt just so," Yasuoka recounts (BSS 3: 124). The rest of the country is left far behind; there is no equivalent to Yamaguchi in Chad. The Chadian Minister of Education asks for a copy of the film, that they might someday, in the future, build venues such as that even in the rural areas of their country.

The narrative Yasuoka and his crew intend to develop in *Tokyo Olympiad* has been thoroughly upset by the reality of the Chad delegation. They are not interested in the extraordinary documentary in progress, or even in the city hosting these Olympics or the facilities designed to great acclaim by Tange Kenzō. They have come to the Summer Olympics, a symbol of the metropole (because, unlike the Winter Olympics, the summer version is always held in a major city), seeking a way to revitalize the provinces. Although Yasuoka's narrative of the events is somewhat othering, he is sympathetic to them. In the April 1965 *Bessatsu kinema junpō* roundtable, one participant suggests that Yasuoka must have been assigned to the Chad unit on purpose, to which Yasuoka replies, "I have no idea why" ("Orinpikku eiga shindan" 177). It was probably no coincidence that Yasuoka was assigned this particular project, considering his background on issues of race and social justice. He had spent time in Nashville in 1960–1961 and was therefore one of the few Japanese people to witness the American Civil Rights Movement first-hand. His American experience made him something of an authority on discrimination in Japan upon his return, merited or not. We can also perhaps see a bit of Yasuoka's own feelings of isolation in Nashville in the Olympic narrative he helped to construct.

Yasuoka's crew decides to focus exclusively on Ahamed Isa, culling his companions from the segment entirely. In the documentary's final form, Isa takes on the appearance of the original script, and there can be little doubt that his narrative is constructed; Isa indeed encounters the Japanese boy as promised in the original script, he practices alone, he dines alone. The narrator introduces Isa by saying that he is older than his own country, a fact that the initial Japanese viewers of the film would compare to the circumstances of their own country; earlier in the film the Olympic flame is lit by a Japanese youth of a similar age to Isa who had been born near Hiroshima on the day the bomb fell on August 6, 1945—that is, at the moment Japan itself went through a rebirth of sorts. Even after Isa was aware he was being filmed and clearly participated to some extent in the effort, the filmmakers continued to use a zoom lens to capture him. Isa is shown going for a training run and encountering a group of Japanese runners; he comes toward the camera as they—the faceless fraternity—casually jog into the background. Throughout his sequence, Isa is given the same treatment as the track-and-field competitors: He is viewed from afar, kept in focus and near the center of the frame—high honor for a mere participant in the Olympics, but also an alienating device as other athletes run through the frame or remain fuzzy at different planes of depth. Isa eats alone in the cafeteria, facing the wall away from the camera, while a horde of white athletes eat together in friendly camaraderie, facing inward and framing Isa. The loneliness he is purported to feel at the Olympic Games becomes a direct consequence of nationalist impulses and, we are clearly encouraged to believe from the demographics of the other athletes in these shots, his race—of the inability of certain athletes at this most social of gatherings to gain entrance to the international community. The aesthetics of the long shot, used throughout the documentary as a matter of necessity, are here employed deliberately to different ends—to visually isolate an emotionally isolated figure. It is a long shot for a long shot.

In this way, Ahamed Isa is the true Jesse Owens figure of *Tokyo Olympiad*, as is everyone else in the stadium; the aesthetics of the long shot democratize the film and valorize all of us. The effect the encounter with the Chad delegation had on the composition of the film as a whole is unknown. What does

Ahamed Isa, an isolated figure.

seem fairly clear, however, is that the story Yasuoka and Ichikawa created from Yasuoka's crew's footage of the Chad delegation is in sympathy with their desires and concerns in the film as a whole. Tange Kenzō's Olympic arenas, of no concern to the Chadians, are largely missing from the final cut. Almost as much screen time is given to the architecture of the developing world through which the Olympic torch passes, from Tehran to Lahore to Southeast Asia, as well as to Tange's other great work, the Peace Memorial Museum in Hiroshima. Isa is shown as an isolated figure, but he is also the most carefully detailed example of a type celebrated throughout the film: common participants, in the widest sense of the term, be they athletes, spectators, or passersby.

We need not wonder what might have happened had *Tokyo Olympiad* fallen to less capable hands; we can see it for ourselves in the pedestrian film subsequently made from Ichikawa's footage, *Sensation of the Century* (*Seiki no kandō*, 1966),[7] ostensibly directed by Kawamoto Nobumasa. *Sensation* is a paint-by-numbers Olympic film, dutifully filling its memory palace, showing events and their winners in a straightforward manner. We can compare the last jarring moment of the Ichikawa film, the closing ceremony of October 24, to the portrayal in *Sensation*. Unlike the orderly opening ceremony, the closing ceremony fell apart as the athletes took the field; in the exuberance of the moment, many athletes ran wild in celebration as they made their way around the track. Ichikawa Kon's version captures the shock of the unexpected revolt. It begins with a long take of the digital scoreboard announcing the closing ceremony, that oracle of the digital age engaged in its perpetual "overwriting and reconstruction of memory." From the slightly-too-long shot of the digital display, the scene abruptly cuts to a horde of foreign athletes pouring down the track in medias res, with the abducted Japanese flagbearer on their shoulders. Lest anyone think this was choreographed, subsequent shots show some delegations attempting to maintain their

Isa, again in the center of a long shot, framed by Western athletes.

ranks while others run merrily around them. In a beautiful moment of performance art, one athlete in full racing gear, number on his chest, majestically trots down the track, dodging all of the others in their formal dress. A few athletes drag what appears to be a stolen wheelbarrow, and the national flag of New Zealand has been attached to a broom, probably from the same grounds-keeping collection. An athlete conducts the orchestra with his umbrella, a group of New Zealand athletes performs the traditional Maori war dance, the haka, in front of the Emperor (they were subsequently scolded by a New Zealand newspaper for doing so), and various other hijinks ensue.

The scene is recut to make it less jarring in *Sensation of the Century*, itself an electronic overwriting of the Ichikawa film, but all of the reportage from the closing ceremony indicates that Ichikawa's film better captures the unnerving effect the scene had on those observing it from the stands. In the moment that the Japanese delegation was swarmed, Yasuoka felt something menacing in the scene: "Was this dissatisfaction on the part of the foreign athletes? For the past two weeks, they had been separated by gender and walled off in the athletes' village; their contact with the outside world had been strictly monitored. We, too, felt the unfairness and frustration of this inflexible system of regulation" (BSS 3: 129). His trepidation at the thought that the foreign athletes had decided to lash out at their captors dissipated the moment the flagbearer went up on their shoulders.

Could it possibly be part of the design, Inoue Yasushi wondered. It seemed unlikely—some of the athletes were in uniform, but some of them were dressed as though they were headed to Haneda Airport right after the ceremony (*Tokyo Orinpikku: Bungakusha*, 211). Kita Morio found the athlete running in mock competition worthy of note (together with his race, used to describe him in nearly every Japanese essay that mentions him), along with the athletes' shouting "sayonara, sayonara" and a hat-stealing incident—a Japanese athlete's hat was stolen off of her head, and she was wearing one of a different color borrowed from another athlete (220). Mishima Yukio also saw someone steal a pink hat, put it on his head, and run away (216). For Mishima, the athletes' wild entrance was the best moment of the ceremony, offering "the beauty of chaos" (*muchitsujo no utsukushisa*) (215).

Both Yasuoka's Isa sequence and the closing-ceremony sequence call attention to the predicament in which the filmmakers find themselves. The Tokyo Olympics are often referred to as the event that brought Japan back into the fraternity of nations, but *Tokyo Olympiad* probably comes closer to capturing the event's true atmosphere. It has surprisingly few scenes of Japanese citizens interacting with their guests. The marginalized athlete from a postcolonial country stands in for the industrialized host country, as well as for the marginalized filmmakers, themselves unable to do anything but capture the action as best they can from a distance. However imperfectly, the subaltern speaks. By reading the film through the circumstances of its production, we can see both Isa and Yasuoka as figures of resistance to auteurist readings of what is commonly referred to as Ichikawa Kon's documentary, just as the film itself stands in resistance to dominant narratives of the Olympics. If the Olympics are about ordinary strugglers and not superstar victors, the documentary making that claim was in the same way a *collective* genius that managed to capture the quotidian ordinarily lost amid the supposed splendor. The memory it creates belongs not to the state, but to the everyday viewers and participants. They may have nothing to offer that is thought particularly worthy of recording. For that reason, their narrative is perpetually in danger of being overwritten. And for that reason, it is all the more crucial to preserve it.

5

Bakumatsu, Postwar, and Memories of Survival

Surely any list of privileged historical settings for postwar Japanese literature and film would start with two time periods: the *bakumatsu*, the period between the arrival of the American black ships in 1853 and the so-called restoration of the emperor to political power in 1868, and "the postwar," meaning in this context the long period of recovery stretching from the end of World War II to the onset of the high-growth economy of the 1960s. As we have seen, for Yasuoka Shōtarō there is a sense that the *bakumatsu* and the early postwar are connected, that the two occupy a shared space in which an old order lies in ruins and a new one is yet to rise. Although Yasuoka made the connection explicit, we can also see it in the historical fiction of the postwar, which ostensibly may be set in the maelstrom of the mid-nineteenth century but is always commenting on contemporary life. Two lodestars of this underexplored literary space are Shiba Ryōtarō's massively popular *Ryōma on the Move* (*Ryōma ga yuku*, 1962–1966), and Yasuoka's prize-winning *A Tale of Wanderers* (*Ryūritan*, 1976–1981). Shiba (1923–1996) and Yasuoka (1920–2013) were near contemporaries. They both served in the army during World War II, and they claimed numerous literary prizes between the two of them, beginning with an Akutagawa Prize for Yasuoka in 1953 and a Naoki Prize for Shiba in 1960. Both of these works treat *bakumatsu* legend Sakamoto Ryōma (1835–1867), a minor samurai from the Tosa domain (*han*), present-day Kōchi Prefecture, who negotiated an alliance between the Satsuma and Chōshū domains that ultimately brought down the Tokugawa Shogunate. In Shiba's novel, Ryōma (as he is familiarly known today) commands center stage even in scenes where he is not present. In Yasuoka's extended essay and family history, Ryōma is merely present in the background of a story which predominantly treats two generations of Yasuokas: the first consists of Yasuoka's great-great-grandfather Genzaemon and his brothers Shunzō and Bunsuke, and the second consists of Genzaemon's sons, Tsunenoshin, Gonma, and Kakuma, and Bunsuke's sons, Kakunosuke, Kasuke, and Michinosuke. By the time of the *bakumatsu*, the Yasuoka family had grown to four estates a short distance from Kōchi City in Yamagita Village: the Main House (*honke*), the Upper House (*o-ue*), the Lower House (*o-shita*), and the West House (*o-nishi*).¹ In order to protect the inheritance of each estate (and presumably, their samurai status), the family used a combined strategy of adoption and intermarriage. Sons from large families were often adopted as needed by the other houses. During the *bakumatsu*, as the main narrative starts, two households are maintained by sons born into them: Bunsuke is master of the West House, and Tsunenoshin of the Lower House. The other two houses have received sons from the West and Lower Houses; Bunsuke's son Kakunosuke was adopted into the Main House, of which he is the master, and Tsunenoshin's younger brother Gonma was sent to the Upper House, where he became the master. To a lesser extent, first cousins and first-cousins-once-removed intermarried to the same end, and they continued to do so at least through Yasuoka's generation.²

Of the masters of the various houses, Bunsuke was thus a generation older than the others. He maintained the households while his sons and nephews engaged in the ferment that ended in the overthrow of the shogunate, first as rebels in league with groups such as the pro-Imperial-restoration Tosa Loyalist Party and the tragically ineffective anti-shogunate Tenchūgumi army and operating under the slogan of "revere the emperor, expel the barbarians" (*sonnō joi*), and later in service to the new Meiji government. Their role in the history of the *bakumatsu* and Meiji Restoration, as minor agitators rather than heroes, is clear from the start: "Kasuke stabbed the chief administrator of Tosa, Yoshida Tōyō, and was involved in the Tenchūgumi; he was apprehended and beheaded in Kyoto. His older brother Kakunosuke, of course, joined the Tosa Loyalist Party and served as a lieutenant under Itagaki Taisuke during the Boshin War; he was hit by a stray bullet and killed at Aizu. And so, the story goes, this Kakunosuke's surviving child moved to Fukushima Prefecture to attend to the father's grave" (YSS 8: 9–10).

A generation of Yasuokas was decimated by the unrest of the *bakumatsu* and the first decade of the Meiji period. In addition to those mentioned at the beginning, there are other deaths: Tsunenoshin died in Osaka in 1862, possibly of measles (YSS 8: 205-6). Kakuma died of unknown causes, probably illness, in 1866 (YSS 9: 396). Gonma died, in prison, in 1878 (YSS 9: 343), and

Yasuoka in the family cemetery in what was once Yamagita Village, present-day Kōnan City in Kōchi Prefecture. The graves are systematically arranged by generation, with the youngest generations in the background of the shot. Although Kakunosuke and Kasuke's graves were there, their father Bunsuke's was not, initiating Yasuoka's long search for answers in *A Tale of Wanderers*. Photograph courtesy of Yasuoka Haruko.

Michinosuke, later Michitarō, died of illness at the age of forty in 1886, working for the People's Rights Movement in Kōchi (YSS 9: 382). All six cousins who made up this generation of Yasuokas died young, spending their short lives in service of political causes. Thus, a generation was erased from the land they had worked for generations, and because they died in relative obscurity, until *A Tale of Wanderers* they only appeared in the background of narratives of the time, strutting and fretting their hour upon the stage. Neither Yasuoka nor Shiba is a historian, and neither claims to be writing a history in these works; Shiba is firmly ensconced in the genre of historical fiction, and Yasuoka's work is an extended essay on family history. That being said, it is undeniable that readers turn to Shiba's novels to understand a history that has been recorded elsewhere, one that they already know in at least rough outline. Kobayashi Hideo has pointed out that in *A Tale of Wanderers* Yasuoka performs the work of a historian (Kobayashi 14: 713–14), but even if one chooses to read the text as history, the nature of Yasuoka's work is fundamentally different: Yasuoka is piecing together a narrative between modes.

In his essay "The Value of Narrativity in the Representation of Reality," Hayden White distinguishes between annals, chronicles, and "history proper" (White, *Content*, 4). In annals White sees the recorder's "apparent refusal, inability, or unwillingness" to turn a sequence of factual events into a narrative (6). In chronicles, there is a narrative, but it doesn't fulfill "normal narratological expectations": there is no meaning assigned to the narrative; it abruptly ends without necessarily concluding (17). A search for closure in historical narrative is a search for moral meaning; it may be perceived as "real," but "this value attached to narrativity in the representation of real events arises out of a desire to have real events display the coherence, integrity, fullness, and closure of an image of life that is and can only be imaginary" (24). For Shiba, this is perhaps not so problematic; in one sense, historical fiction is simply a hyperextension of a historical narrative that already exists. Yasuoka, on the other hand, is attempting to piece together a full narrative from annals and chronicles. And in some cases, the spaces in between: Bunsuke keeps a diary, and his sons send letters to him, but they live under surveillance by the *han*, and Yasuoka must read between the lines to find actual intent. During a time when Kasuke is hiding out in Kyoto and Kakunosuke is still faithfully discharging his duties as a member of the *han* guard, their father Bunsuke notes in his diary that he has received two missives. Surely, Yasuoka argues, they must be from Kakunosuke, and surely they must contain guarded news of Kasuke (YSS 8: 219–21). From his own experience, Yasuoka knows of the tangled relationships between fathers and sons, and of lives disrupted by war and defeat; in *A Tale of Wanderers*, Yasuoka casts his own awareness of the world over the lives of his ancestors. "Yasuoka's own feeling of being a wanderer is highlighted here," one critic avers (Sakai 173).

There is another tension at work in these stories, to be found in the temporal distance between Yasuoka's ancestors and Yasuoka himself. Jan Assmann, in his seminal work "Collective Memory and Cultural Identity," distinguishes between two realms of memory: communicative and cultural. *Communicative memory* is that of people alive right now. It is marked by "a high degree of formlessness, willfulness, and disorganization"—our individual memories come into contact with one another and find common ground, disagree, harmonize, fragment, evolve over time (127). It belongs to the contemporary, a limited, moving window of

Bakumatsu, Postwar, and Memories of Survival

Bunsuke's diary, written from 1834 to 1865, one of the main source documents for *A Tale of Wanderers*. Photograph courtesy of Yasuoka Masatoshi.

time that Assmann puts at eighty to one hundred years at its maximum. Beyond that, only cultural memory operates. In Assmann's construction, *cultural memory* produces a group identity, but that identity will be different for each group: "One group remembers the past in fear of deviating from its model, the next for fear of repeating the past" (133). Cultural memory is independent from the work of archaeologists and historians in that it is tied to identity: "Cultural memory reaches back into the past only so far as the past can be reclaimed as 'ours.' This is why we refer to this form of historical consciousness as 'memory' and not just as knowledge about the past" (Erll and Nünning 113). Organizations from nation-states to families have memories that go further into the past than the individual memory of any living member.

The question of what happens when memory moves out of the realm of communicative memory and into the realm of cultural memory is unresolved to some extent. The anthropologist Jan Vansina, in *Oral Tradition as History*, refers to a "floating gap" in oral history, and Assmann has borrowed the term and modified it for his conceptualization of collective memory (Vansina 23, Erll 28). With the progress of time, the gap between those memories that belong to the living and those that are reconstructions by the living about the dead slides forward, perpetually eighty to one hundred years before the present. We can problematize this in two major ways. For one, such a gap would depend on active participation in the construction of collective understanding by society's oldest members, as well as active communication between them and the "generations" (already a shaky term) that follow. At the same time, it would require forbearance from those who would move to possess historical events before everyone involved had passed on. Clearly, however, the struggle for control over history and memory in every epoch begins long before events pass out of living memory; the "floating gap" is thus an abstraction of a much more complicated process that is perpetually playing out in millions of different ways in any given moment, and the distinction between communicative and cultural memory cannot be established with any certainty. It is in fact their uneasy coexistence, the frisson as memories pass uncertainly from one realm to the other, that makes works focusing on the "floating gap" of such interest to us here.

Rather than attempting to define Yasuoka's works about his ancestors as history or fiction, this reading attempts to show that there is no easy line that can be drawn between the two modes of writing; in fact, both works treated below were written as part of a long-standing memory tradition that refuses to distinguish between fiction and history.[3] Rather than observing the role of narrative in the writing of history, in this chapter I observe the roles of history and memory in the writing of narrative, putting aside questions of genre or mode of writing and looking at how these writers used conceptions of history and literariness to craft works that could be conceived as historical or fictional, depending on parameters the individual reader will have to set.

Meiji as Origin, Meiji as Parallel

From June 21, 1962, to May 21, 1966, Shiba Ryōtarō (1923–1996), already a rising star among writers of historical fiction, serialized the first of the massive novels for which he is best known, *Ryōma on the Move* (*Ryōma ga yuku*), in the *Sankei shinbun*. After winning the Naoki Prize in 1960 for his novel *The Owl Castle* (*Fukurō no shiro*), he quit his job as a newspaper reporter in 1961 to concentrate on writing full time. The decision to base a novel around the brief life of Tosa Restoration figure Sakamoto Ryōma wasn't a completely outlandish choice, but the Ryōma of 1960 was not the Ryōma of today; it is perhaps forgotten even by Japanese fans of historical fiction just how much of Ryōma's larger-than-life presence on the historical stage is owed to Shiba's novel.

It wasn't only public estimation of Ryōma that changed in the postwar, however; the *bakumatsu*, which had been seen "as prelude to the ruinous rounds of militarism and war that had dominated their lives and destroyed their cities" (Jansen ix), became a privileged period for fictional narratives in a new way. Shiba alone would return to the *bakumatsu* over and over again in his fiction.[4] Until the end of World War II many Japanese intellectuals had seen the Meiji Restoration as an unfinished project. Political theorist Kita Ikki (1883–1937) had a plan that "called for dismantling the structure of privilege that had been sustained by the

Bakumatsu, Postwar, and Memories of Survival 161

Meiji state. The peerage would be abolished, and universal manhood suffrage would be instituted. Surplus land would be redistributed among the landless according to size and need of each household" (Najita 720). For Yasuda Yojūrō (1910–1981) and the writers of the Japan Romantic School (*Romanha*) in the late 1930s, "intelligence in modern Japan referred to a theory of civilization and enlightenment, which he identified with the new Meiji bureaucratism and the men who founded it" (Najita 757); he valorized Saigō Takamori's principled resistance to the Meiji government and "saw the romantics as inheritors of this tradition of critical idealism directed against rationalistic modernism and the tyranny of the self" (758). Thinking such as this led to the well-documented arguments on "overcoming modernity" during World War II.[5]

After the war, Japan's defeat was naturally considered the devastating, logical end of the *bakumatsu* and Meiji Restoration; they were viewed as being of the same continuum. From August 15, 1945, John Dower suggests, the "post-surrender fixation on 'enduring the unendurable' was rooted in a sense of vulnerability and victimization that predated the China and Pacific wars and traced back, in its modern guise, to the gunboat diplomacy and unequal treaties with which the Western powers had forced Japan out of its feudal isolation" (Dower, *Embracing*, 179). Much of this had to do with the personage of the one encouraging the enduring, the emperor himself; after a brief period in which popular opinion ran against—or at least indifferent to—the imperial household, it soon became clear that Hirohito would remain on his throne as a symbol, not only of the nation-state but also of the lineage in whose name it had been fought. The Declaration of Humanity (*Ningen Sengen*) that Hirohito read on January 1, 1946, actually opened with the Meiji Emperor's Charter Oath of 1868, which, Herbert Bix has pointed out, was "the oath Meiji had sworn not to the Japanese people but to Amaterasu Ōmikami" (561), a move which Bix sees as "Hirohito's attempt to integrate the concept of democracy with Japanese history, thus avoiding a break with the past that the Japanese enemies of democracy could seize on and later use to argue that democracy was a foreign importation" (562). Despite questions of how much anyone understood of the nuances of Hirohito's grandiloquent speeches, his very hold on his position was a compelling marker of continuity.

In many ways, the common conception of the *bakumatsu* as a point of origin (for the nation, for modernity, for militarism) ended along with the Occupation in 1952, perhaps because of the momentousness of the period the Japanese had just experienced; 1950s and 1960s Japan felt not so much like a continuation of a timeline that had begun with the *bakumatsu* as it did a *parallel* of the extraordinary events that occurred between Perry's arrival in 1853 and the Meiji

Restoration in 1868. In his biography of postwar Prime Minister Yoshida Shigeru (himself the son of a Restoration-era Tosa Loyalist), Dower claims that the decade after Japan's surrender "was a period as dramatic and turbulent as that of the Restoration, beginning with occupation and reformism and ending with restoration of sovereignty, the reconsolidation of conservative elites, and the establishment of new structures of security and overseas expansion" (Dower, *Empire*, 14).

Given the affinities between these periods of great change, it is no wonder that writers would write about the end of a political order in history in light of the demise of the political order they themselves had experienced. The Occupation's suppression of "samurai stories"—strictly enforced in film, somewhat less in literature—only added to the pent-up desire to reconsider the *bakumatsu* period, and Yasuoka tells us that after the Occupation ended, stories about the Meiji Restoration were particularly popular (YSS 8: 12). Shiba himself would write many stories set in the *bakumatsu*, as well as many others featuring Tosa figures on all sides of the political arena as his protagonists,[6] but his decision to write his first long novel about Sakamoto Ryōma—who had everything to do with the Restoration but nothing to do with the Meiji period that followed it—seems worthy of examination.

Shiba Ryōtarō and the Postwar Hero

Shiba's lengthy novel—over three thousand pages in eight-volume *bunkobon* paperback—obviously includes the most spectacular events of Ryōma's life, such as the legendary (in the sense that it is a central scene in any telling of the Ryōma story) attack at the Teradaya in Fushimi on 1866.1.23 from which Ryōma narrowly escaped and the attack at the Ōmiya in Kyoto in late 1867 that would claim his life together with that of his fellow Tosa loyalist leader, Nakaoka Shintarō.[7] Even more than with these iconic, well-documented events, however, Shiba's lacing of the postwar into the *bakumatsu* is visible in the depiction of minor, half-forgotten events, such as the skirmish in Tosa that later came to be known as the Iguchi-mura Incident, which occurred on the evening of 1861.3.4. A bad-tempered upper samurai known as Yamada the Devil has a run-in with a mysterious figure on a bridge:

> The stars were out.
>
> But a fellow couldn't see very far ahead of himself on the path.
>
> A swordsman suddenly appeared from out of the gloomy darkness and jostled Yamada the Devil.
>
> "Who the hell are you?" Yamada the Devil grumbled.

"Sorry about that," the figure said in the gloom, and made to continue on its way, but Yamada the Devil snapped at him to stop.

"I asked you your name. I'm the one they call Yamada the Devil. Isn't it rude to bump into an upper samurai and not even give your name?"

The figure was silent. Yamada the Devil stared at him for a time, then said derisively, "You're a lower samurai, aren't you?" He was drunk. And there was a codified discrimination in Tosa, not present in other domains, in which a higher-ranking samurai had the right to kill a lower-ranking samurai for any perceived slight, even if they *were* both samurai.

Yamada the devil whipped out his sword. The lower samurai he was confronting was a *gōshi*, or country samurai, whom Ryōma knew well. He was a young *gōshi*, named Nakahira Chūichirō. Nakahira was foolishly hot-tempered, and had a weakness for boys. He was in love with a beautiful youth named Uka something-or-other.

That evening, he was out for a walk along the top of the embankment hand in hand with this Uka, as he was wont to do. Because it was the evening of the Doll Festival,[8] they were off canoodling in the darkness. Perhaps they had been enjoying a secret rendezvous. If at all possible, Nakahira didn't want to give his name, or let anything escalate. And yet, it was just like Nakahira to snap as soon as the other called rank on him. Among Tosa samurai, the fighting spirit belonged to the lower samurai. Not to mention that his beautiful youth was watching.

The lover of boys leaped forward, flushing. "Ya-Yamada, dear sir. Do you think you can just get away with insulting a samurai to his face?"

"Now you've said it, bottom runger." Yamada the Devil deftly slipped forward. As a swordsman, he was among the best the upper samurai had to offer. And there was the inescapable arrogance that came with his class.

He swiftly raised his sword to the upper position.

The lover of boys had no choice but to use a lower block. Lower blocks and the like are generally defensive postures; if one doesn't have great confidence in one's arms, it is difficult to turn it into an attack. The lover of boys didn't know that. (Shiba 2: 193–94)

Yamada the Devil cuts down Nakahira, and tells his own companion, the tea master Matsui Hansai, to fetch a lantern so he can see whom he has killed. The boy Uka also goes running, to the home of Ikeda Toranoshin, Nakahira's older brother. Ikeda runs to the scene faster than Matsui, and strikes down Yamada from behind as Yamada is cleaning the blood off of himself in the river. When Matsui returns with a lantern, Ikeda kills him too.

The lower samurai of Tosa are in an uproar; as the word of what happened spreads, they gather at the home of Sakamoto Ryōma to confer. And to plot:

> As the afternoon came, a group of bristling lower samurai shouted, "Sakamoto, it's finally going to be a fight!"
> "Why is that?"
> "A group of upper samurai have gathered at the estate of that dead Yamada the Devil, and they're going to try to storm Ikeda Toranoshin's. As our leader, you need to come with us to the Ikeda estate right away. When you're mooning around here, everyone runs in circles."
> "I'll be there soon." Ryōma got to his feet. (Shiba 2: 198–99)

Instead of going directly to Ikeda's, however, Ryōma visits the scene of the crime to see for himself what has happened. Later, he goes to Yamada's estate, where he is confronted by angry upper samurai. Ryōma not only holds them off single-handedly, he scolds them for their parochial concerns. "If the American ships push into Katsurahama," the port for Kōchi City, Ryōma asks them, "what will you do about it? Will you still be fighting with your fellow samurai?" (2: 206). By the time Ryōma arrives at the Ikeda compound, Ikeda has committed *seppuku*, disemboweling himself to atone for his part in the dispute; he is still alive and begs for a "second" to cut his head off. Ryōma orders another of their group to kill him. The man brings Ryōma the severed head, and Ryōma loosens his sword and dips it in the blood. "Ikeda, we won't forget you," he promises (2: 211).

The swordplay and honorable, ritualized deaths of classic historical fiction are present in Shiba as well, as is the ubiquitousness of famous historical personages (nothing in the historical record indicates that Ryōma actually had anything to do with the event). Several hallmarks of Shiba's own distinct style are visible even in this short sequence, such as his "bird's-eye view" of the action, offering a distant third-person narration that freely depicts scenes in which Ryōma is not present and of which he would have no knowledge. Historian Narita Ryūichi has noted that for a novel entitled *Ryōma on the Move*, Ryōma doesn't make any sudden moves or significant forays into politics for much of the novel (Narita, *Shiba*, 42). In fact, the well-documented progression of Ryōma's political journey—from firebrand advocating warfare against, alternately, foreign incursion and *bakufu* rule, to determined internationalist—is attenuated in Shiba's telling of the story. Perhaps this is partially the effect of the distant narration, which generally provides Ryōma's physical reactions to the events around him, but doesn't put the reader inside Ryōma's head to any great extent. At the same time, Ryōma's unwillingness to commit too deeply to political causes has a distinctly postwar cast. Shiba's Ryōma does what must be done, but he is cool and collected and has a suspicion of ideologies and their adherents that places him squarely in the generation of writers such as Shiba and Yasuoka, who had seen too many political figures change colors as they moved from wartime to Occupation to post-Occupation. What remained for them was a deeply personal, internal search for self. "'I still don't understand myself,' Ryōma says at one point. The ambition of youth is on display, and Shiba gives us a Ryōma searching for himself. It seems safe to say that this aligns with the sentiments of young men in the early 1960s," Narita writes (58).

If there is a political agenda at work in Shiba's novel, it is perhaps that two-headed hydra known as postwar humanism. On the one hand, Ryōma is a prefiguration of the leveling forces in postwar society, and in *Ryōma* we find a clear criticism of a leadership elite that has led the country to ruins. The Tosa from which Ryōma hails is suffocating from an overabundance of class distinctions. Even by Edo standards, mobility (social as well as physical) is restricted in the extreme, and there was a clear division between samurai of upper and lower ranks (Jansen 26). Starting in early Edo, Tosa's ruling Yamauchi clan found it to their advantage to offer a high-ranking lower-samurai status styled "country samurai" (*gōshi*) to potential political adversaries of samurai class who had been loyal to the Chōsogabe clan that preceded them as rulers of the Tosa domain (27).[9] In 1763, *gōshi* status was offered to people of other classes, farmers and even merchants, who were willing to undertake the task of clearing fields that would add to the domain's arable land (29). Although they were prohibited from rising to the upper-samurai ranks, samurai status of even this limited variety enticed numbers of successful farmers and merchants to accept the domain's offer. And *gōshi* membership had privileges of its own: *gōshi* were allowed to participate in certain Tosa ceremonies, and among the later arrivals were absentee landlords, administering their scattered land holdings from Kōchi City (27, 29). The historical Sakamotos were parvenu *gōshi* who had made their fortune as sake brewers in the city, and Shiba uses this fact to make Ryōma a natural hero for the postwar. Ryōma is lucky to be alive at a time when class distinctions are foundering on the shoals of modernity, and he rises through society not through dint of performing well within the system as it has been prescribed, but by working to change the framework of the system itself.[10] In this way, *Ryōma on the Move* is a "popular fiction" (*taishū bungaku*) complement to "literary fiction" (*junbungaku*) narratives of a ruling class collapsing in the systemic shift brought about by the war and its aftermath: the decorous, genteel lives led just before the coming war by Tanizaki Jun'ichirō's four sisters in *The Makioka Sisters* (*Sasameyuki*, 1943–1948) or the troubled aristocrats who lose their land in Dazai Osamu's *The Setting Sun* (*Shayō*, 1947).

The modern society that Ryōma instigated spurred a process of modernization that didn't always bring with it freedom; among many other things, it stifled individual freedom, perhaps most markedly on a sexual front. As Narita says bluntly, "His dislike of male-male love—his homophobia—marks Shiba as a modern man" (*Shiba*, 64). The samurai Nakahira is essentialized as a "lover of boys" (*danshokuka*) in the above-mentioned passage, and his passionate, impulsive Tosa demeanor appears to be blamed for his relationship. Shiba later makes his disapproval even clearer: "It's an extremely foreign custom, but until even twenty or thirty years ago this wicked tradition continued in Tosa" (Shiba 2: 283). For Narita, the Restoration was the beginning of a "modern" homosocial society, in which bonds between groups of men are privileged and sexual male-male relationships were seen to pose a threat to the system; in this sense, the bands of men competing to control the country in Ryōma's time are forerunners of the repressive "salaryman" society reading Shiba's story a hundred years later. At the same time, much of the novel is surprisingly asexual. The women who appear in the story—Ryōma's older sister Otome and his eventual wife Oryō among them—all emerge as mother figures to Ryōma, whose own mother died when he was young. On his journey out of Tosa, the noblewoman Otazu attempts to get Ryōma to return to an inn with her, but he declines on the grounds that her rank prevents his sleeping under the same roof as she (Shiba 1: 51). Otazu will return to help him, even nurture him. Although Shiba was not a member of the Third Generation of New Writers (*Daisan no Shinjin*) literary coterie, he was roughly the same age as they and appeared on the literary scene at roughly the same time. Perhaps Etō Jun's critique of Yasuoka, Kojima Nobuo, and their generation of writers applies to Shiba as well: "If the left-leaning-university grads of the First Generation of Postwar Writers established their sense of self through a relationship with the father, then the junior-high-good-for-nothings of the Third Generation wrote with the relationship with their mothers in mind" (18). Suffice it to say here that the stifling sexual politics and sexuality of *Ryōma on the Move* more closely resemble the time of writing than the time depicted.

Yasuoka Shōtarō between Fact and Fiction in *A Tale of Wanderers*

As we have seen, for Yasuoka, the road to *A Tale of Wanderers* led through the American South where he witnessed Civil Rights Movement protests during the 1960–1961 academic year at Vanderbilt University. When he arrived in the South, he found it as alienating as he had always found Japan to be. He realized that there was a parallel between the lingering Japanese postwar and the sense of grievance and unresolved problems in the South dating back to Reconstruction and that, furthermore, the antebellum South had a lot in common with pre-Meiji Japan. In this way, the American South became an unexpected link for Yasuoka between the wartime and postwar Japan he had known and Japan during the collapse of the Edo shogunate and the rise of the modern nation-state. It is obvious that by the time he wrote *A Tale of Wanderers* he saw his ancestors' experiences during the *bakumatsu* and early Meiji as resembling his own experiences during the postwar—and perhaps offering a path to redemption. Shinfune Kaisaburō has proposed Yasuoka's book-length essay on the twentieth-century "god of the short story," *On Shiga Naoya* (*Shiga Naoya ron*), as another possible link, pointing out that Yasuoka notes in his study that Shiga's grandfather Naomichi, who had such an effect on the young Naoya, lived half of his life in the Edo Period and the other half in Meiji (Shinfune 47).

A Tale of Wanderers appeared in fifty-five installments in the journal *Shinchō*, from March 1976 to April 1981. In the summer of 1976, Yasuoka went to visit his friend Kenneth Richards, a professor of Japanese at the University of Toronto, on what became "a sort of trip in search of Richards's roots" in the United States and Canada (Haley, *Ruutsu*, 362). There, on the same subject, Richards introduced him to Alex Haley's *Roots*, which had not yet been released as a book but was making waves in pre-publication magazine excerpts. *Roots* would go on win a special Pulitzer Prize in the spring of 1977, and in September and October of that same year, Yasuoka's two-volume Japanese translation (with Matsuda Sen) of Haley's novel would be published—i.e., at the same time as Yasuoka was charting the course his own family followed from the eighteenth century to the present.

Although the beginning of the *A Tale of Wanderers* project predates his reading of *Roots*, there are similarities between the two works that perhaps speak to common postwar cultural moments. Genealogies are products of peacetime; to these two World War II veterans (Yasuoka in Manchuria, Haley in the Pacific theater with the US Coast Guard), researching family history was an opportunity to overcome the trauma of war and displacement. As for so many other North Americans, Haley's work was aimed at crossing a continental gap to find an ancestry on the other side of the ocean, and it benefited from the free movement that modern transportation and treaty agreements made possible. At the same time, *Roots* represents the heroic effort (and equally heroic imagination) necessary for African Americans in particular to trace their heritage over centuries of traumatic upheaval and erasure; Haley claimed that *Roots* was the result of "years of intensive research in fifty-odd libraries, archives, and other repositories on three continents" (*Roots*, 891). For Yasuoka, coincidentally, there was also a gap to be bridged: Yasuoka claims that the impetus for his project is to discover why the main branch of his family had fled to Tōhoku, far from Kōchi City; he remembers a relative from the Tōhoku branch coming to his house when he was a small boy and being surprised that the man spoke their mutual family name with a Kōchi inflection (YSS 8: 10). Kōchi, which had been so difficult to navigate through—and out of—for his *bakumatsu* ancestors, was easily accessible for Yasuoka in terms of transit, if not necessarily culturally (YSS 8: 5–6). Both works are essentially searches for "origins," defined, genealogically speaking, as the furthest extent to which one can trace one's ancestry back in time—and just as often, especially in North America, across a "gap" toward a homeland far from the place one is now. If Haley reached a point of origin by identifying (to his own satisfaction, at least) his great-great-great-great-grandfather Kunta Kinte, who was captured by African slavers and eventually landed in the United States on September 29, 1767, Yasuoka was able to trace his family back to the moment when his farming ancestors were able to acquire their *gōshi* samurai status in 1707.

Put another way, the moment of "origin" in both of these narratives is the intersection of an oral history and a written one. Much has been made of this problematic intersection in *Roots*: Alex Haley's tracing of his connection to Kunta Kinte is one part ship records in Annapolis and one part handed-down narrative of a *griot*, or oral historian, in the Gambia. In Haley's mind, the line between the factual elements and the fictional elements was clear:

> To the best of my knowledge and of my effort, every lineage statement within *Roots* is from either my African or American families' carefully preserved oral history, much of which I have been able conventionally to corroborate with documents. [. . .] Since I wasn't yet around when most of the story occurred, by far most of the dialogue and most of the incidents are of necessity a novelized amalgam of what I *know* took place together with what my researching led me to plausibly *feel* took place. (*Roots*, 884–85)

Even so, the division is not so clear-cut; the *griot*'s information is considered suspect (or, at least, very charitably interpreted) by many, and Haley's borrowing, occasionally verbatim, from Harold Courlander's 1967 novel *The African*, intentional or not, is undeniable.[11]

For Yasuoka, too, the intersection of written and oral history is where his interests lie. One of his main sources is the diary of his ancestor Bunsuke; using clues found therein, Yasuoka attempts to bring in other documents to draw a fuller picture of his family. Like Shiba, Yasuoka writes about the Iguchi-mura Incident, but from a very different perspective. He views the encounter much as Shiba does, after considering a variety of primary sources, but comes across a document that gives him pause: A certification that Uka Kikuma, the boy lover, has committed suicide as ordered by the Tosa *han* officials. It is jarring to Yasuoka for a couple of reasons. He wonders why a boy of thirteen was forced to commit suicide. And he notices that the letter sent to the domain officials is signed by one "Betchaku Shunzō," his own great-grandfather:

> Betchaku Shunzō was Bunsuke's youngest brother, but until I saw his name written on the witness line I hadn't realized that Uka Kikuma was my distant relative. In the previous document related to Ikeda Toranoshin, it had said "Uka Ichiryōhei's third son Kikuma"; Ichiryōhei was Bunsuke's close friend. But because Bunsuke always wrote simply "Ichiryōhei," I had overlooked the fact that Ichiryōhei was actually Shunzō's father-in-law. Because of that, I had a newfound interest in the Iguchi-mura Incident, and I called my cousin thinking that he could give me more details.
>
> "Ah, the Uka *tonto*?" he answered, just as though it were a rumor about someone in the neighborhood. "Tonto" is a Tosa word for a boy lover. Ah, yes, was Kikuma Nakahira Chūjirō's young lover? I felt that I now understood a little better, emotionally, why Nakahira would brandish his sword at Yamada. Wasn't it likely that Yamada saw Nakahira walking with his young love and said something nasty about it? At the time, homosexuality wasn't necessarily prohibited, but it wasn't the kind of thing men wanted to advertise, either.
>
> My cousin went on. "Grandma Betchaku was always going on about the Uka *tonto*'s suicide. 'Everybody said to Kikuma, "You can't cry about the pain when you put the sword in. You can't cry—it would be shameful. If you cry, they'll call you a *tonto* and make fun of you …"'"
>
> As my cousin spoke, the face of this Grandma Betchaku dimly came into my mind, and I began to have the feeling that I, too, may have heard the story as a child.
>
> [. . .]
>
> According to my cousin's telling, Uka Kikuma was thirteen when he committed suicide, and the person who cut off his head was his older brother Terada Toshimasa, sixteen at the time. The people around him had to be worried that a thirteen-year-old child would cry in pain as he cut open his belly. Then again, perhaps Kikuma, owing to a paucity of life experience, would face death with an unexpected composure—but it would be unbearable for the people around him to watch. It's all too easy to imagine Toshimasa's torture in undertaking the role of decapitating his younger brother. Grandma Betchaku was this Terada Toshimasa's daughter. And Terada Torahiko was her younger brother, Toshimasa's first-born son.[12] Thinking that Terada Torahiko

must have written something about his father Toshimasa and his uncle Kikuma, I searched in his collected works, but I didn't find anything of the sort. It didn't seem likely that Torahiko had never heard the story of Kikuma's death, considering that even my cousin had heard it over and over. Or was it that this kind of feudal-era story was too awful, and he just couldn't write about his family? (YSS 8: 83–85)

To wit, Yasuoka's great-grandfather Betchaku Shinzō certified the death of his wife's brother Uka Kikuma, the "Uka something-or-other" of Shiba's telling of the story. Kikuma's older brother Toshimasa (later adopted into the childless Terada family) was responsible for "assisting" him by cutting off his head. Ikeda Toranoshin's valiant self-sacrifice in Shiba's telling of the story is replaced here with something more awful—his young companion Kikuma's pathetic death sentence, which perhaps speaks more to the brutality of Edo Japan that is often erased in historical fiction.

Yasuoka is suspicious of his own narrative, however; far from providing a historian's judicious survey of sources en route to a reasoned interpretation of them, Yasuoka is pleased to call all of his sources into question, and even to explore how they mutually undermine one another, en route to creating a new narrative from them that, as with Haley, is based as much in what he feels must have happened as in what he can logically surmise. Yasuoka turns to Bunsuke's diary, which he would expect to detail what had happened. Instead:

> What on earth is he doing? On the fifth day of the third month, that is, the day following the incident, from early in the morning the upper samurai were heading to Yamada's house, the lower samurai were crowding into Ikeda's house, or giving voice to their passions, or raging on about what course of action they should take from here. In the middle of all that, Bunsuke was casually heading out, just as he always did, to stay over with his friends here and there, plucking the koto, crafting terrible waka, kicking the ball around. It sounds just like when old farming men and women today take their hiking field trips into the mountains. After half a month, he finally visited his younger brother Betchaku Shunzō, but it was only for a night, and then he headed off elsewhere. (YSS 8: 86)

Is it possible that Bunsuke knows nothing of the incident? No; Yasuoka provides a diary from a monk in Usa who knows all about it, and Usa is about as far to the west of Kōchi City as Bunsuke's estate is to the east of it. Oddly, according to his account of his journey, Bunsuke is composing waka with people he has never visited before, people who have connections to the political scene. Clearly, Yasuoka tells us, Bunsuke's diary at this point is a cover; Bunsuke knows that his writing could be read by the authorities, and it is a sign of the tensions in Tosa that Bunsuke speaks in code. Here again, the author's wartime and postwar experiences color his understanding of the *bakumatsu*. In his autobiography-cum-history *My Shōwa History*, Yasuoka writes about being a member of the first "generation" not to remember the relative freedom of "Taishō Democracy," who had always operated under one form of significant censorship or another until the end of the American Occupation. During the war, Yasuoka waited for a knock that never came when he published a literary magazine that he thought might run afoul of the authorities (BSS 1: 169). He wouldn't publish again until the tail end of the Occupation period. Whether Yasuoka's take on Bunsuke's situation is consciously informed by his own personal experiences or not, the parallels between their times exist.

Shiba privileges the story over the factual evidence it is based on, meaning that Shiba has no qualms about rearranging events to fit his narrative. For Alex Haley, this is generally true as well; of the 120 chapters of *Roots*, only the last three, describing Haley's own life and search, are entirely dictated by what the author "knows" to have occurred. For Yasuoka, however, the search is the story. He later finds a short reference by Terada to the incident in a Taishō-era haiku magazine; for Yasuoka it becomes the exception that proves the rule: Now that there is proof that Terada knew about his father's grief, the question becomes why he didn't write *more* about it. The find also highlights the eternal possibility that yet-unfound sources will create a new story:

> In my cousin's version of the incident, Kikuma was thirteen at the time. But in Torahiko's account Kikuma is nineteen. This isn't a deception on Torahiko's part; my cousin was the one who was wrong. And it wasn't only my cousin; in almost every treatment of the incident in histories of the Tosa *gōshi* class and so on, Kikuma is thirteen and his older brother Toshimasa is sixteen. I myself heard it that way, but now that I think about it, a number of elements seem strange. From what we've heard, it is impossible to "assist" someone in seppuku without the requisite skill with a sword; if you bungle it, you're likely to slice into your own leg in the act of taking off the head. Given that, sending out a boy of sixteen by the old reckoning (*kazoe*) to assist his brother's death is more than simply gruesome, it is probably impossible in terms of his proficiency. If there weren't anyone else who would be appropriate, and if they needed to choose his second from among his close family, their brother-in-law Betchaku Shunzō could have done it. But

I have no need to inquire here into reasons why Toshimasa was selected as the second. I should just come out with it: according to the family register of the Terada family, Toshimasa wasn't sixteen at the time. He was twenty-five. (YSS 8: 91–92)

Boys who are thirteen and sixteen in the *kazoedoshi* system, which counts the number of years in which one has lived, would be slightly younger by modern reckoning, still children—eleven or twelve and fourteen or fifteen, respectively. A grown man of (by *mannenrei*, modern count) seventeen or eighteen being implicated in a crime and forced to commit *seppuku* for his part in it, and subsequently killed by his older brother of twenty-three or twenty-four, wouldn't have been as heart-rending an event. Or as salacious to modern eyes. A male-male relationship in the Edo period, by custom between a grown man and his adolescent male lover, called a *wakashu*, does not appear to have been quite as scandalous in its time as Shiba and Yasuoka imply; Paul Gordon Schalow argues that it was "a normal component of male sexuality, [. . .] governed by ethical constraints very much like those governing sexual relations between men and women" (27). Greg Pflugfelder describes the age at which a boy ceased to be a *wakashu* as having had "considerable plasticity because manhood was essentially a social condition, its biological referent far less important than its cultural markings" (32), and Kikuma was still at an age at which he could have been a *wakashu* in the eyes of the community and potential male partners, but even if this was true, it is likely that the change in Kikuma's age was crafted to make the relationship more lurid, a narrative by-product of the modern, socially constructed homophobia that Narita identifies.

The first telling of the story in which Kikuma appears as a boy is also the first novel to star Sakamoto Ryōma, *Heroes of a Thousand Miles of Sweat and Blood* (Kanketsu senri no koma, 1883) by Sakazaki Shiran (1853–1913). The opening scene is of the Iguchi-mura Incident. Kikuma is referred to only by his family name, and his role in the sequence of events clearly influenced Shiba's telling of the story. He is a "youth," too young to participate in the fight:

> Now, it seems that the youth who had been accompanying Nakahira, one Uka, saw that the fight was hopeless and ran for dear life to get Nakahira's older brother by birth, Ikeda Toranoshin in Kodakasa-mura (in present-day Kamiyashiki, Kōchi City). Breathlessly, he told him what had happened. Ikeda had been visiting the house next door, and he virtually flew to the scene with his sword in his hand. At a glance, he could see who had won and who had lost: his younger brother Nakahira, drenched in blood, had

Bakumatsu, Postwar, and Memories of Survival

fallen in a stubbled patch of grain. If only I had been a moment sooner, he cried, gnashing his teeth. (31–32)

Ikeda kills Yamada and his companion, then has the boy pick up the swords and other things that fell during the struggle. Ikeda and the boy are both condemned to death for their actions, but the crowd that gathers for the ritual suicide is moved by the boy's death most of all: "At dawn on the next day, the sixth of the third month, the youth Uka, just about to come into manhood, fell on his own sword with great grace. The samurai were determined not to cry but the tears came to their eyes just as when they ate spiced *koi* in vinegar in the spring. There was no one who was not filled with sorrow" (38–39).

First serialized in one of the predecessors to the modern-day *Kōchi shinbun*, *Heroes of a Thousand Miles* went on to become a bestseller in book form. The power of the breathless narrative was such that by the following generation it replaced whatever personal or family history had existed, and was treated as a source for local histories. Given Terada's general silence on the issue, one can imagine that the topic was taboo among the Teradas, leaving Grandma Betchaku and subsequent storytellers such as Shiba to rely on Sakazaki's version.

Yet, while this may be the origin of the legend that Uka Kikuma was a boy when he committed ritual suicide, there is nothing in *Heroes of a Thousand Miles* that characterizes Nakahira and Kikuma's relationship as romantic. Perhaps it was the kind of thing that was left unsaid, but that readers of the time would understand. This would be in keeping with the increasing repression of male-male sexuality during the Meiji period; by 1889, one writer was able to note that the concept of male prostitution, for example, was considered virtually foreign to contemporary Japanese mores (Pflugfelder 195). By the same token, in the story as it was passed down in Yasuoka's family via Grandma Betchaku, there is nothing that directly implies a sexual relationship. On its face, the family's warning to Kikuma simply asserts that if Kikuma *were* to cry he *would be* called a *tonto*. Is it possible that the notion of Kikuma as Nakahira's young lover was entirely the product of a later age?

Storytelling and Survival

It is very likely that the aporia in Yasuoka's family history, produced by a traumatized silence on the part of those directly involved, were filled in by histories of the events that had been in turn influenced by fictional narratives, including, although Yasuoka never says so directly, Shiba's. It took Yasuoka's work in *A Tale of Wanderers* to set the record straight within his own family. His cousin Yasuoka

Yuki self-published a family history in 1970 that makes no mention of the Iguchi-mura Incident, possibly because of a perceived unseemliness, but her 1988 revision, published after *A Tale of Wanderers*, correctly notes that at the time, "Kikuma was nineteen and Toshimasa was twenty-five" (*Ie o sasaeta*, 50).

The widespread interest on the part of historians in the life of Sakamoto Ryōma is largely owing to Shiba's fictional representation of him. In his 1994 preface to the Columbia University Press reissue of *Sakamoto Ryōma and the Meiji Restoration* (1961), Marius Jansen mentions that Japanese scholars regarded his topic as a curiosity at the time he was researching it, and of the many works about Ryōma that had appeared in the interim, the "widest swath [. . .] was surely that cut by Shiba Ryōtarō's *Ryōma ga yuku*" (Jansen xi). *Ryōma on the Move* was the basis for the 1968 NHK year-long *taiga dorama* ("grand-flow drama," perhaps gesturing at once to the immensity of the cast, the complexity of the plot, and the number of hours of screen time that elapse over the course of a year-long broadcast schedule). By Kōno Kensuke's reckoning, between 1960 and 1970, twelve feature films and twenty-three television dramas based on Shiba's works were produced (294–96). In a 2000 survey, *Ryōma on the Move* was declared to be the most popular work in the Shiba canon (Narita, *Shiba*, 29). At the time of this writing, there are at least three museums and two other points of interest dedicated to Ryōma in the Kōchi City area, which is served by the Kōchi-Ryōma airport. On the bookstore shelves, Ryōma is accorded his own section. In this atmosphere, other figures, major in their time, have been forgotten by popular culture and, in turn, by history. Indeed, the 2010 NHK *taiga* drama *Legend of Ryōma* (*Ryōma-den*) uses as a frame the jealousy that an aging Iwasaki Yatarō, founder of Mitsubishi, feels during the Meiji period for the long-deceased Ryōma's fame.

Take Ryōma's friend and mentor, the swordsman Takechi Zuizan. Both Shiba and Yasuoka depict Takechi Zuizan's men's assassination of Yoshida Tōyō, the chief administrator of the prefecture, on the evening of 1862.4.8. Yoshida had worked at the behest of the daimyo Yamauchi Yōdō to centralize control in the Tosa domain, drawing the ire of both the conservative upper samurai and the restless lower samurai, including the *gōshi* who were drawn to Takechi's Tosa Loyalist Party. Sakamoto Ryōma had fled the *han* the previous month, and in Shiba's telling of the story, before he goes, Ryōma attempts to get Takechi to drop his plan and go away with him. Takechi is not to be dissuaded, however, and he chooses a group of three *gōshi* to carry out his task, among them Bunsuke's son Yasuoka Kasuke. The night he is murdered, Yoshida is returning from the castle, where he was teaching the young daimyo (replacing the retired Yōdō, under house arrest in Edo but still a force behind the scenes) a lesson concerning "the uses of history" (Shiba 2: 416). One of the killers, Nasu Shingo, visits his nineteen-year-old nephew, Tanaka Mitsuaki, who will go on to be one of the important figures in the Meiji government. At this point in the narrative, he is portrayed as a wide-eyed youth:

> "Akisuke," Nasu said, using Mitsuaki's childhood name, "come over here." He had him step down to the earthen floor. "Look, I've come here to say something very important. You're young, but because you're a man, you won't repeat this to anyone. Tonight, I'm going to kill Yoshida Tōyō, the chief administrator."
> "Whaaaa—?"
> "Idiot, keep your voice down." (2: 420)

It is a comic gesture on Shiba's part, depicting the ancient man of Shōwa as a Meiji innocent. As if to emphasize this, Shiba allows Tanaka to describe in his own words the melancholy of the moment he saw Nasu off, quoting from Tanaka's memoirs, "dictated when he was ninety-four years old" (2: 421). The story of the assassination is a harrowing one: the three assassins wait along Yoshida's route home. They ambush him, and, after a brief struggle, Nasu deals the deathblow with the words, "Lord Yoshida, we'll be taking your life for the sake of the country" (2: 430). Kasuke is in charge of the severed head, which they wrap up in one of their cotton loincloths. Takechi is upset with them for treating it with such disrespect, but after all, the reader is reminded, it was Tōyō himself who proclaimed, in effect, "Let the upper samurai indulge in luxuries, and the *gōshi* use nothing but simple cotton" (2: 430). The action turns to Ryōma once again: rumors abound that Ryōma is behind the plot, that he faked his own departure from the *han* in order to kill Yoshida. But indeed Ryōma has fled the *han*, crossing over the spine of Shikoku into neighboring Iyo. In the way that all tangential events in Shiba's story inevitably lead back to Ryōma, however, we are reminded that the path that he took through the mountains "was the same path that Nasu, Yasuoka, and Ōishi, the killers of Yoshida Tōyō, would take when they fled the *han*" (2: 437). Politically or not, Ryōma is on the move, literally as a trailblazer, and others are following him.

Yasuoka Shōtarō's sympathies, however, are with those left behind, who do not or cannot flee Tosa and its politics, who can only be saved by narrative itself. Yasuoka turns to the same source, Tanaka Mitsuaki's memoir, to consider the families and friends, quoting Mitsuaki: "Flight at that time was not what we think of today: a prisoner breaking out of jail and fleeing. It was harsher. It involved not just the person who fled, but all of us at the time; the fugitive was punished, but so were his parents, siblings, and children" (YSS 8: 132). For the Yasuokas, this was an especially frightening proposition: because of their intermarriage and cross-adoption, Kasuke had run the risk of recrimination for all four of the Yasuoka houses. Although they do not appear to have been blamed, the damage Kasuke inflicted is felt by Yasuoka Shōtarō himself: virtually nothing in Kasuke's own hand remains, suggesting that everything that would have connected him to his family—letters, diaries, and so forth—was destroyed to protect them. Moreover, "for the year 1862 (Bunkyū 2) only three lines are recorded in Bunsuke's diary, and it is very possible that at this time he destroyed just the portion for 1862 and later scribbled in the three lines" (YSS 8: 134–35). The families and the Tosa Loyalists, although living with the fear that their entire movement would be purged, evade punishment by destroying their documents, and Kasuke himself lives on—for a couple more years. But Kasuke, too, is a forgotten man: The major event of his life, Yoshida's murder, is ultimately a red herring in the long, complicated history of the *bakumatsu*; what happened between the Loyalists and the conservatives in Tosa was rendered moot by the toppling of the shogunate. Kasuke's life must be stitched together from a combination of the fragments that remain and those that *should* remain but inexplicably don't; Yasuoka uses Tanaka Mitsuaki's memoir of the period in a mode of writing wildly different from that of Shiba: if Shiba reads it as history written by the victors, Yasuoka would read it as history written by the survivors—biologically and textually.

The final fifth of *A Tale of Wanderers* turns back to Tosa, which became Kōchi Prefecture in the fourth year of Meiji, 1871, and to Michinosuke's life after the Meiji Restoration. He changed his name to Michitarō and began working for the Freedom and People's Rights Movement. The new government was run by Satsuma and Chōshū figures, largely freezing Tosa out. The Freedom and People's Rights Movement was a movement for greater democratic reforms in early Meiji with a stronghold in Kōchi that played a part in the creation of the Meiji constitution in 1889 and the creation of the Diet in 1890. Michitarō's attempts at writing *dodoitsu*, a comic form of poetry from the Edo period, in support of the cause faced government censorship similar to what Yasuoka himself faced with the Bad Company in wartime Japan (YSS 9: 379). The Freedom and People's Rights Movement was bankrupted during their game of cat-and-mouse with the censors. When the *Kōchi shinbun* newspaper was shut down in 1882, a year after it was founded, an obituary for it appeared in the *Kōchi jiyū shinbun*, and a funeral procession complete with geisha as mourners was held. Less than a week later, the *Kōchi jiyū shinbun* was forced to close, and this time the *Doyō shinbun* served as "chief mourner." (This was not as catastrophic as it sounds; the newspaper industry continued to survive in one form or another, often under

Bakumatsu, Postwar, and Memories of Survival 177

these same names, as we will see below.) Yasuoka, knowing of Michitarō's background writing humorous verse for the cause, wonders if perhaps Michitarō isn't the one behind the sardonic funerals. He had been on staff at the *Kōchi shinbun* and, Yasuoka conjectures, may have been in a gallows mood as he contemplated his own death, which came only four years later, in 1886, at the age of forty (YSS 9: 382).

For Yasuoka, the truth of the matter is the *bakumatsu* and the Freedom and People's Rights Movement bankrupted the family. "What we can surmise is this: The three sons of the West House, Kakunosuke, Kasuke, and Michinosuke, devoted themselves to the overthrow of the shogunate and the Freedom and People's Rights Movement, and the cost of this may well have destroyed the finances not only of the West House, but also the Main House, into which Kakunosuke was adopted. If this is true, then it follows that the early deaths of Tsunenoshin and Kakuma in the Lower House and the illness and death of Gonma in the Upper House allowed them to survive without any serious risk to their finances" (YSS 9: 455). Meaning, better to die young and create a succession problem than to live long enough to become entangled in national affairs and bankrupt the family in support of a cause that, ultimately, did not reward those who suffered the most to bring it to fruition. Indeed, today only the Upper and Lower Houses are still standing. The Lower House has been named an Important Cultural Property and both are still owned by members of the Yasuoka family at the time of writing.

Not all was lost, however. The survival of the generation of wanderers, long gone from the face of the earth, is made possible in memory by Yasuoka's narration. He started writing *A Tale of Wanderers* decades before it was finally published, in the darkest hours of World War II. In 1941, as the prospects for any fast end to the war turned bleak following the attack on Pearl Harbor, Yasuoka holed up in the Keiō library in Hiroshi and attempted to write a fictional version of his ancestor Kasuke's life. Yasuoka was in school only to avoid the draft, and even as he wrote about Kasuke in a similar situation, hiding from the authorities in Satsuma after the assassination of Yoshida Tōyō, he realized he didn't have the endurance to finish the work (BSS 1: 160). In that sense, *A Tale of Wanderers* was a work conceived in wartime, with a gestation period that spanned nearly the first forty years of the postwar. Its survival—and thus, the wanderers' survival—depended on Yasuoka's own.

At the same time, perhaps we can say that Yasuoka's survival depended on the survival of their narrative. History or historical fiction or—as is always the case—somewhere in between, all of these works (including *Roots*) are marked by displacement and movement. The word "wanderer" (*ryūri*) was used for those who wandered away from their hometowns and homelands, and in all of these works the protagonists are displaced by war and violence (Sakai 211). Here, too, the postwar parallel is clear. Like his ancestors, Yasuoka dreamed of escaping his cruel regiment in World War II, a dream depicted in his 1957 novel *Flight* (*Tonsō*). They are the only terms in which he can imagine his ancestor Kasuke's flight through the mountains to Iyo:

> They would have been moving for fifteen or sixteen hours, at the rate of about eight kilometers an hour. When I was in the military, we sometimes moved at six kilometers an hour, but this was very nearly a running pace. To move at eight kilometers an hour, you would have to take no breaks and you would have to run. And the route was along rough mountain paths. The strength they had is difficult for us to imagine today. To be that excited, and pursued by fear—I imagine they simply didn't have time to feel fatigued. (YSS 8: 143)

Is it any wonder that Yasuoka, Shiba, and all the other indefatigable postwar writers-as-historians saw in their forerunners shades of themselves? Shiba never wrote anything major with a contemporary setting, and Yasuoka turned away from the autobiographical stories that had brought him to fame, but perhaps it was to make sense of their own experiences that they cast their attentions into the past. The difference between the two, however, is that Shiba's narrative revolves around that most tragic of figures, Sakamoto Ryōma, who did not survive to see the new world he envisioned; Shiba's narrative, like his protagonist, stops short of the Meiji Restoration. For all of the deaths along the way in *A Tale of Wanderers*, the children survive and have children of their own, and the family name and two of the estates are handed down to Yasuoka's generation, through modernity and into the postwar. For Yasuoka, the *bakumatsu* offers a key to deliverance from the postwar, and the narrative Yasuoka produces about the former offers a way forward through the latter—tentative, hardscrabble, but a path nonetheless, slipping through the spaces between fiction, history, and memory.

The Kagami River and the Mirror of Memory

Yasuoka wasn't done with his Tosa ancestry. In 2000, Yasuoka published his history of his mother's side of the family, *The Kagami River* (*Kagamigawa*). According to Sakagami Hiroshi, Yasuoka Shōtarō had already conceived of the project while still serializing *A Tale of Wanderers* two decades earlier (Sakagami, "Kaisetsu," 203).

The Kagami River flows through central Kōchi City, the prefectural capital of Kōchi-ken. It is one of several rivers that enter the city from the east and west,

Bakumatsu, Postwar, and Memories of Survival

join in the center, and flow southward via Urado Bay out into the sweep of Tosa Bay in the Pacific Ocean. The Kagami, meaning "mirror," has long reflected the lives of the population. It was along the banks of the Kagami that Tosa Province's most famous son, Sakamoto Ryōma, spent his childhood, and it is here that Yasuoka's ancestors on his mother's side lived much of their lives.

While his father's side of the family found their moment at the end of the shogunate and during the opening of Japan and the transition to the modern nation-state, his mother's side of the family tree contains a roster of important figures of the Meiji Period. His maternal aunt Mika's husband Shigehiko was the nephew of Terada Torahiko, the prominent physicist and man of letters who can be traced through Yasuoka's father's lineage as well. His maternal grandfather Irimajiri Chiwaki's sister Shukuko was married to Kataoka Naoharu (1859–1934), the Minister of Commerce and Industry and Minister of Finance for Japan during the 1920s. Irimajiri Chiwaki's father's cousin was Maruoka Kanji (1836–1898), who served as both governor of Okinawa (1888–1892) and governor of Kōchi (1892). At a time when governors were appointed by the government, Maruoka's selection—the first Kōchi native to serve as governor of that prefecture—was a thrilling moment for the entire extended family.

In *The Kagami River*, Yasuoka pieces together the lives of these well-known men through a combination of historical records and family memories—pointing out, as he did in *Ryūritan*, where the two differ. In addition to the roster of famous figures, however, he gives prominence to his distant relative and Maruoka Kanji's nephew, Nishiyama Fumoto. When Yasuoka was a child, Fumoto was used by the women in his family as a constant warning against idleness and lack of ambition: "My mother had gone on about Fumoto to me since I was a child, mainly about how Fumoto was hopelessly, irretrievably lazy: 'At this rate, you're going to end up just like Fumoto in the future, no real job to speak of, carrying the banner at funerals just to scrape by,' she would say" (34).

Late in life, having aspired to nothing in particular, Fumoto found work as an attendant in funeral processions, considered dirty work by Yasuoka's mother and aunts. The novelist Maruoka Akira (1907–1968), the grandson of Maruoka Kanji, told Yasuoka that when he failed the entrance exams to the national high schools multiple times, just as Yasuoka would go on to do, he gave up his dreams of entering the foreign service. He decided he would become a writer, and his grandmother scolded him by saying, "You're the second coming of Fumoto, aren't you?" (36).

In the family's telling of the tale, Kataoka Naoharu, Maruoka Kanji, and Nishiyama Fumoto all lived through difficult times. Kataoka Naoharu was born the same year as Fumoto, 1859, to a rural family. When his father fell ill, Kataoka's mother did piecework for years to pay off the family debts, and the family was so poor that Kataoka was shipped off to a mountain temple for two or three years, where he did both menial labor and filled in for the priest reading sutras as needed (40), incredibly humble beginnings for a future cabinet minister. As a young man, Maruoka had been involved with the Tosa Loyalist party, and fled the province during the height of their tensions with the government following the assassination of Yoshida Tōyō in 1862, making his return as governor three decades later all the more extraordinary. There was no blaming Fumoto's wastrel life on a lack of opportunities.

On the contrary, Fumoto and his mother were supported throughout much of their lives by his uncle Maruoka Kanji. When Kanji went to work for the Imperial Household Ministry (*Kunaishō*), his sister Chika and her son Fumoto joined him there at some point. When Kanji went to Okinawa and then back to Kōchi, the two were with him. As with Yasuoka's ancestors in *A Tale of Wanderers*, the movements of the family members is speculative. Here, it is not intrigue that prevented Fumoto from keeping a record of his journey, it is simply the fact that Fumoto didn't merit the attention of anyone who would keep such records. Maruoka Akira had put together a chronology of his grandfather's life, perhaps as part of his own desire to someday write about Fumoto, but surprisingly, Fumoto doesn't even appear in it (52).

Yasuoka is able to piece Fumoto's life together to a limited extent based on the very thing that he finds interesting about him: Fumoto wrote *kanshi*, Chinese poetry, under the pen name Shōyō. Yasuoka finds a poem about Fumoto's life in Tokyo, placing him there with his uncle (58). When Maruoka Kanji serves as governor of Okinawa, Fumoto works with him; Kanji appreciated his poetry, and Fumoto drank with the locals, which Kanji found politically useful (69). It was hard for Fumoto to become a fully-functioning adult, Yasuoka imagines: his father died when he was young, and he was his mother's only child. After Kanji's death in 1898, Fumoto and his mother Chika are the only members of their family left in Kōchi (91). In some ways, the family has mistaken the responsibility Fumoto feels toward his mother for dereliction of duty. In other ways, Fumoto's life of profligacy is a function of his artistry. Fumoto, despite the barest of formal education, managed to become so proficient in kanshi that he was hailed as a master of the art form by his contemporaries. The time that others spent at work, Fumoto spent in the service of his art; Yasuoka decides that someone like this is far from the lazy good-for-nothing that Yasuoka's mother and others had made him out to be. Even Fumoto's job as a flag-bearer for funeral processions came about because he pointed out an orthographic error on a passing flag and was given work creating and carrying the banners.

Fumoto's later life was hard. After his mother died near the end of the Meiji period, he brought a woman home from the red-light district to live with him. She left him, taking everything of value in the house, including his false teeth and even the single light bulb, which she took "in lieu of alimony" (128). Still, his production of poetry for Kōchi's *Doyō shinbun* increased as he grew older. The poem Yasuoka finds most interesting is one Fumoto wrote for the death of the Meiji emperor in 1915, three years after the emperor's death. Yasuoka wonders if perhaps the poem isn't really Fumoto's way of mourning the loss of his mother at roughly the same time (109–10). If so, Fumoto, already a beacon for Yasuoka for having been a misunderstood man of letters, was a forerunner in another way, in that he approached the collective experience of losing an emperor through the lens of his own individual loss of his mother, much as Yasuoka approached the collective understanding of the Shōwa period through his own personal experiences.

For Yasuoka, Fumoto appears to be both historical figure and metaphor, a prime example of the imbrication of communicative and cultural memory. This is fertile ground for a writer who has always operated between history, literature, and memory to plant stakes. The end of Fumoto's life roughly corresponded to the beginnings of Yasuoka's own memory, in the late 1920s and early 1930s. For Yasuoka, the span of his own childhood was entering the floating gap between communicative and cultural memory when he published this work about Fumoto in 2000. In recuperating Fumoto in *The Kagami River*, doesn't Yasuoka in some respects reclaim something of his own life? The "mirror river" is, in the end, a metaphor for the way that understanding Fumoto—slandered, out of place, out of time Fumoto—is a way of understanding oneself. This figure from the very edge of cultural memory, nearly lost, is tethered to what was then becoming the farthest reaches of communicative memory.

Jan Vansina's original conception of the "floating gap" is broader than the Assmanns' take on it. Rather than a moment of rupture, the floating gap is an attempt in oral traditions to reconcile a lived present and mythic past despite the paucity of information for all that lies between them: "For recent times there is plenty of information which tapers off as one moves back through time. For earlier periods one finds either a hiatus or just one or a few names, given with some hesitation. There is a gap in the accounts, which I will call the floating gap. For still earlier periods one finds again a wealth of information and one deals here with traditions of origin" (Vansina 23). Within living memory, there is a surfeit of information that the community is able to share about the recent past. In the distant past, there is again a great deal of information, for these origin stories, often centering on legendary heroes, have accrued over generations and acquired prestige within the society as being integral to the group's understanding of itself.

Between them, however, in all the generations down to the one that has just slipped out of living memory, is little other than a name here and there. The floating gap, in Vansina's conception, begins eighty to one hundred years in the past and continues into the recesses of time to the age of the gods. Rather than being a break between one form of collective memory and another, it is something that must be sutured, in order to create a continuous narrative of the society: "Sometimes, especially in genealogies, the recent past and origins are run together as a succession of a single generation. [. . .] Accounts fuse and are thrown back into the period of origin—typically under a culture hero—or are forgotten" (23–24).

Vansina is describing societies that rely primarily, if not exclusively, on oral traditions, but Yasuoka's work is a reminder of the ways that oral traditions continue to play a role in literate societies. Sakamoto Ryōma and his compatriots, legendary gods in the history of modern Japan, were invented from a fusion of local legend, popular storytelling, and scattered written evidence. Yasuoka himself used textual evidence in conjunction with oral family history to reshape the narrative of his family. At times the written record tainted a more accurate oral one; Yasuoka's family, knowingly or not, allowed fictional texts to corrupt what they believed to be transmitted memory. Narratives create history anew, establishing chronologies and temporal boundaries, limiting the possibilities of existence. But they can also expand these boundaries and re-envision them; through Yasuoka's creative efforts, the also-rans of the *bakumatsu* and the forgotten poets of the early twentieth century are rendered as heroes of a different order in cultural memory and carried into the present.

In the end, both the Assmanns' and Vansina's conceptions of the floating gap capture it in stasis in order to describe it, but in applying it to Yasuoka's work we can see that the concept is only valid because the floating gap is in perpetual motion. For Yasuoka as a boy in the 1920s and 1930s, the floating gap would have been situated over a period of seventy or eighty years prior to that, namely, the 1850s and 1860s—the *bakumatsu*. Perhaps for Yasuoka this earlier positioning of the floating gap, as living memory of pre-Meiji Japan faded away over the course of his childhood, holds the key to the one that hovers over the memory of his own childhood toward the end of his life. His attempt to suture the loss he is feeling about his childhood demands that he in turn suture the loss he felt as a child about the earlier epoch. The floating gaps, plural, extend into the past in a recursive chain, and we go on attempting to make sense of the present by coming to terms with a past that slips away even as we grasp it.

Conclusion

Ultimately, any single-author study will end up following one path out of many possible routes through the writer's oeuvre; the possibilities are compounded when confronted by a writer as prolific as Yasuoka. Yasuoka's work on the *bakumatsu* and early Meiji is even more substantial than the long, carefully constructed family histories treated here. During a long hospitalization in the mid-1980s, a Kōdansha editor presented him with a set of Nakazato Kaizan's massive serialized novel set in the *bakumatsu*, *Great Bodhisattva Pass* (*Daibosatsu tōge*, 1913–1941). Yasuoka worked his way through the entire series of books and wrote *A Record of the Endless Journey* (*Hate mo nai dōchūki*, 1995). Yasuoka's love for circuses, exemplified by the 1955 Yasuoka short story that generations of Japanese schoolchildren encountered in their textbooks, "The Circus Horse" ("Saakasu no uma"),[1] led him to write *The Circus at the End of the Era* (*Daiseikimatsu saakasu*, 1984, in YSS, vol. 10), his history of a little-known troupe of Japanese circus performers who traveled America and Europe from 1866 to 1869. The book renewed interest in this forgotten troupe in Japan and abroad; Frederik L. Schodt built on work by Yasuoka and others to produce his book *Professor Risley and the Imperial Japanese Troupe* (2012).

Other engagements with literature include *On Shiga Naoya* (*Shiga Naoya ron*, 1968, in YSZ, vol. 6), Yasuoka's treatment of the work of Shiga (1883–1971), the "god of the short story"; *My Own Strange Tales from a Chinese Studio* (*Shisetsu ryōsai shii*, 1975, in YSS vol. 6), an exploration of Pu Songling's (1640–1715) *Strange Tales from a Chinese Studio* (in Japanese pronunciation, Ryōsai shii, c. 1740); and *My Strange Tale from East of the River* (*Watashi no bokutō kitan*,

1999), an homage to his boyhood hero, the writer Nagai Kafū and his "A Strange Tale from East of the River" ("Bokutō kidan," 1937), about the Tamanoi pleasure quarters they both frequented before it was destroyed during the war (Seidensticker 156). The child protagonist in Yasuoka's *Flower Festival* (*Hana matsuri*, 1962, in YSZ, vol. 2), a boy at a temple school who finds himself in a constant state of arousal about the maid, perhaps owes something to Shiga's *Ōtsu Junkichi* (1912) and other works.

In later years, Yasuoka thought about his own mortality. In 1988, Yasuoka converted to Catholicism under the guidance of his old friend Endō Shūsaku. Yasuoka wrote an apologia, together with Inoue Yōji, entitled *Why We Became Christians* (*Warera naze Kirisuto-kyōto to narishi ka*, 1999), a title that clearly alludes in its classical diction to the Japanese title of Uchimura Kanzō's classic work, written in English and originally published in Tokyo as *How I Became a Christian* (*Yo wa ika ni shite Kirisuto-shinto to narishi ka*, 1895.[2] In 1998, Yasuoka published a collection of thoughts about aging and death, *Staring Death in the Face* (*Shi to no taimen*). In 2001, a collection of Yasuoka's conversations with the only member of the Third Generation of New Writers who was his exact age, Kondō Keitarō (1920–2002), *Things Left to Learn at Eighty* (*Yowai hachijū ima nao benkyō*), appeared. In that conversation, Yasuoka admitted that he felt himself slip a little the moment his manuscript of *The Kagami River* was delivered to his publishers (Yasuoka and Kondō 27). At least six collections of essays new and old appeared between 2000 and 2005.

I met Yasuoka Shōtarō only once, at his home in Tokyo in the summer of 2006, around the time the last of his work was published after a postwar writing career of nearly sixty years. His daughter Haruko had arranged the meeting. Yasuoka had been ill and had been awake through the night and sleeping during the day; during his long career, this had been how he worked, but such a schedule was hardly welcome at this point. After a few emails back and forth, she kindly invited me over for lunch on a day when her father appeared to be rested and at his peak. Thanks to this timing, the Yasuoka that I met was friendly and lucid. For two hours, we discussed his life and career. I mentioned that I, too, had spent time in Kōchi Prefecture, and we discussed the mystifying ways of the local dialect, Tosa-ben. He talked about his time in Nashville and how crucial it had been to his career. I asked him who came to visit him now, and he said no one. I tried again by asking which of his friends stopped by, and he said, with a quiet laugh, "All of my friends are gone."

When he passed away on January 26, 2013, at the age of ninety-two, indeed, few writers of his generation were left. The NHK News Web article posted on January 29 began with the works he would likely be remembered for: *A View of*

At home with younger writers. Left to right: Abe Akira, Yasuoka Shōtarō, Sakagami Hiroshi. Photograph courtesy of Yasuoka Haruko.

the Sea and "Bad Company." For the *Mainichi shinbun*, it was *A View of the Sea* and *A Tale of Wanderers*. For the *Asahi shinbun*, it was *A Tale of Wanderers*. In the *Asahi* article, the literary scholar and translator Donald Keene was quoted as saying that he had hoped to translate *The Circus at the End of the Era* while Yasuoka was still alive. In the fall of 2016, the Kanagawa Museum of Modern Literature in Yokohama hosted a Yasuoka exhibit, *Yasuoka Shōtarō: From "Me" to "History"* (*Yasuoka Shōtarō ten: "Watashi" kara "rekishi" e*). (The exhibit was revived, with some variations, in early 2019 at the Kōchi Museum of Literature.) Among those gathered for the opening reception in 2016 were younger writers influenced by Yasuoka, among them Sakagami Hiroshi and Kuroi Senji, who both wrote short essays for the exhibit catalog. The foreword to the catalog was written by Murakami Haruki, a rare gesture of respect from a man who ordinarily keeps the Japanese literary establishment at arm's length. Among the most touching juxtaposition of items on display was Bunsuke's diary, a smaller book than one might imagine, dwarfed by the handwritten manuscript of *A Tale of Wanderers*, a stack of paper about a foot high. I was gratified to see among the trove of personal items on display a DVD I had sent to Yasuoka shortly after our meeting of Jean Renoir's *Grand Illusion* (*La grande illusion*), the 1937 film he was so disappointed in when he finally saw it after the war, because he felt that the moment for it had passed during the time its screening was censored by the wartime authorities. Yasuoka Haruko had told me that he had appreciated it more seeing it decades later.

Yasuoka's importance to Japanese literature continues. Murakami Haruki, who has expressed his admiration for the Third Generation in a series of essays, occasionally uses a motif that seems to be channeling Yasuoka. The Japanese title for *Kafka on the Shore* (*Umibe no Kafuka*, 2002) parallels Yasuoka's for *A View of the Sea* (*Kaihen no kōkei*, but originally titled *Umibe no kōkei*); the two titles shares the initial word "seashore" (*umibe*, alternately pronounced *kaihen*) and a cluster of k- sounds (*kōkei*, versus *Kafuka*), but whether deliberate or dredged from his subconscious, like most things Murakami, it appears to be a reference without any particular meaning. Naoki Prize-winner Nakajima Kyōko, in writing two books about wartime and early postwar Japan, *The Maid's Tales* (*Jochūtan*, 2009) and *The Little House* (*Chiisai ouchi*, 2010), referred to various materials written by people who lived through the period to make her works come alive, and considered Yasuoka's *My Shōwa History* crucial to her work.[3]

The ostensible gap between communicative memory and cultural memory now hangs roughly over Japan's wartime and early postwar period, the central event of Yasuoka's lifetime. Narita Ryūichi has created his own paradigm in which, over time, the war has changed from a "situation" to an "experience" to a "testimony" to a "memory" (Narita, *Sensō keiken*). In spite of this—or perhaps because of it—the urge to write about World War II is as strong as ever in Japan. Writers at the center of the literary establishment who were too young to have experienced the war first-hand continue to write about the war and early postwar. Just among the current judges of the Akutagawa Prize—a very imperfect measure of the center of the literary world in Japan, but one that at least mimics Yasuoka's own time on the committee—nearly all have written novellas, novels, or nonfiction that revisit World War II, including Okuizumi Hikaru, with *The Stones Cry Out* (*Ishi no raireki*, 1993), a second-generation *Fires on the Plain*; Murakami Ryū, with a parallel world in which the war never ended in *The World Five Minutes from Now* (*Gofungo no sekai*, 1994);[4] and Shimada Masahiko, with the wartime and early postwar pastiche *Sisters of Decadence* (*Taihai shimai*, 2005). Younger writers, too, find themselves drawn to the war in an attempt to intercede in the historic moment as it passes from one form of memory to another, including Takahashi Hiroki, a 2018 winner of the Akutagawa Prize. That they are able to do so is surely a product of multiple valences of memory—literary, institutional, familial—operating on their creative lives. But it is also made possible by having the space to do so. Some of this is surely thanks to Yasuoka and writers like him. From the earliest stages of their careers, Yasuoka and his peers were writing their memories at the same time they were undermining them, feeling that the memory of the war and postwar would generate far beyond them. For Yasuoka, it meant finding his way through another long postwar into the liminal space between Edo-period and modern Japan. Other writers, in turn, will be the ones to guide Shōwa Japan toward cultural memory, where the contested space of the war—over territory, treasure, and responsibility and reconciliation—will either be resolved or, more likely, continue to be disputed in very different ways. Yasuoka's work to endure the postwar has helped ensure that the postwar will endure.

Appendix

Works by Yasuoka Shōtarō in English Translation

In *Japan Quarterly* 8 (1961):
"The Pawnbroker's Wife" ("Shichiya no nyōbō," 1960), translated by Edward Seidensticker
"The Glass Slipper" ("Garasu no kutsu," 1950), translated by Edward Seidensticker

In *Contemporary Japanese Literature: An Anthology of Fiction, Film, and Other Writing since 1945*. Edited by Howard Hibbett, New York, Knopf, 1977:
"Prized Possessions" ("Aigan," 1952), translated by Edwin McClellan

In *A View By the Sea*. Translated by Kären Wigen. 1984. Reprint. New York, Columbia UP, 1992:
"Bad Company" ("Warui nakama," 1953)
"Thick the New Leaves" ("Aoba shigereru," 1958)
"The Moth" ("Ga," 1953)
"Gloomy Pleasures" ("Inki na tanoshimi," 1953)
"Rain" ("Ame," 1959)
A View by the Sea (*Kaihen no kōkei*, 1959)

In *Stories from* The East. Edited by Burritt Sabin, Tokyo, The East Publications, 1997:
"The Circus Horse" ("Saakasu no uma," 1955), translated by Leon Zolbrod

In *The Glass Slipper and Other Stories*. Translated by Royall Tyler. Champaign and London, Dalkey Archive Press, 2008:

"The Wandering Minstrel" ("Gin'yū shijin," 1954)
"The Glass Slipper" ("Garasu no kutsu," 1950)
"Homework" ("Shukudai," 1952)
"The House Guard" ("Hausu gaado," 1953)
"Jingle Bells" ("Jinguru beru," 1951)
"The King's Ears" ("Ōsama no mimi," 1954)
"The Sword Dance" ("Kenbu," 1953)
"The Medal" ("Kunshō," 1953)
"A Room in Tsukiji" ("Tsukiji Odawara-chō," 1953)

Notes

Introduction

1. See Van C. Gessel, *The Sting of Life: Four Contemporary Japanese Novelists* (New York: Columbia UP, 1989).
2. For memories of major events—often quite accurate—that capture other mundane memories with them, called "flashbulb memories," see Schacter (195–201).
3. From the time the first Japanese residents of Seoul arrived in 1880, they tended to live together in carefully demarcated communities (Duus 325).
4. In *Murō Saisei zenshū*, vol. 1.
5. In *Teihon Satō Haruo zenshū*, vol. 15.
6. For Hiroshima, see John Treat, *Writing Ground Zero* (1995) and Lisa Yoneyama, *Hiroshima Traces* (1999). For Okinawa, see Davinder Bhowmik, *Writing Okinawa* (2008) and Kyle Ikeda, *Okinawan War Memory* (2014). Reiko Tachibana's *Narrative as Counter-Memory: A Half-Century of Postwar Writing in Germany and Japan* (1998) focuses on Hiroshima stories more than any other subject, demonstrating the central place of Hiroshima in attempts to discuss memory and war in Japanese literature.
7. For Endō, see Mark Williams, *Endō Shūsaku* (1999). For Shimao Toshio, see Philip Gabriel, *Mad Wives and Island Dreams* (1999).

Chapter 1

1. For the origins of the Akutagawa and Naoki prizes, see Edward Mack, *Manufacturing Modern Japanese Literature*. For an analysis of how the prize functions today, see Heitzman (2015), indebted to Mack's study.
2. The source of record for the Akutagawa Prize and Naoki Prize is the *Akutagawa shō Naoki shō 150-kai zenkiroku*.

3. The relationship between *Shin nihon bungaku* writers and *Kindai bungaku* writers, not as confrontational as it is often portrayed, is discussed in Ueda et al., pp. xi–xxxv.
4. Hotta Yoshie and Yoshiyuki Junnosuke are the only others to have multiple works cited.
5. The winning stories are reprinted in the general-interest magazine *Bungei shunjū* together with statements from each judge. From this, we know that Yasuoka's chief supporter was Satō Haruo. Although other judges felt that these two stories were inferior to the previously nominated "The Glass Slipper" ("Garasu no kutsu") and "Prized Possessions" ("Aigan"), in Satō's mind Yasuoka's powers were growing with each story, and he felt that this time, at the very least, something by Yasuoka should be awarded the prize. Other supporters included Niwa Fumio ("Among the authors who have appeared in the postwar, I know of no author as rich in genius, as unique as this one"), Kishida Kunio ("I thought that, generally, it wasn't a mistake for these two stories to receive the prize. But this writer is someone who can write better stories"), Takii Kōsaku ("Since he has a firm grasp on his individual viewpoint, it would be good if, from here on out, his purview were to expand"), Kawabata Yasunari ("I hesitated somewhat in approving a work that I believe to be worse than the one we saw last time, 'Prized Possessions,' but I didn't hesitate to recommend a writer as unusual as Yasuoka"), and Sakaguchi Ango, who also felt Yasuoka had done better work in the past. Uno Kōji and Funabashi Seiichi were lukewarm on the selection, with Ishikawa Tatsuzō the only one vociferously against it. Ishikawa was stunned that the award had gone to Yasuoka, and the day after the decision was reached found him rereading Yasuoka's stories out of a sense of obligation to figure out why they had moved the other judges. "The images in this author's works are crawling in the dirt. No matter where they crawl, they're plain. [. . .] Isn't there a danger, in recommending this kind of work, of making literary fiction (*junbungaku*) boring?" See "Akutagawa Ryūnosuke shō kettei happyō," pp. 258–65. Of the other eight writers nominated, only Shōno Junzō (1921–2009) would go on to win the Akutagawa, a year and a half later.
6. The most noticeable cadre of resisters, members of the Communist Party, was nearly gone by 1936, and the government increasingly turned its attention to other, less obvious targets. See Steinhoff, pp. 202–3.
7. Andrew Gordon writes about a "causal dynamic" in transwar history in "Consumption, Leisure and the Middle Class in Transwar Japan." Gordon has called Chalmers Johnson's *MITI and the Japanese Miracle* the "classic statement of this thesis" (Gordon, *Consumption* 3). See also Sheldon Garon, *Molding Japanese Minds*.
8. For Tanizaki's run-ins with censors who delayed publication of *Sasameyuki* (*The Makioka Sisters*, 1948) until after the war, see Ken K. Ito, *Visions of Desire: Tanizaki's Fictional Worlds*, pp. 188–90. On Kafū's turn from fiction to diary writing during the war, see Donald Keene, *So Lovely a Country Will Never Perish*, pp.

3–4. For Ibuse's silence toward the end of the war and the first year of the postwar, see John Treat, *Pools of Water, Pillars of Fire: The Literature of Ibuse Masuji*, pp. 129–33.

9. Even this—the literature of August 15, 1945—is such a wide-ranging topic that it merits an entire seven hundred-page volume in the collection *Sensō to bungaku* (*War and Literature*), titled *Samazama na 8.15* (*Experiences of August 15*).
10. Unbracketed ellipses exist in the original. Ellipses in brackets indicate omissions in my citations.
11. See maps on pp. 72–77 of Ōta, *Kasane chizu shiriizu Tōkyō: Makkaasaa no jidai-hen* for a visual layover showing the district's escape from the firebombing, as well as its largely unchanged street design.
12. "Civilian control over all Tsukiji facilities resumed in the summer of 1955," i.e., after the initial publication of Yasuoka's story (Bestor 117).
13. Edward Seidensticker discusses Kafū's antimilitarism as reflected in his diaries in *Kafū the Scribbler*, pp. 94 and 347–49. Kafū's success after the war is noted on pp. 170–71.
14. Yasuoka here appears to have, perhaps for dramatic effect, stretched out his four failures over three years into four failures in four years.
15. A chart demonstrating this somewhat convoluted system is in Roden, *Schooldays in Imperial Japan*, p. 255.
16. For psychoanalytic readings of Yasuoka Shōtarō, see Andra Alvis, "Fantasies of Guilt in the Autobiographical Fiction of Yasuoka Shōtarō," PhD dissertation, 1996. Alvis looks at a very limited selection of Yasuoka's short stories set in the postwar and the novella *A View of the Sea* (*Kaihen no kōkei*, 1959) using a psychoanalytic framework but does not address Yasuoka's stories set in wartime.
17. See also Isolde Standish, *Myth and Masculinity in the Japanese Cinema*, pp. 119–41, in which she argues along similar lines that "despite Kaji's conscience and his active resistance, he becomes a mere pawn in the greater movement of power relations" (133).
18. For a summary treatment of Japanese-Russian relations toward the end of the war, see James L. McClain, *Japan: A Modern History*, pp. 510–15.
19. For the despair the Soviet entry into the war precipitated, see Bix, pp. 502–11.
20. A collection of them, including *Flight*, has been gathered for the first time in *Yasuoka Shōtarō sensō shōsetsu shūsei* (Chūkō Bunko, 2018).
21. Although he does not comment on war literature per se, Edward Fowler considers an essentially serious-minded approach to postwar Japanese literature in the English-speaking world in general to be a product of what is available and in print in translation from major publishing houses; as of 1992, he took that to be the "triumvirate" of Kawabata, Mishima, and "the more somber writings" of Tanizaki. See Fowler, "Rendering Words, Traversing Cultures: On the Art and Politics of Translating Modern Japanese Fiction," p. 9. Howard Hibbett sees a change in the literature itself, as "leading novelists since Meiji (with the notable exception of Tanizaki) seemed to lose their sense of humor under the influence

194 Notes to pages 54–69

of nineteenth-century Western novels, and of twentieth-century realities" (*Chrysanthemum* 41).

22. In her excellent translation into English, Kären Wigen has translated the title as *A View by the Sea*, but I have chosen to render it as *A View of the Sea*, for reasons that will become clear.
23. Yasuoka's own mother was born in Tokyo and spent time as a child in Osaka, but her family, the Irimajiris, were also from Kōchi Prefecture.
24. In addition to *A View of the Sea*, Etō analyzes Kojima Nobuo's *Embracing Family* (*Hōyō kazoku*, 1965), Endō Shūsaku's *Silence* (*Chinmoku*, 1966), Yoshiyuki Junnosuke's *The Stars and the Moon are Holes in the Sky* (*Hoshi to tsuki wa ten no ana*, 1967), and Shōno Junzō's *Evening Clouds* (*Yūbe no kumo*, 1965).
25. Tokushima Takayoshi, the editor assigned to *A View of the Sea*, told me that he also had always thought this must be the case. Personal interview, September 30, 2016.

Chapter 2

1. See Tachibana, pp. 14–15, for an overview of the standard generational schema of Japanese wartime and postwar writers that moves seamlessly from arranging writers by first publication to date of birth.
2. Yoshiyuki's brief military experience is listed in the chronology at the back of Takahashi Hiromitsu's *Yoshiyuki Junnosuke: Hito to bungaku*, p. 221. Endō's health waiver exempting him from military service and his first encounter with Yasuoka Shōtarō on the Keiō University campus are both mentioned in the chronology in *Endō Shūsaku bungaku zenshū* 15, p. 335. Endō's multiple encounters with TB are discussed in Williams, pp. 76–77.
3. Kojima's graduation and war experiences are detailed in the chronology at the back of *Kojima Nobuo hihyō shūsei* 8, p. 634. Kathryn Sparling discusses Shimao Toshio's education and war experiences in her brief introduction to his life and works; see Shimao, pp. 2–3. Van Gessel discusses the war experiences of Kojima, Shimao, Yasuoka, and Endō in Gessel, pp. 15–21.
4. One can speak of a "long Taishō" that runs from the end of the Russo-Japanese war in 1905 to the beginning of the Manchurian Incident in 1931.
5. Roman Rosenbaum has written about four rather disparate writers in terms of their membership in the *yakeato sedai*: Oda Makoto, Nosaka Akiyuki, Ōe Kenzaburō, and Ishihara Shintarō. See "The 'Generation of the Burnt-out Ruins,'" pp. 281–93.
6. Ōoka Shōhei's *Fires on the Plain* (1951) is perhaps the most famous example.
7. See my article on the contemporary literary establishment, Heitzman 2015.
8. See Ishiyama Kōichi, "Higurashi," for his version of this.
9. A copy of *Pale Horse* is in the collection of the Kanagawa Museum of Modern Literature. Yasuoka Haruko confirms that "Aouma" is the pronunciation her father used for the title of the magazine (personal correspondence, October 18, 2018). After consultation with editor Tokushima Takayoshi, she notes that the

same pronunciation applies to the unrelated short story "The Pale Horse Revue" ("Aouma-kan," 1955), perhaps titled in honor of his old literary magazine (personal correspondence, November 4, 2018). The pale horse is what Death rides in the book of Revelations; "The Pale Horse Revue" is a whimsical fantasy in which Mephistopheles visits a lovelorn young woman, but one can imagine that the pale horse meant something rather more serious to young men in wartime.

10. This story is collected in Furuyama Komao, *Nijūsan no sensō tanpen shōsetsu*.
11. Yasuoka's attempts to publish the novel are recorded in BSS 2: 67–71. Satō remembers that the humiliation Yasuoka felt when "Patterns and Adventures" was unceremoniously rejected by Hara Tamiki at the literary journal *Mita bungaku* was ameliorated by the paradigm-shifting inspiration Yasuoka drew from reading Oscar Wilde's criticism (Satō 116).
12. Fowler also notes the number of writers who wrote works purportedly describing their own lives in just the half-decade following the 1907 publication of Tayama Katai's *The Quilt*—Shimazaki Tōson, Iwano Hōmei, Chikamatsu Shūkō, and Tokuda Shūsei among them (112). In 1950, the critic Terada Tōru was able to claim that only three modern writers had not attempted the form: Natsume Sōseki, Kōda Rohan, and Izumi Kyōka (cited in Fowler xvi), while Tomi Suzuki has persuasively argued that even writers involved in writing "anti-I-novels," namely, Nagai Kafū and Tanizaki Jun'ichirō, were influenced by the cultural forces that produced the I-novel paradigm (135–86).
13. Hidaka Shōji, unusually, treats the Third Generation in terms of the fantastic or "fairy-tale quality" of their stories, but he limits his commentary to only representative works (in Yasuoka's case, "The Glass Slipper") (Hidaka 95–120).
14. Whether by coincidence or not, an erotic novel named *Helen and Desire*, written by the Scottish novelist Alexander Trocchi under the pen name Frances Lengel, was published in 1954 by the Paris-based Olympia Press, the original publisher of Nabokov's *Lolita* and the William S. Burroughs novel *Naked Lunch*. A Japanese translation of it, *Heren no yokubō*, was finally published in 1980 by Fujimi Shobō.
15. Theatrical performances involving literary stars have been a mainstay of Japanese culture since the Meiji period. By chance, the amateur troupe Kiza was started through a conversation between two of Yasuoka's friends representing his wartime and postwar cohorts: Furuyama Komao and Endō Shūsaku. See Michimata, pp. 247–59.
16. This is one clue to the story's timeframe: As popularly designated in 1957, the three treasures of the modern household were the washing machine, the vacuum cleaner, and the refrigerator. See Carol Gluck, "The Past in the Present," p. 75.
17. Perhaps owing to their controversial nature, the essays were not collected in book form until 1987, when they were published under the title *Fact and Fiction in Literature: The Truth Will Have Its Revenge* (*Bungaku no kyojitsu: Jijitsu wa fukushū suru*). Subsequent essays take to task Takami Jun, Ōoka Shōhei, Endō Shūsaku, Mishima Yukio, Hirano Ken, and Usui Yoshimi.
18. Published as volume 6 of *Yasuoka Shōtarō zenshū*.

Chapter 3

1. The title is surely a reference to the song made famous by Doris Day, "Sentimental Journey." Released in 1945, it was the number-one song in the United States that summer, as American troops began to make their own sentimental journeys home in large numbers. Here again, the war and postwar make their presence felt. At the same time, the title could very well be in homage to Laurence Sterne's *A Sentimental Journey through France and Italy* (1768), published in Japanese in 1947 as *Kanjō ryokō*. Ostensibly non-fiction, the work traces the dying Sterne's travels southward out of England, but the first-person protagonist identifies himself as Reverend Yorick, whom Sterne's readers would have immediately identified as the parson in Sterne's fictional masterpiece *The Life and Opinions of Tristram Shandy, Gentleman* (1759–1767). Sterne, himself a clergyman, also published some of his own sermons under the name Yorick, so that in the end, Yorick's sentimental journey represents a radical blurring of truth and fiction, of historical fact and literary vision.
2. For an overview of Nashville's moment of centrality in the Civil Rights Movement, see Branch, pp. 272–311.
3. In addition to these six, Kim Jiyoung lists four others who went to the United States on Rockefeller Foundation grants: Fukuda Tsuneari, Ishii Momoko, Nakamura Mitsuo, and Etō Jun, for a total of ten. See Kim, pp. 223–30, for brief descriptions of the seven recipients she does not treat at length in her book, and subsequent individual chapters for the three she focuses on: Agawa, Kojima, and Ariyoshi. Of these ten recipients, Yasuoka was the ninth to study in the United States.
4. The prewar writers Agawa discusses are John Manjirō, Joseph Heco, Fukuzawa Yukichi, Niijima Jō, Tsuda Umeko, Uchimura Kanzō, Katayama Sen, Nitobe Inazō, Asakawa Kan'ichi, Arishima Takeo, and Tani Jōji. All were dead by 1935 save Asakawa, who died in 1948.
5. The wartime and postwar writers Agawa discusses are Tsuru Shigeto, Murata Kiyoaki, Mickey Yasukawa, Morita Akio, Ishii Momoko, Oda Makoto, Yasuoka Shōtarō, Etō Jun, Ishikawa Yoshimi, Kirishima Yōko, Satō Kinko, Fujiwara Masahiko, Yamamoto Shichihei, Nishibe Susumu, Shiba Ryōtarō, and Murakami Haruki. He does not include his own father, Agawa Hiroyuki.
6. Kim Jiyoung has cited these letters extensively and offers the best description of Kojima's movements in the United States during his year abroad; I am indebted to her research for clarifying the Kojima timeline. See Kim, pp. 296–306.
7. I am grateful to Minoo Adenwalla, Professor Emeritus of Lawrence University in Wisconsin, for providing proper spellings and independent verification of many parts of Shōno's memoir.
8. Benjamin Houston mentions the curious case of one of the black student activists being served at a test run at Cain-Sloan department store on December 5, 1959, precisely because the staff thought he was a foreign-exchange student (91).

9. Yasuoka Haruko, Yasuoka's daughter, has identified her father's tutor as Muriel Pilley. I have confirmed the spellings of names from Pilley's obituary in the *Tennessean*, July 12, 2002, p. 23.
10. See Winchell, pp. 282–99, for a carefully detailed if far-too-sympathetic reading of Davidson's retrograde racial views.
11. Nick Kapur examines the political and cultural repercussions of Anpo in *Japan at the Crossroads: Conflict and Compromise after Anpo*.
12. Muriel Pilley wrote about her experiences in China in the self-published *The Hills of T'ang: Forty Years in South China* (2002).
13. *Alt-Heidelberg* was a 1902 play by the German writer Wilhelm Meyer-Förster. It was the source for Sigmund Romberg's 1924 light opera *The Student Prince* and the 1954 MGM musical of the same name.
14. Mizukami also went by Minakami Tsutomu for a good portion of his career.

Chapter 4

1. For these Olympic recollections, I am relying on two large compendiums, both of which seem to offer fairly wide-ranging and representative reactions to the 1964 Summer Olympic Games by major literary figures: Ishii Masami's *1964-nen no Tokyo Orinpikku*, and *Tokyo Orinpikku: Bungakusha no mita sekai no saiten*, published by Kōdansha.
2. See Dower, *Embracing Defeat*, pp. 123–32, for a description of this discourse.
3. These statistics can be found on the official website of the Japanese Olympic Committee: *www.joc.or.jp/english/historyjapan/tokyo1964.html*.
4. For an Edo Period usage of the phrase, warning of the decline of the shogunate, see Teeuwen and Nakai, *Lust, Commerce, and Corruption*, p. 308.
5. For a discussion of the auteurist question, as well as the outcry that ensued after early screenings of the film, see "Tokyo Olympiad: A Symposium," in James Quandt, ed., *Kon Ichikawa*, pp. 315–37. For an excellent compilation of (and resistance to) various critical opinions that Ichikawa's film is a "humanistic" response to Riefenstahl's "fascist" aesthetics, see Sharalyn Orbaugh, "Raced Bodies and the Public Sphere in Ichikawa Kon's *Tokyo Olympiad*," in James Baxter, ed., *Historical Consciousness, Historiography, and Modern Japanese Values*, pp. 297–324.
6. I am using the *Script for the Documentary Film of the Tokyo Olympics, Limited Edition* (*Tokyo Orinpikku kiroku eiga kyakuhon genteiban*), a copy of which is held by the Tsubouchi Memorial Theatre Museum ("Enpaku") at Waseda University in Tokyo. It is dated June 1, 1964. This script was reprinted with no apparent changes in *Kinema junpō* 369 (July 1964). It lists Wada Natto, Shirasaka Yoshio, Tanikawa Shuntarō and Ichikawa Kon as the screenwriters. A later script made to conform to the film as produced, shorter than the original speculative script, was published in *Bessatsu kinema junpō* (April 1965): 182–91, as "Tokyo Olympics" ("Tokyo Orinpikku"). This version names only Wada and Ichikawa as screenwriters.

7. Long unavailable anywhere, in 2017 *Sensation of the Century* was released in the United States on DVD and Blu-ray as part of the Criterion Collection's set *100 Years of Olympic Films: 1912–2012*, together with a re-release of *Tokyo Olympiad*. At the time of publication, both films were available for streaming on The Criterion Channel.

Chapter 5

1. Yamagita Village is located in present-day Kōnan-shi, Kōchi-ken. I am using the traditional pronunciation of the name.
2. Thus, through Yasuoka's paternal grandmother, Bunsuke is Yasuoka's great-great-great uncle, but through his paternal grandfather, Bunsuke is his great-great-uncle.
3. A lineage of major modern literary works in Japanese that blur the line between fiction and history could perhaps start with the historical fiction of Mori Ōgai, and include writers such as Akutagawa Ryūnosuke, Tanizaki Jun'ichirō, Shimazaki Tōson, and Yasuoka and Shiba's contemporary Inoue Yasushi. Tanizaki's narrator's attempt in *Arrowroot* (*Yoshino kuzu*, 1931) to gather materials for a historical novel in the wilds of the Kii peninsula mimics the author's own research, and the novella ends with their mutual realization that the area "may be the site of legends, but not of history" (Tanizaki 198).
4. To name only the major works: *Burn, My Sword* (*Moeyo ken*, 1962–1964), about Hijikata Toshizō (1835–1869) of the Shinsengumi; *The Last Shogun* (*Saigo no shōgun*, 1966, translated into English as *The Last Shogun: The Life of Tokugawa Yoshinobu*); *The Pass* (*Tōge*, 1966–1968), about Kawai Tsugunosuke (1827–1868), a commander for the Nagaoka Domain in the Boshin War; *God of Flowers* (*Kashin*, 1969–1971), about Chōshū military tactician Ōmura Masujirō (1824–1869); *Our Days in This World* (*Yo ni sumu hibi*, 1969–1970), about Yoshida Shōin (1830–1859) and Takasugi Shinsaku (1839–1867); and *Like Flying* (*Tobu ga gotoku*, 1972–1976), about Saigō Takamori (1828–1877) and the Satsuma Domain.
5. See Harry D. Harootunian's *Overcome by Modernity: History, Culture, and Community in Interwar Japan*.
6. To name a few novels and stories: *Dreams of War Clouds* (*Sen'un no yume*, 1961), about Chōsogabe Morichika (1575–1615), the last of the Chōsogabe daimyo of Tosa, displaced by Tokugawa Ieyasu after the battle of Sekigahara in 1600 in favor of the Yamauchi line; *Crossroads of Fame* (*Kōmyō ga tsuji*, 1963–1965), centered around a female protagonist, Chiyo, the wife of Yamauchi Kazutoyo, the first of that line; "Drunk as a Lord" ("Yotte sōrō," 1964, translated into English), about Tosa daimyo Yamauchi Yōdō (Toyoshige), one of the major figures of the *bakumatsu*; and *A Song of Summer Grasses* (*Natsukusa no fu*, 1968), about Chōsogabe Motochika (1539–1599).
7. All dates given in the traditional calendar (used here, as elsewhere, for events before the adoption of the Gregorian calendar by the Meiji government on January 1, 1873) will be rendered by the Western year that most closely corresponds to

the traditional year, followed by the month, followed by the day. Thus, 1866.1.23 for the twenty-third day of the first month of the year that mostly overlapped with 1866.
8. Celebrated on 3.4, instead of 3.3, in Tosa at the time.
9. I am here following the lead of Luke Roberts in using the pronunciations for Chōsogabe and Yamauchi as they were traditionally used in Tosa; I thank Prof. Roberts for his kind explanation of the issues involved. For the transition from Chōsogabe to Yamauchi rule, see Roberts, pp. 32–38.
10. W. G. Beasley has demonstrated how membership in the strata at the very bottom of samurai society, without possibility of promotion, was a powerful incentive for Ryōma and his confederates to operate outside of the strictures of Meiji society; higher-ranking samurai were much more likely to attempt to negotiate smaller changes within the *bakufu* system. See Beasley, pp. 140–71.
11. An article about the settlement between Haley and Courlander appeared on the front page of the *New York Times* on December 15, 1978.
12. Terada Torahiko (1878–1935) was a physicist at Tokyo Imperial University, although he is best remembered today for his essays. Born in Tokyo and raised in Kōchi Prefecture, Terada attended the Fifth High School in Kumamoto, where he was a student of Natsume Sōseki. He was Yasuoka Shōtarō's grandfather's cousin.

Conclusion

1. A translation of "The Circus Horse" by Leon Zolbrod appears in *Stories from The East*, edited by Burritt Sabin. The Japanese original is in YSS, vol. 2.
2. Uchimura's book was published the same year by The Fleming H. Revell Company in New York with the title *The Diary of a Japanese Convert*.
3. Personal communication, December 15, 2014.
4. For an analysis of this novel, see Kendall Heitzman, "Parallel Universes, Vertical Worlds, and the Nation as Palimpsest in Murakami Ryū's *The World Five Minutes from Now*." *Mechademia*, vol. 10, 2015, pp. 252–66.

Bibliography

Abbreviations

BSS   *Boku no Shōwa-shi* (*My Shōwa History*)
NIV   *The Holy Bible, New International Version*
YSS   *Yasuoka Shōtarō shū*
YSZ   *Yasuoka Shōtarō zenshū*

Works Cited

Abe Kōbō. *The Woman in the Dunes*. Translated by E. Dale Saunders, New York, Vintage, 1964.
Agawa Naoyuki. *Amerika ga mitsukarimashita ka*. Tokyo, Toshi Shuppan, 1998, 2001. 2 vols.
Akutagawa shō Naoki shō 150-kai zenkiroku. Tokyo, Bungei Shunjū, 2014.
"Akutagawa Ryūnosuke shō kettei happyō." *Bungei shunjū*, vol. 31, no. 13, 1953, pp. 258–65.
Allison, Gary D. *Japan's Postwar History*. 2nd ed., Ithaca, Cornell UP, 2004.
Alvis, Andra. *Fantasies of Guilt in the Autobiographical Fiction of Yasuoka Shōtarō*. 1996. PhD dissertation. University of California, Berkeley.
Anderson, Sherwood. *Winesburg, Ohio*. 1919. Reprint. New York, Random House, 1947.
Aoki Masami. *"Warui nakama" kō*. Tokyo, Nihon Kosho Tsūshinsha, 2007.
Ara Masato. *Ara Masato chosakushū*. Vol. 1, Tokyo, San'ichi Shobō, 1983.
Assmann, Aleida. *Cultural Memory and Western Civilization*. New York, Cambridge UP, 2011.
———. *Shadows of Trauma: Memory and the Politics of Postwar Identity*. Translated by Sarah Clift, New York, Fordham UP, 2016.

Assmann, Jan. "Collective Memory and Cultural Identity." *New German Critique*, vol. 65, 1995, pp. 125–33.

Aston, W. G. *Nihongi*. London, Kegan Paul, 1896.

Bach, Steven. *Leni: The Life and Work of Leni Riefenstahl*. New York, Alfred A. Knopf, 2007.

Barthes, Roland. *Empire of Signs*. 1970. Reprint. Translated by Richard Howard, New York, Hill and Wang, 1982.

Baxter, James, editor. *Historical Consciousness, Historiography, and Modern Japanese Values*. Kyoto, International Research Center for Japanese Studies, 2006.

Beasley, W. G. *The Meiji Restoration*. Palo Alto, Stanford UP, 1972.

Bestor, Theodore C. *Tsukiji: The Fish Market at the Center of the World*. Berkeley, U of California P, 2004.

Bhowmik, Davinder. *Writing Okinawa: Narrative Acts of Identity and Resistance*. London, Routledge, 2008.

Bix, Herbert P. *Hirohito and the Making of Modern Japan*. New York, HarperCollins, 2000.

Bourdaghs, Michael K. *The Dawn that Never Comes: Shimazaki Tōson and Japanese Nationalism*. New York, Columbia UP, 2003.

Branch, Taylor. *Parting the Waters: America in the King Years, 1954–1963*. New York, Simon and Schuster, 1988.

de Certeau, Michel. *The Writing of History*. Translated by Tom Conley, New York, Columbia UP, 1988.

Daniels, Gordon. "The Great Tokyo Air Raid, 9–10 March 1945." *Modern Japan: Aspects of History, Literature and Society*. Edited by W. G. Beasley, London, George Allen and Unwin, 1975, 113–31.

Dazai Osamu. *The Setting Sun*. Translated by Donald Keene, New York, New Directions, 1956.

Dower, John. *Embracing Defeat: Japan in the Wake of World War II*. New York, WW Norton, 1999.

———. *Empire and Aftermath: Yoshida Shigeru and the Japanese Experience, 1878–1954*. Cambridge, Council on East Asian Studies, Harvard UP, 1979.

Duus, Peter. *The Abacus and the Sword: The Japanese Penetration of Korea, 1895–1910*. Berkeley, U of California P, 1995.

Endō Shūsaku. *Endō Shūsaku bungaku zenshū*. Tokyo, Shinchōsha, 1999–2000. 15 vols.

———. *Foreign Studies*. 1965. Reprint. Translated by Mark Williams, Rutland, Tuttle, 1989.

———. *Silence*. [Chinmoku.] Tokyo, Sophia UP; Rutland, Tuttle, 1969.

Erll, Astrid. *Memory in Culture*. Houndsmills, Basingstoke, Palgrave Macmillan, 2011.

Erll, Astrid, and Ansgar Nünning, eds. *A Companion to Cultural Memory Studies*. Berlin, De Gruyter, 2010.

Etō Jun. *Seijuku to sōshitsu: "Haha" no hōkai*. Tokyo, Kōdansha Bungei Bunko, 1993.

Bibliography

Faulkner, William. *Essays, Speeches, and Public Letters*. London, Chatto & Windus, 1967.
Felman, Shoshana, and Dori Laub. *Testimony: Crises of Witnessing in Literature*. New York, Routledge, 1992.
Figal, Gerald. "How to Jibunshi: Making and Marketing Self-Histories of Showa among the Masses in Postwar Japan." *Journal of Asian Studies*, vol. 55, no. 4, Nov. 1996, pp. 902–33.
Fowler, Edward. "Rendering Words, Traversing Cultures: On the Art and Politics of Translating Modern Japanese Fiction." *Journal of Japanese Studies*, vol. 18, no. 1, 1992, pp. 1–44.
———. *The Rhetoric of Confession:* Shishōsetsu *in Early Twentieth-Century Japanese Fiction*. Berkeley, U of California P, 1988.
Furuyama Komao. *Nijūsan no sensō tanpen shōsetsu*. Tokyo, Bunshun Bunko, 2004.
Fussell, Paul. *The Great War and Modern Memory*. New York, Oxford UP, 1975.
Gabriel, Philip. *Mad Wives and Island Dreams: Shimao Toshio and the Margins of Japanese Literature*. Honolulu, U of Hawai'i P, 1999.
Galbraith, Stuart. *The Emperor and the Wolf: The Lives and Films of Akira Kurosawa and Toshiro Mifune*. New York, Faber and Faber, 2001.
Garon, Sheldon. *Molding Japanese Minds*. Princeton, Princeton UP, 1997.
Gessel, Van C. *The Sting of Life: Four Contemporary Japanese Novelists*. New York, Columbia UP, 1989.
Gluck, Carol. "The 'End' of the Postwar: Japan at the Turn of the Millennium." *States of Memory: Continuities, Conflicts, and Transformations in National Retrospection*. Edited by Jeffrey K. Olick, Durham, Duke UP, 2003, pp. 289–314.
———. "The 'Long Postwar': Japan and Germany in Common and in Contrast." *Legacies and Ambiguities: Postwar Fiction and Culture in West Germany and Japan*. Edited by Ernestine Schlant and J. Thomas Rimer, Washington, Woodrow Wilson Center P; Baltimore, Johns Hopkins UP, 1991, pp. 63–78.
———. "The Past in the Present." *Postwar Japan as History*. Edited by Andrew Gordon, Berkeley, U of California P, 1993, pp. 64–98.
Gordon, Andrew. *A Modern History of Japan: From Tokugawa Times to the Present*. 3rd ed., New York, Oxford UP, 2014.
———. "Consumption, Leisure and the Middle Class in Transwar Japan." *Social Science Japan Journal*, vol. 10, no. 1, 2007, pp. 1–21.
Gordon, Andrew, editor. *Postwar Japan as History*. Berkeley, U of California P, 1993.
Graham, Cooper C. *Leni Riefenstahl and Olympia*. Metuchen, Scarecrow Press, 1986.
Halbwachs, Maurice. *On Collective Memory*. Chicago, U of Chicago P, 1992.
Haley, Alex. *Roots*. 1976. Reprint. New York, Vanguard Books, 2007.
———. *Ruutsu*. Translated by Yasuoka Shōtarō and Matsuda Sen, Tokyo, Shakai Shisōsha, 1977. 2 vols.
Harootunian, Harry D. *Overcome by Modernity: History, Culture, and Community in Interwar Japan*. Princeton, Princeton UP, 2000.
Harvey, David. *The Condition of Postmodernity*. Cambridge, MA, Blackwell, 1990.

Hashimoto, Akiko. *The Long Defeat: Cultural Trauma, Memory, and Identity in Japan.* Oxford, Oxford UP, 2015.
Hasumi Shigehiko. *"Watakushi shōsetsu" o yomu.* Tokyo, Kōdansha Bungei Bunko, 2014.
Hattori Tatsu. "Saigo no nikki." *Chisei*, vol. 3, no. 3, 1956, pp. 274–80.
———. "Shinsedai no sakka-tachi." *Kindai bungaku*, vol. 9, no.1, 1954, pp.18–38.
Hayashi Fumiko. *Floating Clouds.* [Ukigumo.] New York, Columbia UP, 2006.
Heitzman, Kendall. "Parallel Universes, Vertical Worlds, and the Nation as Palimpsest in Murakami Ryū's *The World Five Minutes from Now*." *Mechademia*, vol. 10, 2015, pp. 252–66.
———. "The Rise of Women Writers, the Heisei I-Novel, and the Contemporary Bundan." *The Routledge Handbook of Modern Japanese Literature.* London, Routledge, 2016, pp. 285–98.
Hibbett, Howard. *The Chrysanthemum and the Fish: Japanese Humor since the Age of the Shoguns.* Tokyo, Kodansha International, 2002.
Hidaka Shōji. *Senryō kūkan no naka no bungaku: Konseki, gūi, sai.* Tokyo, Iwanami Shoten, 2015.
Hijiya-Kirschnereit, Irmela. *Rituals of Self-Revelation: Shishōsetsu as Literary Genre and Socio-Cultural Phenomenon.* Harvard East Asian Monographs 164. Cambridge, MA, Council on East Asian Studies, Harvard U, 1996.
Holy Bible, New International Version: Containing the Old Testament and the New Testament. 1978. Reprint. Grand Rapids, Zondervan, 2011.
Houston, Benjamin. *The Nashville Way: Racial Etiquette and the Struggle for Social Justice in a Southern City.* Athens, U of Georgia P, 2012.
Hutchinson, Rachael, and Mark Williams. *Representing the Other in Modern Japanese Literature: A Critical Approach.* Oxford and New York, Routledge, 2007.
Huyssen, Andreas. *Present Pasts: Urban Palimpsests and the Politics of Memory.* Palo Alto, Stanford UP, 2003.
Ichikawa Kon, and Mori Yūki. *Ichikawa Kon no eiga-tachi.* Tokyo, Waizu Shuppan, 1994.
Igarashi, Yoshikuni. *Bodies of Memory: Narratives of War in Postwar Japanese Culture, 1945–1970.* Princeton, Princeton UP, 2000.
Ihara Saikaku. *The Great Mirror of Male Love.* Translated by Paul Gordon Schalow, Palo Alto, Stanford UP, 1990.
Ikeda, Kyle. *Okinawan War Memory: Transgenerational Trauma and the War Fiction of Medoruma Shun.* New York, Routledge, 2014.
Iriye, Akira. "Introduction: Historical Scholarship and Public Memory." *Journal of American-East Asian Relations*, vol. 4, Summer 1995, pp. 89–93.
Ishihara Shintarō. *Season of Violence.* [Taiyō no kisetsu.] Rutland, Tuttle, 1966.
Ishii, Masami, editor. *1964-nen no Tōkyō Orinpikku.* Tokyo, Kawade Shobō Shinsha, 2014.
Ishikawa Jun. "The Legend of Gold." [Ōgon densetsu.] *The Legend of Gold and Other Stories*, Honolulu, U of Hawai'i P, 1998.
Ishikawa Tatsuzō. *Soldiers Alive.* [Ikite iru heitai.] Honolulu, U of Hawai'i P, 2003.

Ishiyama Kōichi. "Higurashi." *Gendai Nihon bungaku taikei geppō*, vol. 75, October 1972, Tokyo, Chikuma Shobō, pp. 4–5.
———. *Senmatsu-ha seishun kōyū nikki*. Tokyo, Ozawa Shoten, 1992.
———. *Shinyaa iin da yo monogatari*. Tokyo, Bokuyōsha, 1988.
Isoda Kōichi. *Sengo-shi no kūkan*. 1983. Reprint. Tokyo, Shinchōsha, 1993.
Ito, Ken K. *Visions of Desire: Tanizaki's Fictional Worlds*. Palo Alto, Stanford UP, 1991.
Jansen, Marius. *Sakamoto Ryōma and the Meiji Restoration*. 1961. Reprint. New York, Columbia UP, 1994.
Japanese Olympic Committee. "Tokyo 1964 Olympic Games," History, *www.joc.or.jp/english/historyjapan/tokyo1964.html*.
Jelliffe, Robert A., editor. *Faulkner at Nagano*. Tokyo, Kenkyūsha, 1956.
Johnson, Chalmers. *MITI and the Japanese Miracle: The Growth of Industrial Policy, 1925–1975*. Palo Alto, Stanford UP, 1982.
Kapur, Nick. *Japan at the Crossroads: Conflict and Compromise after Anpo*. Cambridge, Harvard UP, 2018.
Katō Norihiro. "Kaisetsu." Yasuoka Shōtarō, *Boku no Shōwa-shi*. 1984, 1988. Reprint. Tokyo, Kōdansha Bungei Bunko, 2018.
Kawashima Itaru. *Bungaku no kyojitsu: Jijitsu wa fukushū suru*. Tokyo, Ronsōsha, 1987.
Keene, Donald. *So Lovely a Country Will Never Perish: Wartime Diaries of Japanese Writers*. New York, Columbia UP, 2010.
Keenleyside, Hugh Ll., and A. F. Thomas. *History of Japanese Education and Present Educational System*. Tokyo, Hokuseido Press, 1937.
Kim Jiyoung. *Nihon bungaku no "sengo" to hensō sareru "Amerika": Senryō kara bunka reisen no jidai e*. Tokyo, Mineruva Shobō, 2019.
Kobayashi Hideo. *Kobayashi Hideo zenshū*. Tokyo, Shinchōsha, 2001–2002. 14 vols.
Kojima Nobuo. "American School." [Amerikan sukūru.] In *Contemporary Japanese Literature: An Anthology of Fiction, Film, and Other Writing Since 1945*. Edited by Howard Hibbett, New York, Knopf, 1977, pp. 119–44.
———. *Embracing Family*. [Hōyō kazoku.] Champaign, Dalkey Archive P, 2005.
———. *Ikyō no dōkeshi*. Tokyo, Mikasa Shobō, 1970.
———. *Kojima Nobuo bungaku ronshū*. Tokyo, Shōbunsha, 1966.
———. *Kojima Nobuo hihyō shūsei*. Tokyo, Suiseisha, 2010–2011. 8 vols.
Komada Shinji. "Shi teki *Tonsō* ron." *Kokubungaku*, vol. 22, no. 10, 1977, pp. 31–34.
Kōno Kensuke. "Shiba Ryōtarō to eiga." *Hyōshō no gendai*. Edited by Seki Reiko and Hara Hitoshi, Tokyo, Kanrin Shobō, 2008.
Kōno Kensuke, et al. *Sengo senryōki tanpen shōsetsu korekushon 6: 1952-nen*. Tokyo, Fujiwara Shoten, 2007.
Koschmann, J. Victor. *Revolution and Subjectivity in Postwar Japan*. Chicago, U of Chicago P, 1996.
Mack, Edward. *Manufacturing Modern Japanese Literature: Publishing, Prizes, and the Ascription of Literary Value*. Durham, Duke UP, 2010.
Mannheim, Karl. *Essays on the Sociology of Knowledge*. London, Routledge and Kegan Paul, 1952.

Margalit, Avishai. *The Ethics of Memory*. Cambridge, Harvard UP, 2002.
McClain, James L. *Japan: A Modern History*. New York, Norton, 2002.
McKnight, Anne. *Nakagami, Japan: Buraku and the Writing of Ethnicity*. Minneapolis, U of Minnesota P, 2011.
Michimata Tsutomu. *Shibai o ai shita sakka-tachi*. Tokyo, Bungei Shunjū, 2013.
Minear, Richard. *Hiroshima: Three Witnesses*. Princeton, Princeton UP, 1990.
Miyagawa Kazuo. *Kyameraman ichidai*. Kyoto, PHP, 1985.
Miyoshi, Masao. *As We Saw Them: The First Japanese Embassy to the United States*. 1979. Reprint. New York, Kodansha America, 1994.
Morris-Suzuki, Tessa. *Re-inventing Japan: Time, Space, Nation*. Armonk, NY, ME Sharpe, 1998.
Murakami Haruki. *1Q84*. New York, Alfred A. Knopf, 2011.
———. *Kafka on the Shore*. [Umibe no kafuka.] New York, Knopf, 2005.
———. *Wakai dokusha no tame no tanpen shōsetsu annai*. Tokyo, Bungei Shunjū, 1997.
Murakami Ryū. *Gofungo no sekai*. 1994. Reprint. Tokyo, Gentōsha Bunko, 1997.
Muramatsu Takeshi. "Hattori Tatsu no koto." *Chisei*, vol. 3, no. 3, 1956, pp. 280–81.
Murō Saisei. *Murō Saisei zenshū*. Tokyo, Shinchōsha, 1964–1968. 14 vols.
Najita, Tetsuo, and H. D. Harootunian. "Japanese Revolt against the West: Political and Cultural Criticism in the Twentieth Century." *The Cambridge History of Japan 6: The Twentieth Century*. Cambridge, UK, Cambridge UP, 1988.
Nakaishi Takashi. "Musshu Bovarii." *Bessatsu shinpyō*, vol. 7, no. 1, 1974, pp. 249–51.
Nakajima Kyōko. *The Little House*. [Chiisai ouchi.] London, Darf, 2019.
Narita Ryūichi. *Sensō keiken no sengoshi*. Tokyo, Iwanami Shoten, 2010.
———. *Shiba Ryōtarō no bakumatsu, Meiji: Ryōma ga yuku to Saka no ue no kumo o yomu*. Tokyo, Asahi Shinbunsha, 2003.
Nietzsche, Friedrich. *On the Genealogy of Morality: A Polemic*. Translated by Maudemarie Clark and Alan J. Swensen, Indianapolis, Hackett, 1998.
Noma Hiroshi. *Kanpon Sayama saiban*. Tokyo, Fujiwara Shoten, 1997. 3 vols.
———. *Zone of Emptiness*. [Shinkū chitai.] Cleveland, World Publishing Co., 1956
Noma Hiroshi, and Yasuoka Shōtarō. *Sabetsu: Sono kongen o tou*. Tokyo, Asahi Shinbunsha, 1977.
Nora, Pierre. *Realms of Memory: Rethinking the French Past*. New York, Columbia UP, 1996.
Nosaka Akiyuki. *Amerika hijiki, Hotaru no haka*. Tokyo, Shinchōsha, 1972.
———. *Sensō dōwa shū*. 1975. Reprint. Tokyo, Chūkō Bunko, 2003.
Oda Makoto. *Nandemo mite yarō*. 1961. Reprint. Tokyo, Kōdansha Bunko, 1979.
Ogi Shin'ichirō, et al. *Kōchi-ken no rekishi*. Kenshi 39. Tokyo, Yamakawa Shuppansha, 2001.
Ōkubo Fusao. *Bunshi to wa*. Tokyo, Beni Shobō, 1999.
Okuizumi Hikaru. *The Stones Cry Out*. Orlando, Harcourt, 1999.
Olick, Jeffrey K. "Collective Memory: The Two Cultures." *Sociological Theory*, vol. 17, no. 3, 1999, pp. 338–43.

Bibliography

Ōoka Shōhei. *Fires on the Plain*. [Nobi.] New York, Knopf, 1957.
Ōoka Shōhei, and Yutaka Haniya. *Futatsu no dōjidai-shi*. Tokyo, Iwanami Shoten, 1984.
Orbaugh, Sharalyn. *Japanese Fiction of the Allied Occupation: Vision, Embodiment, Identity*. Leiden, Brill, 2007.
———. "Raced Bodies and the Public Sphere in Ichikawa Kon's *Tokyo Olympiad*." *Historical Consciousness, Historiography, and Modern Japanese Values*. Edited by James C. Baxter, Kyoto, International Research Center for Japanese Studies, 2007. 297–324.
"Orinpikku eiga shindan." *Bessatsu kinema junpō: Tokyo Orinpikku* (April 1965), pp. 176–80.
Orr, James J. *The Victim as Hero: Ideologies of Peace and National Identity in Postwar Japan*. Honolulu, U of Hawai'i P, 2001.
Osaragi Jirō. *The Homecoming*. [Kikyō.] New York, Knopf, 1954.
Ōta Minoru. *Kasane chizu shiriizu Tōkyō: Makkaasaa no jidai-hen*. Tokyo, Mitsumura Suiko Shoin, 2015.
Ozaki Kazuo. *Rosy Glasses*. [Nonki megane.] Woodchurch, P. Norbury, 1988.
Patrick, Hugh T. *Monetary Policy and Central Banking in Contemporary Japan*. Series in Monetary and International Economics, vol. 5. Bombay, U of Bombay, 1962.
Pflugfelder, Gregory M. *Cartographies of Desire: Male-Male Sexuality in Japanese Discourse, 1600–1950*. Berkeley, U of California P, 1999.
Pilley, Muriel. *The Hills of T'ang: Forty Years in South China*. Self-published, 2002.
Philippi, Donald L., translator. *Kojiki*. Tokyo, Princeton UP, U of Tokyo P, 1969.
Quandt, James, editor. *Kon Ichikawa*. Cinematheque Ontario Monographs 4. Toronto, Toronto International Film Festival Group, 2001.
Roberts, Luke S. *Mercantilism in a Japanese Domain: The Merchant Origins of Economic Nationalism in 18th-Century Tosa*. Cambridge, Cambridge UP, 1998.
Rodd, Laurel Rasplica, translator. *Shinkokinshū: New Collection of Poems Ancient and Modern*. Leiden, Brill, 2015. 2 vols.
Roden, Donald. *Schooldays in Imperial Japan: A Study in the Culture of a Student Elite*. Berkeley, U of California P, 1980.
Rothberg, Michael. *Multidirectional Memory: Remembering the Holocaust in the Age of Decolonization*. Palo Alto, Stanford UP, 2009.
Rosenbaum, Roman. "The 'Generation of the Burnt-Out Ruins.'" *Japanese Studies*, vol. 27, no. 3, 2007, pp. 281–93.
Sabin, Burritt, editor. *Stories from The East*. Tokyo, The East Publications, 1997.
Sakagami Hiroshi. "*Kaihen no kōkei* saidoku." *Kokubungaku*, vol. 22, no. 10, 1977, pp. 35–37.
———. "Kaisetsu." Yasuoka Shōtarō, *Kagamigawa*. 2000. Reprint. Tokyo, Shinchō Bunko, 2004.
Sakai Toshio. *Aru "sengo" no henreki: Yasuoka Shōtarō o yomu*. Tokyo, Dōbutsusha, 2006.
Sakazaki Shiran. *Kanketsu senri no koma*. In *Shin nihon koten bungaku taikei* 16. Tokyo, Iwanami Shoten, 2003.

Samazama na 8.15. Sensō to bungaku 9. Tokyo, Shūeisha, 2012.
Sand, Jordan. *Tokyo Vernacular: Common Spaces, Local Histories, Found Objects.* Berkeley, U of California P, 2013.
Satō Haruo. *Teihon Satō Haruo zenshū.* Kyoto, Rinsen Shoten, 1998–2001. 38 vols.
Satō Morio. *Magarikado de.* Self-published, 1983.
Sawaki Kōtarō. *Orinpia: Nachisu no mori de.* 1998. Reprint. Tokyo, Shūeisha Bunko, 2007.
Schacter, Daniel L. *Searching for Memory: The Brain, the Mind, and the Past.* New York, Basic Books, 1996.
Schalow, Paul Gordon, trans. Introduction to *The Great Mirror of Male Love*, by Ihara Saikaku. Palo Alto, Stanford UP, 1990.
Schodt, Frederik L. *Professor Risley and the Imperial Japanese Troupe.* Berkeley, Stone Bridge Press, 2012.
Seidensticker, Edward. *Kafū the Scribbler: The Life and Writings of Nagai Kafū, 1879–1959.* 1965. Reprint. Ann Arbor, U of Michigan, Center for Japanese Studies, 1990.
Shiba Ryōtarō. "Drunk as a Lord." [Yotte sōrō.] *Drunk as a Lord: Samurai Stories.* Tokyo, Kodansha International, 2001.
———. *Ryōma ga yuku.* Tokyo, Bunshun Bunko, 1998. 8 vols.
———. *The Last Shogun: The Life of Tokugawa Yoshinobu.* [Saigo no shogun.] New York: Kodansha International, 1998.
Shimada Masahiko. *Taihai shimai.* Tokyo, Bungei Shunjū, 2005.
Shimao Toshio. *The Sting of Death and Other Stories.* Translated by Kathryn Sparling, Ann Arbor, Center for Japanese Studies, University of Michigan, 1985.
Shimao Toshio, et al. *Shimao Toshio, Yasuoka Shōtarō, Kojima Nobuo, Yoshiyuki Junnosuke shū.* Gendai Nihon bungaku taikei 90. Tokyo, Chikuma Shobō, 1972.
Shinfune Kaisaburō. *Fudōchō no onshoku.* Tokyo, Hon no Izumi-sha, 2013.
Shōno Junzō. *Evening Clouds.* [Yūbe no kumo.] Berkeley, Stone Bridge Press, 2000.
———. *Ganbia taizaiki.* 1959. Reprint. Tokyo, Misuzu Shobō, 2005.
Slaymaker, Douglas N. *The Body in Postwar Japanese Fiction.* London, RoutledgeCurzon, 2004.
———. "Yokomitsu Riichi's Others: Paris and Shanghai." In *Representing the Other in Modern Japanese Literature: A Critical Approach.* Edited by Rachael Hutchinson and Mark Williams, New York, Routledge, 2007, pp. 109–24.
Standish, Isolde. *A New History of Japanese Cinema: A Century of Narrative Film.* New York, Continuum Books, 2005.
Steinhoff, Patricia. *Tenkō: Ideology and Societal Integration in Prewar Japan.* New York, Garland, 1991.
Suzuki, Tomi. *Narrating the Self: Fictions of Japanese Modernity.* Palo Alto, Stanford UP, 1996.
Tachibana, Reiko. *Narrative as Counter-Memory: A Half-Century of Postwar Writing in Germany and Japan.* Albany, State U of New York P, 1998.
Tahara Sōichirō. "Shōwa wa moete ita." *Bungei shunjū*, vol. 90, no. 2, 2012, pp. 276–79.
Takahashi Hiromitsu. *Yoshiyuki Junnosuke: Hito to bungaku.* Tokyo, Bensei, 2007.

Takeyama Michio. *Harp of Burma*. [Biruma no tategoto.] Rutland, Tuttle, 1966.
Tanikawa Shuntarō. "Orinpikku zakki." *Bessatsu kinema junpō: Tokyo Orinpikku* (April 1965), pp. 170–72.
Tanizaki Jun'ichirō. *The Key*. [Kagi.] New York, Knopf, 1961.
———. *The Makioka Sisters*. [Sasameyuki.] New York, Knopf, 1957.
———. *The Secret History of the Lord of Musashi* and *Arrowroot*. Translated by Anthony Chambers, New York, Perigee, 1983.
Tatar, Maria. *The Annotated Classic Fairy Tales*. New York, Norton, 2002.
———. *Secrets Beyond the Door: The Story of Bluebeard and His Wives*. Princeton, Princeton UP, 2004.
Teeuwen, Mark, and Kate Wildman Nakai. *Lust, Commerce, and Corruption: An Account of What I Have Seen and Heard, by an Edo Samurai*. New York, Columbia UP, 2017.
Toba Kōji. *1950-nendai: "Kiroku" no jidai*. Tokyo, Kawade Shobō Shinsha, 2010.
Toeda Hirokazu. "From the God of Literature to War Criminal: The Media and the Shifting Image of Yokomitsu Riichi from Prewar and Wartime to the Postwar Era." Translated by Atsuko Ueda. *Literature among the Ruins, 1945–1955*. Edited by Atsuko Ueda, Michael K. Bourdaghs, Richi Sakakibara, and Hirokazu Toeda, Lanham, Lexington Books, 2018, pp. 177–89.
Tokushima Takayoshi. "Yasuoka Shōtarō *Kaihen no kōkei* no koro." *Kikan bunka*, vol. 61, 2014, pp. 152–56.
Tokyo Orinpikku: Bungakusha no mita sekai no saiten. 1964. Reprint. Tokyo, Kōdansha, 2014.
Treat, John Whittier. *Pools of Water, Pillars of Fire: The Literature of Ibuse Masuji*. Seattle, U of Washington P, 1988.
———. *Writing Ground Zero: Japanese Literature and the Atomic Bomb*. Chicago: U of Chicago P, 1995.
Trouillot, Michel-Rolph. *Silencing the Past: Power and the Production of History*. Boston, Beacon Press, 1995.
Tsuboi Sakae. *Twenty-Four Eyes*. [Nijūshi no hitomi.] Tokyo, Kenkyūsha, 1957.
Uchida, Jun. *Brokers of Empire: Japanese Settler Colonialism in Korea, 1876–1945*. Cambridge, Harvard University Asia Center, 2011.
Ueda, Atsuko, Michael K. Bourdaghs, Richi Sakakibara, and Hirokazu Toeda. *The Politics and Literature Debate in Postwar Japanese Criticism, 1945–52*. Lanham, Lexington Books, 2017.
Vansina, Jan. *Oral Tradition as History*. Madison, U of Wisconsin P, 1985.
Vildrac, Charles. *Chants du désespéré*. 1920. Reprint. Paris, Gallimard, 1946.
Wada Natto, and Ichikawa Kon. "Tokyo Orinpikku." *Bessatsu kinema junpō*, April 1965, pp. 182–91.
White, Hayden. *The Content of the Form: Narrative Discourse and Historical Representation*. Baltimore, Johns Hopkins UP, 1987.
Wigen, Kären, translator. *A View by the Sea*. By Yasuoka Shōtarō. 1984. Reprint. New York, Columbia UP, 1992.

Williams, Mark. *Endō Shūsaku: A Literature of Reconciliation*. London, Routledge, 1999.
Winchell, Mark Royden. *Where No Flag Flies: Donald Davidson and the Southern Resistance*. Columbia, U of Missouri P, 2000.
Winter, Jay. *Remembering War: The Great War Between Memory and History in the Twentieth Century*. New Haven, Yale UP, 2006.
Yasukawa Minoru [Mickey Yasukawa]. *Furaibō ryūgakuki: Nihon seinen Amerika o arasu*. Tokyo, Kōbunsha, 1960.
Yasuoka Shōtarō. *Amerika kanjō ryokō*. Tokyo, Iwanami Shinsho, 1962.
———. *Amerika-jin no chi to kishitsu*. Tokyo, Shūeisha, 1977.
———. *Boku no Shōwa-shi*. Tokyo, Kōdansha, 1984, 1988. 3 vols.
———. *Boku no Tokyo chizu*. Tokyo, Sekai Bunkasha, 2006.
———. *Eiga no kanjō kyōiku*. Tokyo, Kōdansha, 1964.
———. *Hate mo nai dōchūki*. Tokyo, Kōdansha, 1995.
———. *Jijoden ryokō*. Tokyo, Bungei Shunjū, 1973.
———. *Kagamigawa*. Tokyo, Shinchō Bunko, 2004.
———. *Saru ga ki kara oriru toki*. Tokyo, Asahi Shinbunsha, 1971.
———. *Shi to no taimen*. 1998. Reprint. Tokyo, Kōbunsha Chie no Mori Bunko, 2012.
———. *Shisetsu ryōsai shii*. Tokyo, Asahi Shinbunsha, 1975.
———. *Watashi no nijū-seiki*. Tokyo, Asahi Shinbunsha, 1999.
———. *Yasuoka Shōtarō sensō shōsetsu shūsei*. Tokyo, Chūkō Bunko, 2018.
———. *Yasuoka Shōtarō shū*. Tokyo, Iwanami Shoten, 1986–1988. 10 vols.
———. *Yasuoka Shōtarō zenshū*. Tokyo, Kōdansha, 1971. 7 vols.
———. *Yasuoka Shōtarō zuihitsu shū*. Tokyo, Iwanami Shoten, 1991. 8 vols.
Yasuoka Shōtarō, and Inoue Yōji. *Warera naze Kirisuto-kyōto to narishi ka*. Tokyo, Kōbunsha, 1999.
Yasuoka Shōtarō, and Kondō Keitarō. *Yowai hachijū ima nao benkyō*. Tokyo, Kōbunsha, 2001.
Yasuoka Yuki. *Ie o sasaeta senjintachi*. Self-published, 1988.
———. *Yasuoka-ke no rekishi*. Self-published, 1970.
Yates, Frances A. *The Art of Memory*. Chicago, U of Chicago P, 1966.
Yoneyama, Lisa. *Hiroshima Traces: Time, Space, and the Dialectics of Memory*. Berkeley, U of California P, 1999.
Yoshida Hiroo. "*Kaihen no kōkei*." *Kokubungaku kaishaku to kanshō*, vol. 37, no. 2, 1972, pp. 134–37.
Yoshimoto, Mitsuhiro. *Kurosawa: Film Studies and Japanese Cinema*. Durham, Duke UP, 2000.

Index

À nous la liberté (film), 135
Abe Akira, *185*
Abe Kōbō, 137
Adenwalla, June, 105
Adenwalla, Minoo, 105–6
Africa, 126–27
After the Curtain Falls (*Maku ga orite kara*) (Yasuoka), 86–94, 95, 96
Agawa Hiroyuki, 99, *99*
Agawa Naoyuki, 101
Agrarian literary movement, 105, 113
Akutagawa Prize
    current judges of, 186
    Endō and, 23, 82, 101–2
    Furuyama and, 69
    Kojima and, 23
    Kondō and, 23
    Ozaki and, 134
    Shōno and, 23
    Takahashi and, 186
    Yasuoka and, 1, 2, 23, 26, 101–2, 155
Akutagawa Ryūnosuke, 3, 7, 198n3
Alexander, Lamar, 112–13
Ali, Muhammad (Cassius Clay), 124–25
Alt-Heidelberg (Meyer-Förster), 197n13
Alvis, Andra, 193n16
American Blood and Temperament (*Amerikajin no chi to kishitsu*) (Yasuoka), 126–27

"American School" ("Amerikan sukūru") (Kojima), 45, 103
Anderson, Sherwood, 105
Angel of Mockery, The (*Shitadashi tenshi*) (Yasuoka), 54, 83–86
Aoki Eigorō, 127
Aoki Masami, 70
Ara Masahito, 28
archive, 67–69, 93–94
Ariyoshi Sawako, 99, 102, 139
Arrowroot (*Yoshino kuzu*) (Tanizaki), 198n3
Art of Memory, The (Yates), 131
Asahi Journal (magazine), 127–29
Asahi shinbun (newspaper), 139, 185
Assmann, Aleida, 19, 25, 67, 100, 131–32, 182
Assmann, Jan, 19, 158–59, 182
At a Crossroads (*Magarikado de*) (Satō), 69–70
Autobiographical Journey, An (*Jijoden ryokō*) (Yasuoka), 5

Bach, Steven, 142
Bad Company (group), 68–75, 176
"Bad Company" ("Warui nakama") (Yasuoka), 23, 26–27, 33, 42, 69, 184–85

bakumatsu period
  Perry expedition and, 114, 161–62
  postwar and, 155, 160–62
  in *Sentimental Journey to the United States, A* (*Amerika kanjō ryokō*), 119–20
  See also *Ryōma on the Move* (*Ryōma ga yuku*) (Shiba); Sakamoto Ryōma; *Tale of Wanderers, A* (*Ryūritan*) (Yasuoka)
Barthes, Roland, 107
Bastille Day (*Quatorze juillet*) (film), 136
Beasley, W. G., 199n10
Beat Generation, 106–7
Berlin Olympics (1936), 137. See also *Olympia* (documentary)
Bessatsu kinema junpō (magazine), 132, 197n6
Betchaku Shunzō, 156, 169–70
Biblical narratives, 75–76, 78–81
Bikila, Abebe, 130–31
Bix, Herbert, 161
"Bluebeard" ("Aohige") (Yasuoka), 76–78, 79–80
body, 40–45
Bolváry, Géza von, 135
Bourdaghs, Michael, 72
Brown v. Board of Education (1954), 98, 110
Brundage, Avery, 139
Buck, Pearl S., 106–7
bundan (literary establishment), 2, 70–72
Bungaku jihyō (literary journal), 28
Bungakukai (literary journal), 1–2, 23–24, 82
Bungei shunjū (journal), 26, 66, 90, 192n5
burakumin, 2, 127–29
Burn, My Sword (*Moeyo ken*) (Shiba), 198n4

Cameraman's Life, A (*Kyameraman ichidai*) (Miyagawa), 144
Canada, 126–27, 167
canon, 67–69, 93–94
Carné, Marcel, 136
Catcher in the Rye, The (Salinger), 50
Catholicism, 101–2, 184
Certeau, Michel de, 100
Chad, 132–33, 148–52
Chaplin, Charlie, 132
Charter Oath (1868), 161
Chenal, Pierre, 134

Chiang Kai-shek, 9
Chikamatsu Shūkō, 195n12
Childhood (*Yōnen jidai*) (Murō), 7
childhood memoirs, 7
"China Incident" (1937), 16, 26
Chisei (journal), 81–82
Cicero, Marcus Tullius, 131
circus, 183
Circus at the End of the Era, The (*Daiseikimatsu saakasu*) (Yasuoka), 183, 185
"Circus Horse, The" ("Saakasu no uma") (story), 183
City of Corpses (*Shikabane no machi*) (Ōta), 30
Civil Rights Act (1964), 98, 125
Civil Rights Movement
  Nashville and, 98, 109–11, 112–13, 125
  Yasuoka and, 100, 109, 116–19, 151, 166–67
Clair, René, 134, 135, 136
Clay, Cassius (Muhammad Ali), 124–25
Clown in a Foreign Land, A (*Ikyō no dōkeshi*) (Kojima), 103
collected memory, 25
collective memory, 17–19, 25–26, 42
"Collective Memory and Cultural Identity" (J. Assmann), 158–59
communicative memory, 158–59, 181–82, 186
Communist Party, 112, 192n6
Conceptions of Youth (*Seinen no kōsō*) (literary journal), 69
Conceptions Society (*Kōsō no Kai*), 24
Contes (Perrault), 76–77
Convention of Kanagawa (1854), 114
Coubertin, Pierre de, 137, 138
Crime and Punishment (*Crime et chatiment*) (film), 134
Crime and Punishment (Dostoyevsky), 134
Crossroads of Fame (*Kōmyō ga tsuji*) (Shiba), 198n6
cultural memory, 19, 25, 67, 158–59, 181–82, 186–87

"Dangers of English, The" ("Abunai eigo") (Maruya), 138

Index 213

Davidson, Donald, 113
"Dawn in *Préau Huit*" (*Pureo yuitto no yoake*) (Furuyama), 69
Day, Doris, 196n1
Days with Friends Who Came of Age toward the End of the War (*Senmatsu-ha seishun koyu nikki*) (Ishiyama), 70
Dazai Osamu, 7, 14, 33–34, 35, 116, 165
de Havilland, Olivia, 79–80
deception
   in *After the Curtain Falls* (*Maku ga orite kara*), 86–94
   in *Angel of Mockery, The* (*Shitadashi tenshi*), 83–86
   in "Bluebeard" ("Aohige"), 76–78, 79–80
   as dominating theme in Yasuoka's writing, 63
   in "Glass Slipper, The" ("Garasu no kutsu"), 80
   in "House Guard, The" ("Hausu gaado"), 80
   in "Martha's Lament" ("Maruta no nageki"), 78–80
   in *Moon Is in the East, The* (*Tsuki wa higashi ni*), 94–97
   in "In a Neighborhood with Pine Trees" ("Matsu no ki no aru machi de"), 90
   in "Woman Who Had Dreams, The" ("Yume miru onna"), 75–76
Declaration of Humanity (*Ningen Sengen*), 161
Delinquent Club (*Fūten kurabu*) (literary journal), 68
Democracy in America (de Tocqueville), 117
Did You Find America? (*Amerika ga mitsukarimashita ka*) (Agawa), 101
digital revolution, 132
Dinshaw, Piroja, 105
dodoitsu (comic poetry), 176
Doolittle Raid (1942), 10–11
Dostoyevsky, Fyodor, 134
"Double-Layered Occupation, The" ("Senryō no nijū kōzō") (Isoda), 33–34
Dower, John, 161–62
Doyō shinbun (newspaper), 176–77, 181
Dreams of War Clouds (*Sen'un no yume*) (Shiba), 198n6

"Drunk as a Lord" ("Yotte sōrō") (Shiba), 198n6
Du Bois, W. E. B., 112
Duvivier, Julien, 134, 136

Edo period (1603–1868), 38–39, 165, 172, 176. See also *bakumatsu* period
emasculation narratives, 25–26, 45–49
Embracing Family (*Hōyō kazoku*) (Kojima), 103
Empire of Signs (*L'Empire des signes*) (Barthes), 107
Endō Shūsaku
   Akutagawa Prize and, 23
   Conceptions Society and, 24
   in France, 99, 101–2
   Hattori and, 82
   Kiza and, 195n15
   on Olympics, 137, 139
   research on, 18
   Third Generation of New Writers and, 63
   Yasuoka and, 61–62, 101–2, 184
English language, 101, 105, 111
Erll, Astrid, 25
Etō Jun, 55–56, 67, 166, 196n3
"expel the barbarians" (*jōi*) movement, 114

Fact and Fiction in Literature (*Bungaku no kyojitsu*) (Kawashima), 195n17
fairy tales, 75–78
Faulkner, William, 13, 114–15
Feyder, Jacques, 134
Figal, Gerald, 15
Fires on the Plain (*Nobi*) (Ōoka), 49–50, 186, 194n6
Flight (*Tonsō*) (Yasuoka), 26, 49–51, 178
Floating Clouds (*Ukigumo*) (Hayashi), 35
Flower Festival (*Hana matsuri*) (Yasuoka), 184
"Fly, Tomahawk!" ("Hashire tomahōku") (Yasuoka), 39–40
Fontaine, Joan, 79–80
Ford, John, 134
Foreign Studies (*Ryūgaku*) (Endō), 102
"Fortune Teller, The" ("Uranaishi") (Yasuoka), 39, 90
Foucault, Michel, 42

Fowler, Edward, 71, 193n21
France
 Endō in, 99, 101–2
 Yasuoka in, 11–12, 136
Freak (*Kikei*) (literary journal), 69
Freedom and People's Rights Movement, 176–77
"From Rome to Tokyo" ("Rōma kara Tokyo e") (Inoue), 138
Fugitives (literary movement), 113
Fujin kōron (magazine), 138, 148
Fukuda Tsuneari, 196n3
Fukuzawa Yukichi, 126
Fulbright scholarships, 99, 101
Funabashi Seiichi, 192n5
Furuyama Komao
 Akutagawa Prize and, 69
 Bad Company and, 68–69, 70, *73*
 Kiza and, 195n15
 Yasuoka and, 68–69, 70, 134, 144–45
Fussell, Paul, 17–18

Gandhi, Mahatma, 100
Geesink, Anton, 140–41
Gekkan asahi sonorama (magazine), 137
generations, 62, 63–67, 159–60. *See also* Third Generation of New Writers (*Daisan no Shinjin*)
Gessel, Van C., 2, 23–24, 42, 70, 96
Gide, André, 148
"Glass Slipper, The" ("Garasu no kutsu") (Yasuoka), 23, 46–48, *47*, 67, 68, 80
"Gloomy Pleasures" ("Inki na tanoshimi") (Yasuoka), 23, 27, 33, 50
Gluck, Carol, 14
Go-Ahead-and-Die Stories (*Shinyaa iin da yo monogatari*) (Ishiyama), 70
God of Flowers (*Kashin*) (Shiba), 198n4
Go-Daigo, Emperor, 9
Gomikawa Junpei, 45–46
Gordon, Andrew, 130, 192n6
Gorky, Maxim, 134
Gosho Heinosuke, 135
Government Aid and Relief in Occupied Areas (GARIOA), 101
Grand Illusion (*La Grande Illusion*) (film), 15, 135, 136, 185–86

Grant, Cary, 148
Grass, Günter, 49–50
"Grave of the Fireflies" ("Hotaru no haka") (Nosaka), 64
Great Bodhisattva Pass (*Daibosatsu tōge*) (Nakazato), 183
"'Great Expectations' of the Tokyo Olympics, The" ("Tokyo Gorin no 'Ōinaru isan'") (Sono), 139–40
Great War and Modern Memory, The (Fussell), 17–18
Guide to the Short Story for Young Readers, A (*Wakai dokusha no tame no tanpen shosetsu annai*) (Murakami H.), 67–68

hahamono (mother films), 45
Halbwachs, Maurice, 17–18, 25
Haley, Alex. See *Roots* (Haley)
"Handstand" ("Sakadachi") (Yasuoka), 36, 39
Haniya Yutaka, 23, 66
Hara Tamiki, 29, 120–21, 195n11
Harp of Burma (*Biruma no tategoto*) (Takeyama), 35
Harris, Townsend, 114
Harvey, David, 33, 34, 35
Hashimoto, Akiko, 14–15
Hasumi Shigehiko, 67
Hattori Tatsu, 14, 24, 64–65, 81–83, 85
Hayashi Fumiko, 35
Hayes, Bob, 145–46
Helen and Desire (Lengel), 195n14
Heroes of a Thousand Miles of Sweat and Blood (*Kanketsu senri no koma*) (Sakazaki), 172–73
Hibbett, Howard, 108, 193–94n21
Hidaka Shōji, 195n13
Hijiya-Kirschnereit, Irmela, 72
"Hills of a Foreign Land" ("Ikoku no oka") (song), 122–23
Hino Ashihei, 49–50
Hirabayashi Taiko, 140–41
Hirohito, Emperor, 161
"History within Me, The" ("Watashi no naka no rekishi") (Yasuoka), 15
Hitchcock, Alfred, 79–80, 134
Hitler, Adolf, 135

Index

Holocaust, 18, 100, 125–26
Homecoming, The (*Kikyō*) (Osaragi), 35
"Homework" ("Shukudai") (Yasuoka), 23, 35–36, 58
homosexuality and homophobia, 166, 172, 173
Hosoe Eikō, 144
Hôtel du nord (film), 136
Hotta Yoshie, 120
"House Guard, The" ("Hausu gaado") (Yasuoka), 47–48, 80
Houston, Benjamin, 109–10, 196n8
How I Became a Christian (*Yo wa ika ni shite Kirisuto-shinto to narishi ka*) (Uchimura), 184
"How to Jibunshi" (Figal), 15
Human Condition, The (*Ningen no jōken*) (Gomikawa), 45–46
"Humid Morning" ("Mushiatsui asa") (Yasuoka), 31–32, 33, 73, 74–75
Huyssen, Andreas, 14

I Want to be a Shellfish (*Watashi wa kai ni naritai*) (television drama and film), 46
Ibuse Masuji, 28–29
Ichikawa Kon, 127, 131, 141–44, 145
Igarashi Yoshikuni, 130
Iguchi-mura Incident, 162–64, 168–74
I'll See It All (*Nan demo mite yarō*) (Oda), 106
Imai Tadashi, 135
Imai Tatsuo, 92
Immortal Love (*Eien no hito*) (Kinoshita), 135
"In a Neighborhood with Pine Trees" ("Matsu no ki no aru machi de") (Yasuoka), 90
Inoue Yasushi, 138, 153, 198n3
Inoue Yōji, 184
I-novels (*shishōsetsu*), 61, 70–75, 92–93
Iowa Writers' Workshop, 102–3
Irimajiri Chiwaki, 179
Irimajiri Shukuko, 179
Iriye, Akira, 14
Isa, Ahamed, 148, 151–52, *152–53*
Ishihara Shintarō, 24, 64, 82, 141, 194n5
Ishihara Yūjirō, 66
Ishii Momoko, 196n3
Ishikawa Jun, 28, 64

Ishikawa Kazuo, 127–28
Ishikawa Tatsuzō, 49–50, 134, 192n5
Ishiyama Kōichi, 69, 70, 71, 92, 134–35
Ishizaka Yōjirō, 134
Isoda Kōichi, 33–34, 95
Ito, Ken, 32
Iwano Hōmei, 195n12
Izumi Kyōka, 195n12

Jackson, Andrew, 119
Jäger, Ernst, 142
Jansen, Marius, 174
Japan Romantic School (*Romanha*), 161
Japanese Olympic Committee (JOC), 130–31, 139–40, 141, 145
Japanese Tragedy, A (*Nihon no higeki*) (film), 45
"Jesus of the Ruins, The" ("Yakeato no iesu") (Ishikawa), 64
jibunshi ("self-history"), 15
"Jingle Bells" ("Jinguru beru") (Yasuoka), 32–33
Johnson, Lyndon B., 125
judo, 140–41, 145
July, Robert W., 103
junbungaku (literary fiction), 165

Kafka on the Shore (*Umibe no Kafuka*) (Murakami H.), 186
Kagami River, The (*Kagamigawa*) (Yasuoka), 178–82
Kaikō Takeshi, 24, 120
Kamei Fumio, 137
Kaminaga Akio, 140–41
Kanagawa Treaty (1854), 114
Kataoka Naoharu, 179–80
Katō Norihiro, 50
Kawabata Yasunari, 7, 192n5, 193n21
Kawamoto Nobumasa, 152
Kawashima Itaru, 70–71, 92–93
kazoedoshi system, 5, 172
Keene, Donald, 185
Key, The (*Kagi*) (Tanizaki), 108
Kim Jiyoung, 196n3, 196n6
Kim Shi-jong, 127
Kindai bungaku (literary journal), 23, 24, 28, 64–65

Kinema junpō (film magazine), 145
King, Martin Luther, Jr., 112, 118
"King's Ears, The" ("Ōsama no mimi") (Yasuoka), 73, 74
Kinoshita Keisuke, 35, 38, 45, 135
Kishida Kunio, 192n5
Kita Ikki, 160–61
Kita Morio, 153–54
Kiza (amateur troupe), 195n15
Kobayashi Hideo, 120–21, *121*, 158
Kobayashi Masaki, 45–46
Kobori Nobujirō, 12, 69
Kōchi jiyū shinbun (newspaper), 176–77
Kōchi shinbun (newspaper), 176–77
Kōda Rohan, 195n12
Kōdansha, 2, 54, 183
Koizumi Junsaku, 69
Kojiki ("Records of Ancient Matters"), 140
Kojima Nobuo
    Akutagawa Prize and, 23
    emasculation narratives and, 45
    Rockefeller Foundation grant and, 99, 102–3
    Third Generation of New Writers and, 1–2, 61, 62, *63*, 166
Kojima Nobuo: works
    "American School" ("Amerikan sukūru"), 45, 103
    Clown in a Foreign Land, A (*Ikyō no dōkeshi*), 103
    Embracing Family (*Hōyō kazoku*), 103
    "Regarding Creative Writing Courses in the Academy" ("Daigakunai no sōsaku kōsu ni tsuite"), 103
    "On the Tragic Ground" ("Yogoreta tochi ni te"), 103
Kondō Keitarō, 23, *63*, 184
Kōno Kensuke, 174
Korean War, 13
Kumagai Hisatora, 134
Kurahara Korehito, 28
Kurata Hiromitsu, 12, 68, 72–75, *73*
Kuroda Tatsuo, 120–21
Kuroi Senji, 185
Kurosawa Akira, 141, 143
Kurosawa Akira: films
    Rashōmon, 13, 107
    Seven Samurai, The, 132
    Stray Dog (*Norainu*), 45, 75
Kusunoki Masashige, 9

"Last Journal Entry, The" ("Saigo no nikki") (Hattori), 81–82
Last Shogun, The (*Saigo no shōgun*) (Shiba), 198n4
Lawson, James, 110, 112
League of Nations, 101
"Legend of Gold, The" ("Ogon densetsu") (Ishikawa), 28
Legend of Ryōma (*Ryōma-den*) (NHK *taiga* drama), 174
Lengel, Frances, 195n14
Levi, Primo, 50
lieux de mémoire, 18
Life and Opinions of Tristram Shandy, Gentleman, The (Sterne), 196n1
Like Flying (*Tobu ga gotoku*) (Shiba), 198n4
literary fiction (*junbungaku*), 165
literature of the flesh (*nikutai bungaku*), 40
Little House, The (*Chiisai ouchi*) (Nakajima), 186
logic of scarcity, 125–26
Lower Depths, The (Gorky), 134
Lower Depths, The (*Les bas-fonds*) (film), 134

Maid's Tales, The (*Jochūtan*) (Nakajima), 186
Mainichi shinbun (newspaper), 138, 185
Makioka Sisters, The (*Sasameyuki*) (Tanizaki), 32, 165
Manchurian Incident (1931), 16
mannenrei system, 5, 172
Mannheim, Karl, 62
Marco Polo Bridge Incident (1937), 16
Margalit, Avishai, 100, 118–19
"Martha's Lament" ("Maruta no nageki") (Yasuoka), 78–80
Maruoka Akira, 179, 180
Maruoka Kanji, 179–80
Maruya Sai'ichi, 138
Matsuda Sen, 167
Matsumoto Seichō, 137
Maturity and Loss (*Seijuku to soshitsu*) (Etō), 55–56
McClain, Yoko, 102

Index

McKnight, Anne, 128
Meadows, Earle, 143
"Medal, The" ("Kunshō") (Shōtarō), 30, 31, 48–49
Meiji Restoration, 63–64, 156, 160–62
Mein Kampf (Hitler), 135
memory
  archive and, 67–69, 93–94
  digital revolution and, 132
  dimensions of, 19
  history and, 5
  mnemotechnics and, 131–32
  as multidirectional, 125–27
  in *My Shōwa History*, 5, 10–12
  as public, 14–16
  trauma and, 13–14, 16–17
  See also collective memory; cultural memory; social memory
Meyer-Förster, Wilhelm, 197n13
Michiko, Empress, 66
Mishima Yukio, 7, 14, 138–39, 154, 193n21
Mita bungaku (literary journal), 195n11
Mitsuhiro Yoshimoto, 45, 75
Miura Shumon, 61, *99*
Miyagawa Kazuo, 144
Miyamoto Tsuneichi, 127
Miyoshi, Masao, 126
Mizoguchi Kenji, 134
Mizukami Tsutomu, 127
mnemotechnics, 131–32
Montgomery, Alabama, bus boycott (1955–1956), 98
Moon Is in the East, The (*Tsuki wa higashi ni*) (Yasuoka), 92–93, 94–97
Mori Ōgai, 198n3
Mori Yūki, 142, 143
Morning for the Osone Family (*Ōsone-ke no ashita*) (film), 35
Morris-Suzuki, Tessa, 33, 34
mother films (*hahamono*), 45
Mountain House (writers' retreat), 54
multidirectional memory, 125–27
Multidirectional Memory (Rothberg), 125–26
Murakami Haruki, 67–68, 185, 186
Murakami Ryū, 186

Murō Saisei, 7
"Music Class" ("Ongaku no jugyō") (Yasuoka), 37–38
My Alt Heidelberg (*Waga Aruto-Heideruberuhi*) (Yoshida), 124–25
My Map of Tokyo (*Boku no Tokyo chizu*) (Yasuoka), 5–6
My Own Strange Tales from a Chinese Studio (*Shisetsu ryōsai shii*) (Yasuoka), 183–84
My Shōwa History (*Boku no Shōwa-shi*) (Yasuoka)
  on books, 44
  covers of, *3*
  on Faulkner, 115
  importance of, 2
  memory in, 10–12, 15–17
  Nakajima and, 186
  Olympia in, 144–45
  personal and national narratives in, 7–10
  postwar in, 12–14
  on Rockefeller grant, 109
  on Taishō Democracy, 171
  time and space in, 3–7
  on war, 42
  war's end in, 30–31
My Strange Tale from East of the River (*Watashi no bokutō kitan*) (Yasuoka), 183–84
My Twentieth Century (*Watashi no nijū-seiki*) (Yasuoka), 134

Nagai Kafū, 28, 40, 183–84, 195n12
Nakagami Kenji, 127, 128–29, *128*
Nakaishi Takashi, 93
Nakajima Kyōko, 186
Nakamura Kōzō, 122
Nakamura Mitsuo, 196n3
Nakaoka Shintarō, 162
Nakazato Kaizan, 183
Naoki Prize, 155, 160
Narita Ryūichi, 164–65, 166, 186
Nashville, Tennessee
  Civil Rights Movement and, 98, 109–11, 112–13, 125
  Yasuoka in, 98–101, *110*, 124–25, 126–27, 151
  See also Vanderbilt University

Nasu Shingo, 175
National Diet Library, 70
National Sports Festival, 150
nationalism, 136–37, 141
Natsume Sōseki, 195n12
Nazi Germany, 135
neural memory, 19
New Criticism, 105
New Life (*Shinsei*) (Shimazaki), 72
New York Times (newspaper), 105
NHK News Web, 184–85
Nietzsche, Friedrich, 10
Nihon Shoki (*Nihongi*) (*Chronicles of Japan*), 140
nikutai bungaku (literature of the flesh), 40
Nintoku, Emperor, 140
Nishida Shūhei, 143
Nishiyama Fumoto, 179–81
Niwa Fumio, 192n5
Noma Hiroshi, 23, 49–50, 61, 127–29
Nora, Pierre, 18
Nosaka Akiyuki, 29, 64, 194n5
Not Because of Color (*Hishoku*) (Ariyoshi), 102

Ōba Hideo, 35, 135–36
Oda Makoto, 99, 103, 106–9, 130, 139, 194n5
Odagiri Hideo, 137
Ōe Kenzaburō, 24, 64, 194n5
Ōe Sueo, 143
Okada Michiyo, 72
Ōkubo Fusao, 61, 92
Okuizumi Hikaru, 186
Olick, Jeffrey, 25
Olympia (documentary), 132–33, 141–43, 144–46
Olympia: In the Realm of the Nazis (*Orinpia: Nachisu no mori de*) (Sawaki), 142
Olympics, 136–37. *See also* Rome Olympics (1960); Tokyo Olympics (1964)
On Collective Memory (*Les cadres sociaux de la mémoire*) (Halbwachs), 17–18, 25
On Shiga Naoya (*Shiga Naoya ron*) (Yasuoka), 92–93, 167, 183–84
On the Genealogy of Morality (*Zur genealogie der moral*) (Nietzsche), 10

"On the Tragic Ground" ("Yogoreta tochi ni te") (Kojima), 103
Once More (*Ima hitotabi no*) (film), 135
One-Two Association (*Ichi-ni-kai*), 24
Ōoka Shōhei, 66, 99, 120, 127. *See also Fires on the Plain* (*Nobi*) (Ōoka)
oral history, 19, 159, 168–69
Oral Tradition as History (Vansina), 159
Orbaugh, Sharalyn, 42, 148
Orr, James J., 38
Osaragi Jirō, 35
Ōta Yōko, 30
Ōtsu Junkichi (Shiga), 184
Our Days in This World (*Yo ni sumu hibi*) (Shiba), 198n4
Owens, Jesse, 145–46, *147*
Owl Castle, The (*Fukurō no shiro*) (Shiba), 160
Ozaki Kazuo, 134
Ozaki Shirō, 134

Pale Horse (*Aouma*) (literary journal), 69
"Pale Horse Revue, The" ("Aouma-kan") (Yasuoka), 194–95n9
panopticon, 136
Paris, France, 11–12, 136
Pass, The (*Tōge*) (Shiba), 198n4
"Past in the Present, The" (Gluck), 14
"Patterns and Adventures" ("Ishō to bōken") (Yasuoka), 70
"Pawnbroker's Wife, The" ("Shichiya no nyōbō") (Yasuoka), 42–45, 90
Perrault, Charles, 76–77
Perry, Matthew, 114, 161–62
Pflugfelder, Greg, 172
plagiarism, 9–10
popular fiction (*taishū bungaku*), 165
postwar humanism, 165
postwar Japan
  bakumatsu period and, 155, 160–62
  emasculation narratives and, 45–49
  generations in, 63–67
  public memory in, 14–16
  war's end in narratives and, 27–31
  in Yasuoka's writing, 12–14, 30–33, 115–20, 123
  See also US Occupation of Japan (1945–1952)

"Prized Possessions" ("Aigan") (Yasuoka), 23, 89
Professor Risley and the Imperial Japanese Troupe (Schodt), 183
Proud of My Voice (*Nodo jiman*) (NHK program), 122
Pu Songling, 183–84
public memory, 14–16
Pulitzer Prize, 167

Quilt, The (*Futon*) (Tayama), 70, 72

race and racial segregation
  burakumin and, 127–29
  Japanese writers in the United States and, 102, 104, 105–6, 108
  Yasuoka and, 111–13, 116–19, 124–25, 148–52
  See also *Brown v. Board of Education* (1954); Civil Rights Movement
race walking, 146–48
Ransom, John Crowe, 105, 113
Rashōmon (film), 13, 107
"Razor, The" ("Kamisori hanashi") (Yasuoka), 68
Record of My Stay in Gambier, A (*Ganbia taizaiki*) (Shōno), 104–5
Record of the Endless Journey, A (*Hate mo nai dōchūki*) (Yasuoka), 183
"Record of the Olympic Film Struggles, A" ("Orinpikku eiga-zukuri funsenki") (Yasuoka), 148
"Regarding Creative Writing Courses in the Academy" ("Daigakunai no sōsaku kōsu ni tsuite") (Kojima), 103
Re-Inventing Japan (Morris-Suzuki), 33
Reischauer, Edwin, 106–7, 108
religion. See Catholicism; Zen Buddhism
Renoir, Jean, 15, 134, 135, 136, 185–86
Richards, Kenneth, 167
Riefenstahl, Leni, 132–33, 141–43, 144–46
Rilke, Rainer Maria, 136
Roberts, Luke, 199n9
Rockefeller Foundation
  Japanese writers and, 99, 101, 103
  Shōno and, 104–6
  Yasuoka and, 2, 10, 13, 98–101, *99*, 109, 113, 120
Romanha (Japan Romantic School), 161
Romberg, Sigmund, 197n13
Rome Olympics (1960), 13, 143
rōnin (masterless samurai), 66–67
"Room in Tsukiji, A" ("Tsukiji Odawara-chō") (Yasuoka), 38–39
Roots (Haley)
  history and, 171
  Nakagami and, 129
  Pulitzer Prize and, 167–68
  Yasuoka and, 2, 127, 129, 167–68
Rosenbaum, Roman, 194n5
Rosy Glasses (*Nonki megane*) (film), 134
"Rosy Glasses" (Ozaki), 134
Rothberg, Michael, 125–26
Ryōma on the Move (*Ryōma ga yuku*) (Shiba)
  as historical fiction, 157–59, 171
  Ryōma in, 155–56, 160, 162–66, 174–75, 178
  Tale of Wanderers, A (*Ryūritan*) (Yasuoka) and, 168–70

Saigō Takamori, 161
Sakagami Hiroshi, 57, 178, 185, *185*
Sakaguchi Angō, 192n5
Sakamoto Ryōma
  in *Heroes of a Thousand Miles of Sweat and Blood* (*Kanketsu senri no koma*) (Sakazaki), 172–73
  in *Ryōma on the Move* (*Ryōma ga yuku*) (Shiba), 155–56, 160, 162–66, 174–75, 178
  in *Tale of Wanderers, A* (*Ryūritan*) (Yasuoka), 155–56, 174–75
Sakamoto Ryōma and the Meiji Restoration (Jansen), 174
Sakazaki Shiran, 172–73
Salinger, J. D., 50
"Same Old, Same Old" ("Ai mo kawarazu") (Yasuoka), 36–37, 41, 66–67, 73–74
Sand, Jordan, 131
Sankei shinbun (newspaper), 160
Sasaki Kiichi, 120–21, *121*
Satō Haruo, 7, 192n5
Satō Morio, 68, 69–70, 145

Sawaki Kōtarō, 142–43
Sayama Incident (1963), 127–28
"Scar Left by a Twisted Truth, The" ("Waikyoku sareta jijitsu no kizuato") (Kawashima), 70–71, 92
Schalow, Paul Gordon, 172
Schodt, Frederik L., 183
Season of the Sun (*Taiyō no kisetsu*) (Ishihara), 24, 82
Second Sino-Japanese War, 16, 26
"Secret of the Trade" ("Shokugyō no himitsu") (Yasuoka), 53–54
Sekai (journal), 127, 132
Sengo-ha ("postwar writers"), 23
Sensation of the Century (*Seiki no kandō*) (documentary), 152–54
Sensō to bungaku (*War and Literature*) (collection), 193n9
Sentimental Education in Film, A (*Eiga no kanjō kyōiku*) (Yasuoka), 132
"Sentimental Journey" (song), 196n1
Sentimental Journey through France and Italy, A (Sterne), 196n1
Sentimental Journey to the Soviet Union, A (*Sobieto kanjō ryokō*), 120–23
Sentimental Journey to the United States, A (*Amerika kanjō ryokō*) (Yasuoka), 13, 98, 115–20
Seoul (Keijō), 3, 6
Setting Sun, The (*Shayō*) (Dazai), 35, 116, 165
Seven Samurai, The (film), 132
Shiba Ryōtarō, 160, 178. See also *Ryōma on the Move* (*Ryōma ga yuku*) (Shiba)
Shiga, Naoya, 183–84
Shima Kōji, 134
Shimada Masahiko, 186
Shimao Toshio, 1–2, 18, 29, 62, 92
Shimazaki Tōson, 72, 195n12, 198n3
Shin nihon bungaku (literary journal), 24
Shin Nihon Bungakukai (New Japan Literary Society), 28
Shinchō (literary journal), 34, 167
Shindō Junkō, 81
Shinfune Kaisaburō, 167
Shinkokinshū (anthology of poetry), 140
Shinsei (magazine), 28
Shirasaka Yoshio, 197n6

shishōsetsu (I-novels), 61, 70–75, 92–93
Shōno Junzō, 23, 63, 99, 103, 104–6, 109
Shōwa single-digits (*Shōwa hitoketa*), 64
Sisters of Decadence (*Taihai shimai*) (Shimada), 186
Slaughterhouse-Five (Vonnegut), 49–50
Slaymaker, Douglas, 40, 102
social memory, 19, 25
"Sociological Problem of Generations, The" ("Das problem der generationen") (Mannheim), 62
Soldiers Alive (*Ikite iru heitai*) (Ishikawa), 49–50
Song of Summer Grasses, A (*Natsukusa no fu*) (Shiba), 198n6
Sono Ayako, 139–40
South Korea, 6
Southern Agrarians (literary movement), 105, 113
Soviet Union
  World War II and, 48
  Yasuoka in, 120–23, 121
space, 3–7, 33–40, 54–58
Space of Postwar History, The (*Sengoshi no kūkan*) (Isoda), 34
Standish, Isolde, 136, 193n17
Staring Death in the Face (*Shi to no taimen*) (Yasuoka), 184
Sterne, Laurence, 196n1
Sting of Death, The (*Shi no toge*) (Shimao), 92
Stockholm Games (1912), 136
Stones Cry Out, The (*Ishi no raireki*) (Okuizumi), 186
storytelling, 75–81
"Strange Tale from East of the River, A" ("Bokutō kidan") (Nagai), 183–84
Strange Tales from a Chinese Studio (Pu), 183–84
Stray Dog (*Norainu*) (film), 45, 75
Student Prince, The (opera and musical), 197n13
Sugiura Minpei, 127
suicide
  Hattori and, 81–83
  in *Heroes of a Thousand Miles of Sweat and Blood* (*Kanketsu senri no koma*) (Sakazaki), 173

Index   221

in *My Shōwa History* (Yasuoka), 3, 7, 13, 14
in *Tale of Wanderers, A* (*Ryūritan*) (Yasuoka), 168–72
Summer Flowers (*Natsu no hana*) (Hara), 29
Supreme Court. See *Brown v. Board of Education* (1954)
Suspicion (film), 79–80
"Sutra Case, The" ("Kyozutsu") (Ibuse), 28–29
Suzuki, Tomi, 72, 195n12
"Sword Dance, The" ("Kenbu") (Yasuoka), 89

Tahara Sōichirō, 66
Taishō Democracy, 64, 69, 72, 171
taishū bungaku (popular fiction), 165
Tajima Naoto, 143
Takahashi Hiroki, 186
Takatori Masao, 127
Takayama Akira, 12, 68
Takechi Zuizan, 174
Takeyama Michio, 35
Takii Kōsaku, 192n5
Tale of Wanderers, A (*Ryūritan*) (Yasuoka), 2, 155–60, *159*, 166–72, 173–78, 185
Tamura Taijirō, 40
Tanaka Mitsuaki, 175–76
Tange Kenzō, 150, 152
Tanikawa Shuntarō, 144, 197n6
Tanizaki Jun'ichirō, 28, 32, 108, 165, 193n21, 195n12, 198n3
Tatar, Maria, 77
Tate, Allen, 113
Tayama Katai, 70, 72
Terada Torahiko, 169–70, 179
Terada Tōru, 195n12
Theft of the Mona Lisa, The (*Der raub der Mona Lisa*) (film), 135
"Thick the New Leaves" ("Aoba Shigereru") (Yasuoka), 40–42
Things Left to Learn at Eighty (*Yowai hachijū ima nao benkyō*) (Yasuoka and Kondō), 184
Third Generation of New Writers (*Daisan no Shinjin*)
  Hattori and, 81, 82
  I-novels and, 70
  Murakami on, 186

overview of, 1–2, 23–24, 61–63, *63*
Shiba and, 166
Yasuoka and, 1–2, 23–24, 61–63
"This Time That Summer" ("Sono natsu no ima wa") (Shimao), 29
time, 3–7, 33–40, 54–58
Tin Drum, The (Grass), 49–50
"To the Youth of Japan" (Faulkner), 115
Tocqueville, Alexis de, 117
Toeda Hirokazu, 137
Tokuda Shūsei, 195n12
Tokushima Takayoshi, 54, 194–95n9, 194n25
Tokyo nichinichi (newspaper), 137
Tokyo Olympiad (*Tokyo Orinpikku*) (documentary)
  Chad delegation in, 132–33, 148–52, *152–53*
  closing ceremony in, 152–54
  digital revolution and, 132
  Japanese Olympic Committee and, 131, 141, 145
  Olympia and, 141–43, 144–46
  opening ceremony in, *149*
  Owens in, 145–46, *147*
  production of, 141, 143–44
  script of, 145–48
  Sensation of the Century and, 152–54
  Yasuoka and, 127, 132–34, 144–45, 148–52, 154
Tokyo Olympics (1964), 130–31, 137–41. See also *Sensation of the Century* (*Seiki no kandō*) (documentary); *Tokyo Olympiad* (*Tokyo Orinpikku*) (documentary)
Tokyo shinbun (newspaper), 28
Tōmatsu Shōmei, 144
trauma, 13–14, 16–17
Treat, John, 29
Treaty of Amity and Commerce (1858), 114
Treaty of Mutual Cooperation and Security between the United States and Japan (Anpo Jōyaku) (1960), 13
Treaty of San Francisco (1952), 103
Trocchi, Alexander, 195n14
Trouillot, Michel-Rolph, 15
Truce, The (Levi), 50

Tsuboi Sakae, 37–38
Turner, Frederick Jackson, 55–56
Twenty-Four Eyes (*Nijūshi no hitomi*) (Tsuboi), 37–38
Two Contemporaneous Histories (*Futatsu no dōjidai-shi*), 66

Uchida Tomu, 134
Uchimura Kanzō, 184
Uehara Ken, 122
Uka Kikuma
  in *Heroes of a Thousand Miles of Sweat and Blood* (*Kanketsu senri no koma*) (Sakazaki), 172–73
  in *Ryōma on the Move* (*Ryōma ga yuku*) (Shiba), 163
  in *Tale of Wanderers, A* (*Ryūritan*) (Yasuoka), 168–72
Under the Paris Sky (*Sous le ciel de Paris*) (film), 136
Under the Roofs of Paris (*Sous les toits de Paris*) (film), 135, 136
United States
  "Japan boom" in, 107–8
  Japanese students and writers in, 99, 101, 102–9
  Perry expedition and, 114, 161–62
  Yasuoka in, 2, 109–20, *110*, 124–25, 126–27, 166–68
  See also *Sentimental Journey to the United States, A* (*Amerika kanjō ryokō*) (Yasuoka); US Occupation of Japan (1945–1952)
Uno Kōji, 192n5
Until the Day We Meet Again (*Mata au hi made*) (Imai), 135
US Occupation of Japan (1945–1952)
  bakumatsu period and, 161–62
  Dazai on, 33–34
  end of, 103
  English language and, 101
  in "House Guard, The" ("Hausu gaado") (Yasuoka), 48
  in *My Shōwa History*, 13
US–Japan Security Treaty (1951), 16
US–Japan Security Treaty (1960), 13, 114
Usui Yoshimi, 23

Vagabond Student (*Furaibō ryūgakuki*) (Yasukawa), 104
"Value of Narrativity in the Representation of Reality, The" (White), 158
Vanderbilt Foreign Student Association, 113
Vanderbilt Hustler (student newspaper), 112–13
Vanderbilt University, 98–101, 112–13
Vansina, Jan, 159, 181–82
Vietnam War, 125
View of the Sea, A (*Kaihen no kōkei*) (Yasuoka)
  After the Curtain Falls (*Maku ga orite kara*) and, 89
  Alvis on, 193n16
  biographical reading of, 58–59
  importance of, 2, 26, 184–85
  Murakami and, 67–68, 186
  space and time in, 54–58
  as war novel, 54–60
  writing of, 54
Vildrac, Charles, 138
Vonnegut, Kurt, 49–50
Voting Rights Act (1965), 98

Wada Natto, 197n6
wakashu (adolescent male lover), 172
Walk, Don't Run (film), 148
"Wandering Minstrel, The" ("Gin'yū shijin") (Yasuoka), 71
Wang Jingwei, 9
"War Song" ("Gunka") (Yasuoka), 51–53
Warren, Robert Penn, 113
Watanabe Kunio, 122
Waterloo Bridge (film), 136
What Is Your Name? (*Kimi no na wa*) (film), 35, 135–36
Wheat and Soldiers (*Mugi to heitai*) (Hino), 49–50
When Monkeys Came Down from the Trees (*Saru ga ki kara oriru toki*) (Yasuoka), 126–27
"Where the Ball Went" ("Tama no yukue") (Yasuoka), 36, 39
White, Hayden, 158
Why We Became Christians (*Warera naze Kirisuto-kyōto to narishi ka*) (Yasuoka and Inoue), 184

Index

Wigen, Kären, 194n22
Wild Days (*Wanpaku jidai*) (Satō), 7
Winesburg, Ohio (Anderson), 105
Winter, Jay, 5, 18
"Winter Fireworks" ("Fuyu no hanabi") (Dazai), 33–34
"Witches Won, The" ("Majo wa katta") (Ariyoshi), 139
witnessing, 19, 100, 118–19
Woman in the Dunes (*Suna no onna*) (Abe), 137
"Woman Who Had Dreams, The" ("Yume miru onna") (Yasuoka), 75–76
World Five Minutes from Now, The (*Gofungo no sekai*) (Murakami R.), 186
World War I, 17–18
World War II
    collective memory and, 18
    as Fifteen-Year War, 15–16
    generations in Japan and, 3, 66
    narratives of, 49–50. See also *Flight* (*Tonsō*) (Yasuoka)
    narratives of war's end and, 27–31
    Yasuoka and, 1, 9, 16, 49, *51*
"Writers of the New Generation, The" ("Shinsedai no sakka-tachi") (Hattori), 64–65
Writing of History, The (de Certeau), 100
Wyler, William, 134

yakeato sedai (generation of the ruins), 64
Yamaguchi Hitomi, 137
Yamanaka Sadao, 134
Yanagita Kunio, 15
Yasuda Yojūrō, 161
Yasukawa, Mickey (Yasukawa Minoru), 103–4, 111
Yasuoka Bunsuke, 156, 158, *159*, 168–71, 176, 185
Yasuoka family, 155–57
Yasuoka Genzaemon, 156
Yasuoka Gonma, 156–57
Yasuoka Haruko, 184, 186, 194–95n9
Yasuoka Kakuma, 156–57
Yasuoka Kakunosuke, 156–57, *157*, 158
Yasuoka Kasuke, 156–57, *157*, 158, 174, 175–76, 177

Yasuoka Michinosuke (later Michitarō), 156–57, 176–77
Yasuoka Shōtarō
    in Africa, 126–27
    Asahi Journal roundtables and, 127–29, *128*
    Bad Company and, 68–75, *73*, 176
    in Canada, 126–27, 167
    as canonical figure, 67–69
    Catholicism and, 101–2, 184
    cinema and, 15, 79–80, 132, 134–36, 185–86
    death of, 184–85
    education of, 1, 3, 7–10, 66–67, 68–69
    family history and, 129, 155–57, *157*. See also *A Tale of Wanderers* (*Ryūritan*) (Yasuoka)
    family of, 1, 3–5, *4*, *8*, 13
    generations and, 63–67
    Hattori and, 81, 82–84, 85
    health of, 1, 48, 49, 183
    as house guard, 48
    importance and legacy of, 1–3, 184–86, *185*
    interview with, 184
    language and, 6
    photography and, *133*
    as *rōnin*, 1, *8*, 9–10, 66–67, 68–69
    Roots (Haley) and, 2, 127, 128, 129, 167–68
    in the Soviet Union, 120–23, *121*
    Third Generation of New Writers and, 1–2, 23–24, 61–63, *63*, 166
    Tokyo Olympiad and, 132–34, 144–45, 148–52, 154
    at Vanderbilt University, 98–101
    World War II and, 1, 9, 16, 49, *51*
    writing as act of political resistance and, 24
Yasuoka Shōtarō: works
    After the Curtain Falls (*Maku ga orite kara*), 86–94, 95, 96
    American Blood and Temperament (*Amerika-jin no chi to kishitsu*), 126–27
    Angel of Mockery, The (*Shitadashi tenshi*), 54, 83–86
    Autobiographical Journey, An (*Jijoden ryokō*), 5

Yasuoka Shōtarō: works (cont'd)
"Bad Company" ("Warui nakama"), 23, 26–27, 33, 42, 69, 184–85
"Bluebeard" ("Aohige"), 76–78, 79–80
Circus at the End of the Era, The (*Daiseikimatsu saakasu*), 183, 185
Flight (*Tonsō*), 26, 49–51, 178
Flower Festival (*Hana matsuri*), 184
"Fly, Tomahawk!" ("Hashire tomahōku"), 39–40
"Fortune Teller, The" ("Uranaishi"), 39, 90
"Glass Slipper, The" ("Garasu no kutsu"), 23, 46–48, *47*, 67, 68, 80
"Gloomy Pleasures" ("Inki na tanoshimi"), 23, 27, 33, 50
"Handstand" ("Sakadachi"), 36, 39
"History within Me, The" ("Watashi no naka no rekishi"), 15
"Homework" ("Shukudai"), 23, 35–36, 58
"House Guard, The" ("Hausu gaado"), 47–48, 80
"Humid Morning" ("Mushiatsui asa"), 31–32, 33, 73, 74–75
"Jingle Bells" ("Jinguru beru"), 32–33
Kagami River, The (*Kagamigawa*), 178–82
"King's Ears, The" ("Ōsama no mimi"), 73, 74
"Martha's Lament" ("Maruta no nageki"), 78–80
Moon Is in the East, The (*Tsuki wa higashi ni*), 92–93, 94–97
"Music Class" ("Ongaku no jugyō"), 37–38
My Map of Tokyo (*Boku no Tokyo chizu*), 5–6
My Own Strange Tales from a Chinese Studio (*Shisetsu ryōsai shii*), 183–84
My Strange Tale from East of the River (*Watashi no bokutō kitan*), 183–84
My Twentieth Century (*Watashi no nijū-seiki*), 134
"In a Neighborhood with Pine Trees" ("Matsu no ki no aru machi de"), 90
"Pale Horse Revue, The" ("Aouma-kan"), 194–95n9
"Patterns and Adventures" ("Ishō to bōken"), 70
"Pawnbroker's Wife, The" ("Shichiya no nyōbō"), 42–45, 90
"Prized Possessions" ("Aigan"), 23, 89
"Razor, The" ("Kamisori hanashi"), 68
Record of the Endless Journey, A (*Hate mo nai dōchūki*), 183
"Record of the Olympic Film Struggles, A" ("Orinpikku eiga-zukuri funsenki"), 148
"Room in Tsukiji, A" ("Tsukiji Odawara-chō"), 38–39
"Same Old, Same Old" ("Ai mo kawarazu"), 36–37, 41, 66–67, 73–74
"Secret of the Trade" ("Shokugyō no himitsu"), 53–54
Sentimental Education in Film, A (*Eiga no kanjō kyōiku*), 132
Sentimental Journey to the United States, A (*Amerika kanjō ryokō*), 13, 98, 115–20
On Shiga Naoya (*Shiga Naoya ron*), 92–93, 167, 183–84
Staring Death in the Face (*Shi to no taimen*), 184
"Sword Dance, The" ("Kenbu"), 89
Tale of Wanderers, A (*Ryūritan*), 2, 155–60, *159*, 166–72, 173–78, 185
"Thick the New Leaves" ("Aoba Shigereru"), 40–42
Things Left to Learn at Eighty (*Yowai hachijū ima nao benkyō*), 184
"Wandering Minstrel, The" ("Gin'yū shijin"), 71
"War Song" ("Gunka"), 51–53
When Monkeys Came Down from the Trees (*Saru ga ki kara oriru toki*), 126–27
"Where the Ball Went" ("Tama no yukue"), 36, 39
"Woman Who Had Dreams, The" ("Yume miru onna"), 75–76
See also *My Shōwa History* (*Boku no Shōwa-shi*) (Yasuoka); *View of the Sea, A* (*Kaihen no kōkei*) (Yasuoka)
Yasuoka Shōtarō: From "Me" to "History" (*Yasuoka Shōtarō ten: "Watashi" kara "rekishi" e*) (exhibition), 185

Yasuoka Shunzō. *See* Betchaku Shunzō
Yasuoka Tsunenoshin, 156–57
Yasuoka Yuki, 173–74
Yates, Frances, 131
Yokomitsu Riichi, 137
Yomiuri shinbun (newspaper), 139–40
Yosa Buson, 96
Yoshida Hiroo, 58–59

Yoshida Tadashi, 122–23
Yoshida Tōyō, 174–75, 180
Yoshiyuki Junnosuke, 1–2, 23, 61–62, *63*, *99*

Zen Buddhism, 108
Zone of Emptiness (*Shinkū chitai*) (Noma), 49–50

www.ingramcontent.com/pod-product-compliance
Lightning Source LLC
Chambersburg PA
CBHW031435160426
43195CB00010BB/737